AN AMERICAN ARTIST'S STORY

An American

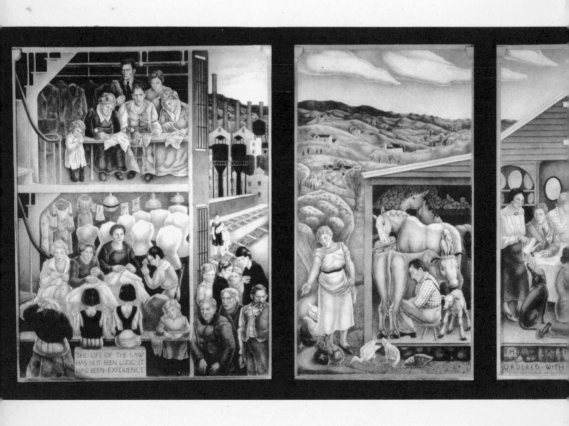

BOSTON LITTLE, BROWN AND COMPANY 1939

Artist's Story

GEORGE BIDDLE

TO HELENE SARDEAU

The author begs to acknowledge his indebtedness to *The Arts, Groton School Quarterly* and the *American Magazine of Art* for permission to include articles or parts of articles printed in these magazines and to *Arts and Decoration* for permission to print photographs which appeared in this magazine.

Contents

Illustrations

Illustrations

AN AMERICAN ARTIST'S STORY

Those Golden Days

1885-1898

Quant' è bella giovinezza
Che si fugge tuttavia!
Chi vuol esser lieto, sia:
Di doman non c'è certezza.

LORENZO DE' MEDICI

WHEN I was about four and a half years old and Francis three, we decided at the latter's instigation to kill the baby. A sequence of events led up to this resolution. Francis had stolen the baby's rubber doll. The doll was forcibly expropriated from Francis by Irish Mary and returned to the baby. Francis snatched the doll back and slugged the baby in the face with it. For this he was formally punished. We talked things over later and decided that the easiest way was to drop him out onto Spruce Street. We got the cradle as far as the third-floor window and were working on the latch when Irish Mary again intervened and we were spared a further humiliation.

From that day and for many years to come Francis and I grew up together. I was the more prudent, he the more lively of the two. I had greater scruples and he a swifter imagination. I think of myself as the balance wheel and of him as the accelerator of this two-cylindered combination. His ardor often led him into crooked paths and consequently he was spanked more often. Although I always followed, somewhat timidly perhaps, in his wake, I never seem to have been much punished. I was essentially good — too good, without any question. I was a little smug and a little priggish. I tried very hard to do the right thing, but until well on in life was never very successful. I wanted very much the approbation of older and successful people. Life for me was a contest rather than a holiday. I was earnest and mild and very forgiving. I had one other offensive trait. When I had done any-thing particularly aggravating and hazardous — like holding a giant firecracker between my teeth while Francis lit it — I always admitted that I was in the wrong if I really thought so. That was the Quaker in me.

I had one redeeming quality, a vast curiosity about life; and I was willing to try anything once, just for the experience.

At night I lay awake and watched lights dance and zigzag an established course across the nursery ceiling. They were reflected from the headlights of the horse cars as they jogged their way down Spruce Street.

In the spring I used to walk to Rittenhouse Square with Irish Mary. What trees grew along the way I cannot say, but they dropped long cattails of rotting flowers. I crushed them in my hands. They had a rank, fetid, pungent odor, which fifty years later I can still remember.

Once Irish Mary bought me a few cents' worth of tinware kitchen toys: little spoons, dishes, dessert molds. I can recall, too, the piercing shock of happiness I experienced in their possession.

One Easter I was driven to the Park where I met my cousin Philip. We both had Easter bunnies. I hated to leave the fields of waving grass and kept stroking the yellow dandelions.

When I was about four years old my father had rented a small house near Haverford College. On a June morning we three, Francis, Moncure and I, were taken out by Irish Mary and played all morning at prisoner's base in and out of the shrubbery. The lawn was carpeted with Quaker ladies. Eventually we were summoned back and asked if we cared to see the baby. I don't remember him so much, but my mother impressed me. She was lying all in white propped up on numberless pillows. The baby was somewhere beside her. I don't think we said anything but just stared at Mother.

Father had been ill and it was decided the following winter that he and my mother would go to Switzerland. White-haired Nana, who was the same age and height as Queen Victoria, and who had nursed my mother as a child, was to take Moncure and myself to winter in Atlantic City. Before that time I cannot particularly recall the turbulence of my older brother. Turbulent indeed is too temperate a word for him. He flashed through childhood like some tempestuous meteor, searing anything that crossed his path. He was vivid, black-haired, black-eyed, high-colored; seething with energy and deviltry. Passionate, emotional, warm in his affections and high-spirited, he had an ungovernable temper. One could not indeed envisage a probable career for him. One could have pictured him best in the role of a fifteenth-century condottiere. One could hardly foresee him as a successful investment banker and a leading authority on Philadelphia municipal bonds.

I was charmed and awed by his refractory and tumultuous violence, but my admiration was tempered with disapproval. I never wholeheartedly took part in his many acts of sedition but observed them with mingled dread and fascination.

I recall one particularly active morning when Nana, to ensure herself a little rest, had locked him in an upper bedroom which overlooked the boardwalk. Imprisoned in the bedroom Moncure, however, hardly wasted a moment. With a ball of knitting yarn he lowered from his window a small basket in which he proceeded to advertise, offer for sale and peddle with some success whatever belongings of Nana's he felt would most readily catch the eye and appeal to the appetite of the passersby. He had stripped the room bare of most of Nana's toilet articles before she was aware of the gathering crowd below his window.

In later years we used to recall his various exploits with successive nurses, governesses and tutors. He had locked the lantern-jawed and sad-eyed Henrietta, who taught us German, all morning in a linen closet. In Switzerland he had bought a small, savage mongrel which he kept on a leash and which at unexpected moments he would unloose upon Mademoiselle Schlumberger. Lastly there was that breathless occasion when Bonne Mama Biddle, who was extremely proud of her oldest grandson, was showing him off to a daughter-in-law who had presented her with only four granddaughters.

"Now your girls are all very backward, Minnie," she was saying. "Moncure, spell a really big word for your Aunt."

"A b — ab," shouted Moncure; "d o m e n — domen. There's your abdomen!" And he gave Bonne Mama a whack which delighted all of us.

When I was seven years old Father died. The Ardmore house on the edge of the Haverford College woods was closed and my mother moved over to live with Grandfather Robinson at Penllyn. Grandfather Robinson was at that time almost ninety. He could remember the War of 1812, and had graduated from William and Mary before the deaths of Thomas Jefferson and John Adams. Grandmother Robinson was a granddaughter of Edmund Randolph, Governor of Virginia and first Attorney General under Washington; and was consequently a cousin of President Jefferson and Robert E. Lee, both of whose mothers were Randolphs. My mother's family were tremendously proud of this connection. They considered themselves something like royalty and looked down on all Philadelphians as rather middle-class and stuffy. Of late years I have grown a little bored with my great-great-grandfather and learned recently with some pleasure from my friend Sam Morison, the historian, that he was apparently a rather shallow person, a little dishonorable in his petty financial dealings, but otherwise a charming and well-dressed fellow.

At a certain period of my childhood, however, I was much given to genealogical research, and derived, as a compensation for a somewhat puny physical frame and a lack of social poise, a sense of power from the thought that the blood of patriots and statesmen flowed through my veins. I learned, then, with some disgust that Edmund Randolph, who had been elected a member of the Constitutional Convention, had, for a certain bias, personal, political or otherwise, packed up his bags in Philadelphia and returned in a huff to Richmond without ever signing the Constitution! Petty, I called it. For some grudge he had let us all down, forever and ever. On my eighth birthday my mother presented me with a pair of cuff links which had belonged to him. She immediately took them back, however, as she feared I might lose them. Quite a hollow gesture, I felt. But I still have them.

As a very young man Grandfather Robinson had moved up from Richmond to Philadelphia. In 1829, at the age of twenty-seven, he had constructed the Pottsville and Danville — the first railroad in America. In 1834 he had surveyed and started building the Philadelphia and Reading; and two years later was sent to England to secure a loan for the completion of the road. He had in Paris presided at a dinner given to Lafayette by the American colony. As a child I saw and spoke to an old man who when he was still young had spoken and broken bread with an old man who was intimate with Washington and a contemporary of Jefferson's and who had played a not insignificant part in the American and French Revolutions.

I associate Grandfather Robinson with his cane and shaggy white eyebrows. He was led about by his private secretary for his eyes were failing him. He did not seem to me so much lacking in cordiality as curiously detached and above not only us boys, but life itself. He never offered us the choice between a nickel and a dime as did our jovial, kindly Grandfather Biddle. I could imagine intimacy with him as easily as intimacy with an ancient spruce tree. One conceived indeed of Grandfather Robinson in terms of mahogany furniture and cut-glass decanters, or of that peculiar odor of an old stone house whose shutters remain always closed to the heat and light of the shimmering Pennsylvania August weather. The more I think of him, indeed, the more he seems a completely disembodied and detached reflection of his own setting. And it is curious that I, who feel so deeply moved by, so loving and possessive of, that Penllyn background, should feel so little moved, so almost hostile to its most real and vital emanation. Later on I realized to what extent he had dominated — through no fault of his own but merely through the force of his personality — all those who sprang from his loins or suffered his impact for nearly a hundred years, for three full generations.

How could a boy not love the Penllyn farmhouse? Washington, it was told us, had spent the night there. Washington had tied his horse under the maple tree that shaded Grandmother Robinson's bedroom window. I saw the tree come down, trembling in safety well beyond the orbit of its power to strike and rend. All morning the men, Negroes and farm hands, had been at it below ground with the shovels and picks, wedging a great gap above the roots with their axes. Seven men, Negroes and farm hands, swayed on the ropes; and gradually the maple swayed, swayed with them, shuddered and came down to earth with a crash that sickened me.

That was annihilation, destruction, the severance of life from life, as I first encountered it.

That summer a Negro killed a snake in the field with his shovel. He slashed and ripped at the snake, which churned and slithered, headless, tailless, de-ossified, truncated, bleeding. The Negro turned to me, smiling: "Ole man snake won't die, though, till de sun goes down." That also I accepted. I too had seen death in the afternoon.

(8)

The house itself had fine solid walls of Pennsylvania masonry, low-ceilinged, cool, white-plastered rooms within. The house nestled under shade maples and firs. A well-banked, shallow brook ran from the springhouse, parting in two the lawn and wandering off into the meadow. There were brick steps leading up to the house and a brick terrace in the rear. Here we lunched on hot summer days. Behind the house were the stables, barns, the colored farmer's cottage, the corncribs and the icehouse.

I stood once in the corncrib with old Ben, an ex-slave of Grandfather's. A rat jumped at him and Ben caught it by the tail and flung it out of the corncrib and the dogs got it. Down by the stables we watched John the Coachman curry the horses in the early morning. With his right hand he scraped and curried the big chestnut's belly, and with the other scratched, slapped and caressed the broad flat croup, blowing air through his teeth, talking to the chestnut. In the afternoon I went driving with Grandmother in the victoria, to the Blue Bell Inn, up the Old Morris Road, to Spring House or the Four Corners. I sat in front with John the Coachman. The chestnuts' quarters were in a lather of white spume. Periodically they would raise their tails and slowly squeeze out the droppings which fell to the breechings and burst into seed on their hocks. John the Coachman talked to the horses through these operations, urging them with a flick of the whip or a shake of the rein, as if to encourage them in the parturition.

Near the railroad track was a squalid settlement of Negro shacks — chickens, goats, cart wheels, clothes lines, privies and children. We chummed with some of the kids and they invited us to a baptism. We drove over to the Wissahickon at Fort Washington. A black girl was screaming and leaping about, up to her waist in the muddy water. Every time she got well out she was shoved down again by the other Negroes, screaming and singing.

One day I climbed to the attic of Grandfather's house. It

was the twenty-third of January, 1893, because the next day was my eighth birthday. From the heat and old trunks and dust I found myself in the tank room, cool and mysterious with the sweating, gurgling water tanks crowded high about me. I heard water running but the top of the tanks was above my eye level. I managed to chin myself and looked down over the edge into one of them. As fast as the water ran in through one pipe it ran out through another vent in the far side. I was fascinated by the dripping tank walls, the pipes and the noise of the water. I seem to have had a corncob with me and I stuffed it securely into the outgoing vent. I had no definite plan or expectation. I acted on the spur of the moment just to see what would happen. Eventually I wandered off in search of further afternoon distractions. The effects of my experimentation were appalling. It was only the next morning that it became evident to what extent the dining room and kitchen were flooded. Grandfather's and Grandmother's bedrooms had absorbed the first impact, but as they had both left the country for the town house, this upper infiltration was not immediately noticed. As a punishment I spent my eighth birthday in bed and was not allowed to see anyone.

I do not recall my mother as being particularly angry. In such situations she concentrated her entire attention in an effort to measure out the strictest discipline, tempered with impartiality rather than mercy. There seemed no room left for any other emotion. On other occasions, however, for what seemed to me no adequate reason, she would explode into the most violent fits of anger. Her mere expression at such moments always shocked me. Francis and Moncure would lose their tempers, too, and scream and stamp in rage. I couldn't. This display of feeling was repugnant to me, undignified and ill-bred. I waited in silence until it was over or I could get away. Until the very end I could never fathom the wellsprings of my mother's emotions. We discussed her together at length as if she were an intricate problem in chess; but no one of us — or anyone else — ever had the satisfaction of really understanding her; of plumbing, of cataloguing, of pigeonholing and rationalizing the currents and crosscurrents of her nature.

The cause of one of these explosions, over which I pondered for years, was that I gave her for a Christmas present a very expensive aquatinted dry point by my beloved Mary Cassatt. At another time she would not speak to me for days — it soured an entire Easter holiday — because I bought her an equally expensive print by my immortal Hokusai, this time for her birthday. I could never seemingly observe any relation of cause and effect between my acts or omissions to act and what we used to describe as my mother's "nerves." My brother Geoff recalls a meeting in a hotel on the Grand Canal at Venice. We two had been on a week's walking trip about the lakes and hill towns of Lombardy. My mother had been waiting for us alone in one of her rare moods of through-shining romantic affection. And this I shattered at a blow by asking her after a week's absence, before indeed she had had time to be kissed, which way it was to the water closet.

Once — I was perhaps eight or nine — my mother had taken me to town and in the confusion on Chestnut Street I seized her arm somewhat roughly as she did not seem aware of an approaching hansom cab. When we crossed the street I noticed that her cheeks were wet and she seemed from some remark she made to love me. For many years I wondered why. Poor Mother! She was in need of so vast a quantity of something which she seemed unable to educate her sons to give her.

Shortly after my eighth birthday my mother took us abroad and settled us for fifteen months at the Pension Sillig at Vevey on the Lake of Geneva. We had crossed on a North German Lloyd boat. I remember the sailors hoisting a shift of mainsail, probably to steady the keel. Traveling through Switzerland in a second-class coach I saw the fields of bright poppies waving under the snow-capped mountains; but even more vividly do I recall a terrible scene enacted between Moncure and a very British tutor which my mother must have annexed in Paris. The tutor started the trouble by forbidding Moncure to swallow the entire contents of a large bottle of sweet pickled walnuts. Moncure said to go to hell in so many different ways that even the Swiss passengers pricked up their ears. The tutor said in an awfully dignified, English-public-school sort of way for Moncure to come to his chambers later when we reached our hotel and he would give him a caning. Moncure spat the walnuts in his face and all over him. The tutor seized Moncure by the wrists and said he would hold him until the little American bounder came to his senses. Moncure could take this from no man. He bit the tutor till he let go and then raked him fore and aft with his fingernails. I have forgotten who had the best of that particular skirmish. The tutor only lasted ten days and then returned to England, unshaken in his opinion of little American bounders.

At Berne all three of use went to visit the famous bear pits. Dressed in blue serge blouses with cotton collars, black silk scarfs and new straw hats, we stood on either side of my mother, tightly clasping her hands and looking down at the bears. Whether it blew off or whether he threw it in is of little consequence, but before we knew it Moncure's new straw hat was in the center of the pit, with the bears sitting rather nervously in a ring about it. My mother called to a guard and offering him a franc asked him to retrieve it for her. He looked at her and then looked down at the bear pit. He called over to another guard and passed him the franc and said: "Go get the straw hat in the bear pit for the lady." My mother picked him up rather sharply, saying in her not smooth but forceful German that where she came from men were men, and please to keep a civil tongue in your head. By this time we had a dozen guards and many others about us all guffawing in the loudest manner. My mother was tremendously excited. Her lip curled in scorn; her eye flashed with anger. I maneuvered her smoothly but rapidly away from this scene of humiliation, for by now the new straw hat was in shreds and the bears were romping about with the debris. She jerked her arms in irritation, occasionally pausing to shout back that they were ill-bred fellows.

Francis and I ran away and climbed all day through the hills and the cobbled villages above Vevey. We bought sour white wine, black bread and cheese for lunch. There were purple gentians in the fields and the sound of cowbells coming down from the mountains. It was the happiest day we had ever had together.

When we returned to Ardmore, Moncure and I were sent to Haverford School. I was nearly eight. They called us both "Frenchy." We resented it and there were some stiff fights.

One summer we were sent with a tutor for a few weeks to Canada. We were to camp out, cook our own food and learn how to hunt and fish. We got plenty of trout and bass and Moncure and the tutor shot some sandpipers on the edge of the lake, but big game seemed pretty scarce. Moncure always carried the gun. It seemed fair that he should get the first shot if any game were seen, even a fox or a woodchuck. A day or two before we left a shell jammed and the only way to dislodge it was to fire off the shotgun. I was allowed to do this — successfully — at a chipmunk. I was tremendously proud and happy and skinned and cured my game that evening. Home at Ardmore I stuffed and mounted it. I already had a mounted mole and several small songbirds, a white-eyed vireo and a chippy sparrow. I made such a realistic job of the chipmunk that our cat mistook it for live game and mangled it badly. One paw was gone and the lower jawbone. By an extremely delicate operation I grafted one of the mole's paws and part of its face on to the chipmunk. A few weeks later Mrs. Gillespie, a granddaughter of Benjamin Franklin, was visiting my mother. I always considered her a badly-dressed and ugly old woman, although she had the reputation of a great lady, a sharp tongue, a scholar of the humanities; and was over eighty.

Talk drifted to Canada and Mrs. Gillespie asked me very graciously what luck I had had hunting and fishing.

"Not so bad," I said. "As a matter of fact I got a chipmunk."

"Well," she sniffed, "you need hardly have left the Haverford woods, or your own back porch for that matter."

From then on for a few years life seems to have been a series of shocks and adventures. I may as well mention a few of them. They served no educational purpose — either for myself or for my mother. They would seem to indicate the difficulties that even a well-meaning and earnest child under the most favorable circumstances may have in adjusting himself to his physical environment.

I had always wanted a Swedish knife. They were popular in those days. The knife is bodily removed from the handle, which looks like a hollow cigar, open at either end. The blade is unlocked and then thrust back through the handle. By means of some gadget the blade is held firmly in place and can only be released by pressing a concealed spring. In moments of ignorance or indecision in matters strictly masculine, my mother would always consult Uncle Charley Chauncey, who had sabred a rebel cavalryman in the Civil War, or Uncle Harry Boyer, who had shot buffalo in Wyoming. She wanted us to grow up just like other boys, as long as our possessions were not too great a risk to the rest of the household. She accordingly bought on approval a Swedish knife with a three-inch blade and carried it out to Penllyn, for Uncle Harry's inspection and advice. Uncle Harry pronounced it a very safe and prudent investment, since the blade would not snap down and cut off my fingers.

In the train back from Penllyn, curiosity got the better of my mother. She took the Swedish knife out of its smart leather case and opened it without any difficulty. She could not, however, locate the spring to close it, and traveled all day with the open blade and a French novel concealed in her muff. She turned it over to me at once and for a week I did nothing but sharpen it.

I have no explanation of the sequel.

Charles the Coachman was a tiny fellow, not five feet high. I was devoted to him. I used to help him harness Dandy the pony, when he drove down to Ardmore in the little dogcart for the marketing. That morning I stood about watching him adjust the check-straps. I made passes in the air with my Swedish knife. Charles unlooped the reins, hanging from the snaffle, leading them through the terret rings on the saddle. I climbed in ahead and he passed me up the reins. As he jumped in after me I held the knife point up on his seat and said: "Sit, Charles, sit." He was a gentle little fellow and forebearing. "Stop your fooling, George," he said, and brushing aside the knife, started to sit down. I was too quick for him and got it back point up and he sat on it. I don't know which of us was the more distracted. Perhaps he did not realize what had happened for he started to whip up Dandy, then jerked her head round again into the stable. He ran for the water trough bleeding terribly. His idea was to squat over it until he would stop bleeding. In a moment the water trough seemed full of blood. Blood was everywhere. Charles ran up from the stable to the kitchen. I was too frightened to follow him in. I wandered round and round the house, with the Swedish knife in my hand. I traced Charles's bloody trail over the cement area which separated the stable from the kitchen. I went in. They had him lying on his face on the kitchen table. They had his trousers off and were pouring flour over his buttocks from the flour barrel.

But everything turned out pretty well. There was no telephone and I drove down with Dandy and got hold of Dr. Gerhard. He sewed Charles up and had him moved from his room over the stable to a room on the third floor. It must have been in June because I remember bringing him up raspberries every evening from our garden.

I was allowed to keep the Swedish knife but later on that summer up at York Harbor I got remorse and threw it into the river.

Generally speaking, we were nice, well-brought-up kids. Not ornery or quarrelsome. Once in an argument over a game of cricket Francis kicked me in the groin and I was in bed for a week with a swollen testicle. Another time in a croquet match Moncure hit Philip over the head with a croquet mallet. Phil was younger but big and bony and he knocked Moncure down. Moncure lost his temper — one of his real ugly fits — and ran into the house for his shotgun. I loathed these scenes and persuaded Phil to beat it. We got into the hayloft over the stable and well down into the hay. Then we heard them coming, Moncure and Mother, both pretty wild. Mother was screaming, "You murderer! You murderer!"

Moncure was a handful to manage when he got started. Her temper was just as violent and in a crisis she was afraid of nothing. Once a tramp tried to get by her and into the house. Charles the Coachman and the gardener were away. She stood in the door and faced him. He bullied and threatened her. She never said a word and stared at him with all her fury.

After that she bought a pistol. It had a mother-of-pearl handle. She kept it in a little gray suede case on her nightstand. Uncle Charley would ride over from Narbeth, pin a paper bull's-eye on a tree, step off twenty paces and coach her pistol practice. She held her left hand over her left eye and got as far from the pistol as she could. She was quite beautiful in her frightened determination.

As a girl my mother rode well — side-saddle. She had had a bad fall, and from what her nurse told me at her death, it may have accounted for the fact that she spent much of her time in bed or lying on her back. She used to practise archery with an English yew bow that Mrs. Owen Jones Wister had won at a tournament and given her. She never took up bicycling, which just then was coming in.

Upon rare occasions my mother and Annie Deane went into town to shop. Mother wore a small black hat and a long black veil. Annie Deane wore a lavender dress and a shorter purple veil. She bristled in front with whalebone. On one such occasion we three were alone in the nursery. The baby was at the other end of the house. Moncure explained to us that the way to make oil paint was to mix our water colors in a bucket of water and add to it the scrapings from the cracks between the floor boards. We each had a box of water colors and we pooled them for the experiment. It seemed to work perfectly. We had no suitable brushes, however, for the job we had in mind. Francis suggested that we could cut off dogwood twigs and fasten them together. We had tired of the colored supplements of the *London Graphics* which were pasted with flour and water on the nursery walls. They were a nauseating series of Little Boys Blue with Newfoundland dogs, or little girls and Great Danes, or bulldogs and Newfoundland pups, or little girls and boys giving each other oranges. We got a bucket of water from the pump house, filled it with our oil paint and had the nursery walls pretty well covered by lunch time. After lunch, as there was still some paint left, we tackled the stairway and what my mother called the "hall." This was at the bottom of the stairs. There was a fireplace with a coat of chain mail and some crossed swords above it. The swords were supposedly worn by Colonel Clement Biddle, who at the Battle of Trenton was selected by Washington to receive the swords of the Hessian officers; and by his son, Clement Cornell Biddle, who commanded a Pennsylvania regiment of light infantry during the War of 1812. On either side of the chain mail were suspended a bronze copy of a Renaissance helmet and a bronze copy of a Greek shield. There were three mahogany

(17)

chairs that were part of a set given to Clement Biddle by Washington; a Louis XIII stained oak settee with the date carved
on it; some atrocious rococo hand-carved imitation Spanish chairs;
and things done in mosaic, that were copied from something at
the Alhambra in Granada. These were framed in black ebony
and scattered about. At one time there was a plaster cast about
four feet high of Michelangelo's slave, a drawing by Baudry
which I thought very beautiful, of a naked girl looking at herself
in a mirror, and a replica on porcelain in color of the famous
painting by Guido Reni of Aurora — Dawn Driving her Chariot
and Horses across the Firmament. There were also yellow
Moorish ceramics, and Venetian glasses with dragons for handles,
and a tall black thing that looked like a pitcher with an opening
at the bottom but no funnel. I never knew what it was for — perhaps to smoke out of. I still have it. These things Father had
brought back from his trips to Europe and they gave the "hall"
a look of rich and somber dignity. With such accessories and
nothing but our dogwood-twig brushes to do the fine detail
work, it was a slower job than the flat surfaces of the nursery, but
we finished it to our satisfaction before my mother and Annie
Deane returned from the station, loaded down with the marketing baskets and their many purchases.

A year or two later we were being entertained by Poultney
Bigelow on a North German Lloyd steamer. Mr. Bigelow
had been regaling us all morning with anecdotes of all the
naughty things he and Kaiser William had done together as children.

He asked: "And how many times have you boys been
whipped?"

Francis looked at me. I looked at Francis. With the above
house-painting episode perhaps in mind, and exaggerating somewhat for the honor of the family:

"Five times," Francis said with a soldierly air and he drew
himself to attention.

"Mercy," Mr. Bigelow murmured. "At your age I had been whipped twenty-eight times — with a horse whip."

Whenever I could I got down into the cellar of the Ardmore house. It was a place of mystery like the attic at Grandmother Robinson's. There were the great zinc wash tubs with running water, the wine closets and the coalbin, through which the cat could always escape to safety when I chased it down the cellar steps with Fangs. In the center was the furnace with its complicated system of vents, air boxes and pipes, that crisscrossed about the cobwebbed ceiling. I liked to pry open the furnace door. Sometimes the coals were fused in red-white shimmering heat. Sometimes the tiniest tongues of fire licked their way between the coals.

One day I found a box of sawdust near the furnace and threw a handful on the flames. The sawdust flared up so prettily and then sighed itself away to nothingness. Here was a new game. I quenched out all the little flames with sawdust, flinging it in feverishly, handful after handful. I had the whole inside of the furnace banked two inches deep by now, and just to give myself a dare, stuck my head in for a minute. When the explosion occurred I was standing about three feet away. It shook the whole house and tore the cast-iron gate from its hinges. It burnt my eyebrows off clean and my eyelashes and hair. My clothes were singed to the knees. I did the one thing I shouldn't have. I ran to the wash tubs and plunged my head and hands into the cold water. By that time everyone in the house was in the cellar. They seemed glad to find me alive. Dandy and the dogcart were dispatched after Dr. Gerhard, who soon arrived in his break. He was a brisk, efficient little man, drove a single-footer or pacer and looked very much like Lloyd George. He said as long as I wasn't blind there was nothing much to worry about, just as on a former occasion he had dismissed Charles with the remark that it was mighty lucky for both of us that he hadn't sat down half an inch more to one side. When Francis swallowed the shoe-button and one-cent piece, he said it was mighty lucky it hadn't been an English penny. I don't know what he said to Geoff when he came back from Atlantic City with samples of the fifty-seven varieties in his stomach. I suppose it was that it was a mighty lucky thing Heinz didn't manufacture a hundred.

I was in bed for about a month. The backs of my hands rose up first and looked like overdone, charred soufflés. My face came off in patches, here and there at different intervals. The first week was bad as I had to lie with my eyes closed and various sorts of poultices over me, olive oil, vaseline, ice bags. After that it was a long and shining holiday. Aunt Lydia gave me a box of oil paints and my mother bought me Holland's *Butterfly Book*. I was up to my ears then in entomology and ornithology and alternated chapters from Holland's beautiful book and the *Birds of Pennsylvania*. When I went back to school I had to wear some sort of a cloth mask for a month or so and my wrists showed the scars for about ten years.

Francis and I rode all over the country on the ponies. Fangs, John Bull and Jimmy Biddle, the water spaniel, accompanied us. I trained Fangs to dig out field mice, to retrieve small game and to tree cats. He broke the backs of several, catching them on the run before they reached their tree, and I was very proud of him. Fangs and Jimmy Biddle both lived to a ripe age. John Bull had a rather sinister ending. One day he swallowed a toad and soon went about shaking his head, slobbering, frothing at the mouth. We tied him up. Everyone said he was getting rabies. Jenks the Slopman, who had pigs, and who lived near the foot of our avenue and drove up every day to empty our small slop can into one of his great ones, said nonsense, John Bull was all right. We didn't give him enough to eat. That was all the trouble. He took him away and tied him up and fed him raw meat and slops. A week later John Bull almost bit his hand off and they shot him.

On Lancaster and Montgomery Pikes we would edge very

quietly up to the toll houses, and the tollkeepers who sat inside reading newspapers would not notice us. A few yards from the gates we would dig our heels into the ponies, stand up in the stirrups and charge by, shouting: "We skip the toll gate every time!" Eventually my mother would get the bill. It was two or three cents per horse depending on the distance from the preceding toll gate.

Francis and I had lead soldiers. We got most of them at a penny a box in a little dry-goods store on the corner of the Pike and Ardmore Avenue. We had names for all of them, every soldier in the two armies. The generalissimo of Francis' army was Sir Richard of Longsword. Another notable was Sir George of Howeland, whom he had traded in from George Howe for a set of twelve different matchsticks. The leader of my outfit was Sir Olaf of Cedarwood. Our men went through a rather Spartan training before they were conceded any real distinction. We would partially burn them over candles, throw them into snow-drifts to be rescued after the spring thaws, or subject them to some other toughening experience. There was almost nothing left of Sir Olaf. A bit of one thigh, which I soldered to a new leaden charger.

We went into all this with some elaboration. Francis wrote Sir Richard a thirty-four–verse epic, commemorating his exploits as a young man. I find in an old notebook, sandwiched in be-tween two lyrics entitled "Spring" and "Fighting for Liberty," and dated May 26, 1897, the beginning of an Odyssey of "Olaf of Cedarwood, Part I" (in red ink). The third verse (in black ink) I quote, not so much as a thing of any great distinction, but rather as an index of the sort of poetry which apparently children aspired to in May, 1897.

> Remembretht thou the first Iquarub,
> And thine horse Ibantinub?
> A! thou wert born in rough Balcinia,
> Not to befriend but fight the cub!

We invented of course new religions, monetary systems, maps, wars and Nordic aspirations for our heroes. We were somewhat anticipating a similar but less innocent infantilism, which was to a great extent to engage the fantasy of Europe some forty years later.

We began to identify ourselves with our heroes. We had been reading *Robin Hood*. I carved a whole series of hand-chiseled wooden daggers. We cut ourselves hickory and ironwood staves and practised whole mornings rushing at one another, shouting: "Have at you!" Francis appropriated Geoff, who was about five years old, as his "squeer." The squeer was supposed to hold Francis' stirrup when he mounted Dandy, and carry a couple of extra ironwood stakes in case of accident.

We debated some more dramatic pursuit than bloodying each other's knuckles. Francis suggested witch hunting. There were four categories of witches, malevolent and terrifying in progressive order. I can only recall three. The stone witches were the lowest and least significant. They disguised themselves as pebbles and lodged in the ponies' feet, between the frog and the shoe. Their aim, of course, was to throw the ponies, or cause them to stumble and give us a spill on a macadam pike. They never threw us on the soft red dirt roads.

Far more resourceful and ruthless were the corn witches. They could disguise themselves exactly like human beings, like Sir Richard or Sir Olaf. But they could never get rid of their corn-silk mustaches. If a corn witch had his back turned, he looked just like one of us, quite harmless. Then he would whisk about and you saw the horrible tawny, red-tipped, drooping mustache, the ferocious leer, the blood-shot eye, the bared fang.

The three of us went hunting corn witches together. Sir Richard and I crept ahead, crawling cautiously between the tall rows of horse corn on Farmer Grimes's property. The squeer panted behind carrying extra hardwood staves and wooden daggers; and praying to his "huckey" stone which we had given him as a talisman and which he carried, sewed in a little flannel bag, about his neck.

The ripe horse corn waved high above our heads and the August sun sucked the hot rich smells from the Pennsylvania cornfields.

When we had got deep into the field, Sir Richard and Sir Olaf plunged forward. A corn witch had been startled up and the pursuers were after their quarry. We ran, zigzagged and double-tracked. In no time the terrified squeer was left behind, turning this way and that, encumbered with his ironwood staves. He knew he was done for.

We would come back then, taking our time, fastening on our corn-silk mustaches. The squeer was too terrified to run and mumbled prayers to his huckey stone. We led him out of the corn, into the woods, tied him to a tree and started building a fire, reminiscing the while.

"You certainly strangled Sir Olaf between finger and thumb, brother."

"Ah yes! Ah yes! It was great sport. And I fairly laughed my insides out when you had Sir Richard wriggling about on the tip of your spit."

"What wiry old birds! They would surely have been tough eating. All skin and bones and gristle."

"Yes, brother, I always says: 'Eat 'em young and eat 'em tender.'"

This would go on for a while until we thought the squeer had taken enough punishment.

"Listen, brother! Ha! I hear sounds! Someone is approaching!! Quick! Be off!! We're done for!!!"

The corn witches would plunge off through the thorns and spicebush. And a moment later we charged in: "A la rescousse! A la rescousse!" We untied the squeer and he would help us pick up the witches' trail through the broken spicebush. He was proud and grateful and we surely had great times together.

(23)

An American Artist's Story

Wood witches were another matter. Less obvious in their approach and harder to assault in frontal attack, since they protected themselves through spells and incantations. They, too, could disguise themselves — but exactly — like humans. Not even the tell-tale mustaches. There was just one possible give-away, the faintest, most subtle, intangible bit of evidence for all the lurking danger. They could never quite control a certain well-known tendency of witches to tremble. So there was always a slight nervous tic, a certain unsteadiness of the hand, the quivering of an eyelid. As everyone knew, they wormed their way into a household, and over a period of time would poison everything with their foul stinking presence.

About that time Nana was paying my mother her yearly visit. She must have been nearly eighty. In the evenings she would read to us one of Andrew Lang's Red, Green, Yellow or Blue Fairy Books. The squeer would pull out his huckey stone and begin to mumble his prayers to it. Annie Deane grew suspicious. Then one weekend Francis Boyer, who was about the squeer's age, came over from Norristown. All afternoon we had a grand witch hunt — corn witches of course and perhaps a stone witch or two, small game thrown in. Francis Boyer didn't stand the strain so well. He got hysterics undressing, threshed about a good deal in his crib, and shouted in the night. The cat was out of the bag. Francis Biddle and I promised solemnly to organize some new activity for Sir Olaf and Sir Richard.

It would perhaps be unfair to say that my mother disliked children. Sometimes she might give that impression. I think she liked them homeopathically, in small and infrequent doses. She had an excellent palate for wine, and enjoyed her wine in much the same manner. She was fastidious and frugal. Half a glass of old Madeira once in a fortnight. With her children, metaphorically, she was forced to consume gallons and gallons of half-fermented cheap red ink, a lot of which was always spilling over her dresses. She would have preferred to imagine her relations with us like those of a lovely gardener with her rosebushes. Straw-bonneted and blue-ribboned, she gathers her dainty basket and garden scissors, and occasionally toward sundown strolls to the rose beds and snips off a basketful of tender blossoms, trimming away, here a dead leaf, there a faded bud; she returns to the terrace, empties them all about her and then leisurely arranges them in tall vases of majolica. Among her rare papers — for she destroyed most of them — is the following from Cousin Jeff Taylor to Uncle Beverley, her brother:

> St. James' Rectory,
> Accomac, Virginia.
> December 7th, 1911.

My dear Bev:

Your letter of yesterday . . . came to me this morning.

She is a dear indeed, and I cannot express to you how touched I am.

It is now just seventeen years ago since I spent the night with her at Ardmore. Then her boys were all, except her youngest perhaps, going to school or college, and she, another Cornelia, watching over her jewels. If she were a man, I would say she was the most knightly one I ever knew. I see her now as she sat in her sitting room before a suit of old armor that hung on the chimney piece, and the scene recalled to me the stories about young knights watching their armor, the eve before they were dubbed knights. She seemed watching the armor for them until one by one they should, each, take her place. God bless her and give her the comfort in them that she deserves.

> Yours faithfully
> JEFF.

This was by no means an unusual tribute to the effect that my mother produced on those who admired her. It is comforting, too, already in 1894 to have impressed a Virginia clergyman as a jewel and a knight without armor.

We grew and blossomed, much influenced by the directive intent of Mother's calculations and enthusiasms, but quite strictly alone in each other's company. Our personalities expanded in inverse ratio to the pruning and cultivation of our manners.

Something was done, however, about our social obligations apart from the mere necessity of governess or tutor. Occasionally the four Biddle girl cousins were used, like wooden duck decoys to lure us back into a deportment of gentility. We viewed them with curiosity mingled with suspicion. And too often our fears were justified. Events that began auspiciously ended in cloudbursts. One such Sunday visit was the occasion of a feast the memory of which still leaves my glands dripping. Rich oyster soup, speckled with tiny pink crabs; rare roast beef, all dressed in golden crisp, girded with baked potatoes and Yorkshire pudding; tomato pudding sweetened and toasted brown; corn soufflé, slithery okras, rich cakes of rice or hominy; and to cap all a huge dish of "nigger in his shirt," chocolate cornstarch pudding floating in whipped cream. Conversation lagged and we sawed our grinders to good intent. One fixed idea burned in eight breasts. Sixteen jaws were pumping in noisy unison. There was after all a bottom to every dessert bowl of happiness. I worked less noisily but more smoothly than Francis and never wasted a moment. I finished my helping first and shoved my plate silently across to my mother for a second. She took the empty dessert bowl and firmly planted it in front of me. I was too humiliated to speak, nor had I an explosive nature. I suffered a concentration of shame and misery. I bowed my head for a moment, stifled every emotion and then looked about me in dumb suffering. I saw nothing but the crowns of seven heads bent low over the seven plates of what remained of that magnifi-

cent dish. Like a trapped animal I watched and waited. Francis
was the next to lick his plate clean. With the same arm flex with
which he laid down his spoon, and without looking up, he too
slid his plate across to my mother. She reached over, seized the
empty dessert bowl and set it this time in front of Francis. He
gave a startled cry. The four Biddle girls looked up in inquiry.
He let out one loud bellow of rage and disappointment. I
breathed a sigh of relief.

Then and for many subsequent years I cared nothing for
honor, much for appearances.

My motives were usually delicate. My manners were less so.
Moncure, in the role of the elder brother, often admonished and
occasionally prayed for me. He has kept this up for some forty-
five years with, I am afraid, a growing sense of disillusion,
amounting sometimes to bitterness.

Annie Deane used to superintend the ritual of our undressing
and evening prayers. She began by reading to us from *The Back
of the North Wind* or *Mopsie the Fairy*. She ended up by
coaxing, wheedling and threatening Moncure with the Fire
Department. Her technique was a good deal that of a Texan
horse wrangler. First at one and then at another, keeping her
weather eye on the whole outfit. Whoever undressed first
had the privilege of saying his prayers to her. They were a routine affair: Lord's Prayer, Now-I-lay-me-down-to-sleep-I-pray-
the-Lord-my-soul-to-keep stuff, with rare innovations; and ending up all in one breath: "God bless Father and Mother and
little brothers and make George Francis Moncure and Geoff
and Annie and my Nana good boys for Jesus Christ sake
Amen."

One evening I must have been particularly gross in the preparation of my evening toilet. Perhaps Moncure had been smoul-
dering over me for weeks. He undressed rapidly and hurried over
to Annie Deane. When he came to the "And make George

Francis Moncure and Geoff and Annie and my Nana good boys," there was an ominous pause.

"And especially George," he added.

I asked: "What's he praying for me for, Annie?"

"Because, George, you are so bold for Jesus Christ sake Amen."

Certain rich, subtle characters can be presented as clear-cut profiles. There are others, however, of whom an exact simulacrum can never be made. My mother was such a person, many-sided and many-faceted: irrational, unexpected, volatile, vaporish; and upon other occasions just the reverse, being dominant, purposeful, high-minded and high-moraled, undeviating and single-tracked. I conceive of her more as a tremendous flow of energy; generated, as energy is from positive and negative poles, perhaps from many opposing forces, currents, sources, placed in the frame of her social, physical, economic, chronologic environment; and then bursting, exploding, as waves of energy will, upon the rocks, the reefs, into the dreary shallows, through the occasional channels, over the precipices, the cataracts of life.

One is not apt to think of or describe in terms of energy, dynamics, or explosions, a woman who spent much of her life in bed or reclining with closed eyes upon a chaise longue; who conceived of herself as a chronic invalid; and who seemed in a physical sense to possess so little vitality and resilience that her greatest problem in life often became an effort to guard herself against any act which would emotionally drain her; such as a human relation, the display of any warmth of feeling, the reviving of a memory, even the overt participation in the emotions of another; and to guard herself equally against all the physical impingements of life, the presence of children in the room, the household administration, the need of social contacts and the preparation of herself for such social contacts; even, eventually, the retention of her own possessions. All such contacts, emo-

(28)

tional and physical, seemed so completely to drain my mother that she grew more and more to avoid them, cutting herself off almost completely from life itself, until she seemed as if suspended in the vacuum of her own emotions. Yet from this vacuum she continued, almost until the day she died, to scheme, to protect, to direct, to thwart, to untangle — in as far as they affected her children — the threads of destiny. Until the end her motions and gestures seemed as fresh and energetic as a young woman's; her emotions welled up as overflowingly; her handwriting was as round and firm, close, rather heavy, deliberate; up-trailing in energy, optimism and vitality — the handwriting of an active, energized business administrator, never that of an invalid or of a neurotic.

The last letter which I had from her, dated two days before her eightieth birthday, and consequently a fortnight or so before her death, was dictated; and mentioned the fact that she felt too ill to write herself. She continued:

Will you please let me know soon the unpaid balance of your mortgage. I would like to pay it.

Your very loving M.

Then in her own penciled hand, beginning with the slightest hesitancy but ending up round and firm and up-trailing as ever:

I don't believe I shall have so much longer — so please write soon. Dear George. Love. M. I suppose you got the 2000 for wh I have the receipts.

FRANCES BIDDLE.

That short scrawl, the final purposeful, protective burst of energy, was the symbol of her life's intent, the alpha and omega, the only final justification, which my mother could have proffered for whatever reward we four boys might lay at her feet.

I often wondered if destiny had intended her to be solely and so completely a mother. If so destiny had ill-equipped her for

the task. I rather think that by some curious chemical transformation her more general and specific interests, affections and
loves were sublimated and fused by my father's death into one
driving passion, the upbringing and education of her four
children.

At the very end, at that last pagan ritual, when the coffin
glided down the shaft, with the slow inevitable motion of a ship
gliding off its ways into the unknown, her only remaining sister,
my dear Aunt Nathalie, stood beside me. They had long been
separated and had come together during the few happy years
that preceded her death.

"Often I felt I did not understand your mother. Nor did any
of us. Some things about her now I understand. She knew — and
none of us ever quite realized she knew — that after your father's
death she could never again be happy, never again have peace,
never again rest, until she achieved this moment. All her life she
was waiting to die, yet could not die, until she had done with
you all what she felt he would have wanted."

Grandfather Robinson was an old man when the Civil War
broke out, too old at least to fight; but my mother was already
old enough to help cut up the lint and tie it in packages to send
to the Confederate wounded. Her older brother John fought for
the South and ran the blockade to England. Her older brothers
Edmund and Beverley fought for the North, Beverley not so
long out of college. She was too young to remember much about
it all. She did remember, however, that a salesgirl in John
Wanamaker's store had radiantly announced to Grandmother
the news of Lee's surrender at Appomattox; and that Grandmother had loudly denied it and sworn up and down that she
would never again enter John Wanamaker's as long as she lived
— which she never did.

My mother grew up in a large family — eight of them. Two
more had died in infancy. Her sister Agnes was a generation

older. So were some of the others. But there were four of them of an approximate vintage, Moncure, Charley, my mother and Aunt Nathalie. Grandmother adored and spoiled them. Grandfather seems to have been too old to exert much discipline. I have a feeling he spoiled my mother, too, being proudest of her. She was beautiful and spirited and clever. Her upbringing was chaotic. There was no regular schooling, no disciplined routine. Uncle Moncure had unusual gifts but he suffered from weak eyes. Grandfather persuaded him to throw up his studies and gave him horses to keep him out of mischief. Before he was twenty he was a gentleman jockey in the hardest-drinking crowd in America, and had ridden and won steeplechase races in Philadelphia and Baltimore. What my mother knew never came from schooling. She was made much of by Mrs. Owen Jones Wister, who was a daughter of Fanny Kemble; and before her coming out into society was taken abroad by Agnes Irwin, who was a great educator, a profound mind and a forceful personality. Later she was to become Dean of Radcliffe.

In Paris Miss Irwin introduced Father to my mother. He was quite different from what she had known in her own turbulent household. The origin of the one family was tide-water Virginian and of the other Quaker. Father read Horace in the original. Grandfather Biddle had translated and published "The Orations on the Crown" of Æschines and Demosthenes. Grandfather Robinson was an engineer and a railroad man. Grandfather Biddle was a classical scholar, a lawyer of the old school and for years the leader of the Philadelphia Bar. George Wharton Pepper and, over a course of years, some fifty other young law students read Blackstone in his office. He was a Democrat and a States' Rights man and consequently during the early years of the Civil War had been in distinctly bad odor, but when Lee invaded Pennsylvania he clashed with Grandfather's States' Rights principles. So the latter quit his law and his Greek translations and enlisted in a volunteer regiment. His children were

(31)

too young to fight but his brother Chapman distinguished himself as Colonel of a Pennsylvania regiment at the Battle of Gettysburg.

Father was twelve years older than my mother and a brilliant young lawyer. Later he was to teach law, and through Dean Langdell of the Harvard Law School helped to introduce the "case system" at the University of Pennsylvania. One would like to think of him engaged in lighter preoccupations that summer. Surely he and Miss Irwin exchanged Latin quotations from Horace and French maxims from Montaigne, but perhaps he found occasion to initiate my mother into the charm of the Romantic School of German poetry. She told me subsequently that it was he who started her in her German studies. Perhaps he took her to the Louvre, or showed her the antiques he had picked up in Greece or the photographs of Millet and of Guido Reni. They wandered together through the pale pink harmonies of the Place des Vosges — the most Philadelphian bit of color in all of Paris. The Palais Royal of Napoleon had vanished nearly a decade before. *Trilby* was not to be written for another decade. But one had glimpses of Henri Murger's *Bohème*. Americans in Paris still read Victor Hugo and de Musset.

Ah, to meet in the lilac season and to fall in love in Paris!

Grandfather Biddle and Grandfather Robinson were the oldest and best of friends. They were delighted when they heard these rumors from Miss Irwin of their children's expeditions to the Louvre and of their incursions into German lyric poetry.

"Kennst du das Land, wo die Zitronen blühn?"

My mother told Father when she got back from Europe that she would have to come out first and then wait a year before she made up her mind. They were married on the twenty-eighth of June, 1879, at St. Mark's Church in Philadelphia. She went straight home after the ceremony, locked herself in her room and stayed in bed for a week.

If for the next ten years or so she was secure in her happiness and the path she had chosen, it would not be denying the fact that often she led Father a hell of a life. She might be asked to serve as Patroness to the Philadelphia Assembly, and at the last moment refuse to attend. Philadelphia society could politely shudder and go hang. Father might invite some friends a week in advance to dinner. My mother might or might not decide to come down, or just stay in bed. If through perverse and fickle obstinacy she could at the last moment have refused to participate in the births of her own sons I am sure she would have done so. While Father was alive such caprice was made possible by his own forethought or patience, and the solid regularity of his income. When properly bulwarked and safeguarded by a plentiful background of nurses and domestic comfort, the most dutiful mother can afford many gestures of wantonness or irresponsibility. What matter, then, if the parents were away for a winter in Switzerland, off for the summer to the North Shore. Father could anchor his happiness in the knowledge that under the squalls and whitecaps were unplumbed depths of loyalty, love and integrity. My mother could afford such elfin whims as her fancy indulged in, secure in the boundless faith and protection that was lavished on her. Father must have been often sorely tried. They were deeply and completely happy.

With his death every prop that sustained happiness was kicked from under. There was indeed but one prop that sustained the will to live at all. She had four small sons and a slender income, just enough if properly parceled out to pay for everything that four boys' education called for. There would be nothing left over to pay for her own desires. She had no desires. She was dead to life. She was thirty-three years old that spring.

For years my mother dressed in black and wore a long mourning veil. She never mentioned Father's name without the tears immediately welling to her eyes. I never mentioned Father's name to anyone without a deep feeling of abasement and self-pity. Years later a school friend said to me, "My father is a doctor.

What's yours?" "He's a lawyer," I said. Perhaps I was actually ashamed of his death. Perhaps I had been conditioned to feel that a reference to him was too great an evocation of sorrow. In my forty-second year I grew a beard. I had not seen my mother for a year or more. When, on a visit to her in Chestnut Hill, I entered her bedroom, she burst into a flood of tears. It made me rather angry. Several years later she said to me: "You reminded me of your father." She had not had the courage to say so at the time. The day after Father died my mother asked Cecilia Beaux to make a drawing of him. Aunt Nathalie who was in the house arranged matters. While Cecilia Beaux worked my mother paced up and down the room below. For over forty years she never mentioned this to Aunt Nathalie or ever once mentioned my father's name to her. My mother showed me Cecilia Beaux's drawing once and asked me what she should do with it. I begged her to leave it to me, although it was not a fine drawing. She promised to do so but later destroyed it.

Once during these early years she copied into a notebook the following:

If I should never see you again promise me in yr heart that you will not relapse again into slothful slumber, that you will look and listen; face the real light of day, make part of the . . . band of labourers . . . collect the harvest . . . plentiful always to those who do not dream life away.

My mother aroused a feeling of pure idolatry in the hearts of older women, such as Mrs. Gillespie, Agnes Irwin, Mrs. Owen Jones Wister or Bishop Potter's daughter, Clara Davidge — in the last case a contemporary. They worshiped her and their love and fulsome tribute were perhaps a mild substitute for the admiration which she steadfastly refused to exact from men. She must have had admirers. How could she not? My fancy likes to play with the possibility that Henry James was one of them. He had met her in 1910 at a house party at Butler Place. Mrs.

Wister was a bluestocking and took a certain pride in keeping abreast of the current French drama. Her mind was bold and ardent but her moral standards stuck like a balking horse before many a current French idiom. Salacious innuendos and bawdy words threatened to terminate her intimacy with contemporary French literature. My mother, however, belonged to a younger and tougher generation and when intellectually stirred she stopped at nothing. She undertook then literally with a stroke of the pen to shield Mrs. Wister's moral susceptibilities during her digressions into French literature. She read the plays in advance, buttressed up with a dictionary of slang, and underscored whatever obscenities she felt over-ripe for Mrs. Wister's palate.

During the house party in question Henry James had sauntered down ahead of the other guests, and fingering through the various yellow paper volumes on the withdrawing-room table, had come across several comedies, heavily underlined, which seemed much to his fancy. He was deep in one of them when Mrs. Wister came in and presented him to my mother, serious-minded and excited by the prospect of such an encounter.

"And who is it," smiled the great man to Mrs. Wister, "who has been annotating your plays with such literary understanding?"

"Oh," said Mrs. Wister, who was somewhat confused about the method of my mother's editing, "Fanny Biddle has been marking her favorite passages for me to glance through."

This introduction, which he beautifully felt must be met full on without the shadow of a smile or mental deflection, might question the particular epithet of all others which my mother insisted was the one he used in describing her. He had subsequently called her the most elusive — the only elusive — woman he had ever met in America.

It would seem indeed that the impression she made upon him was lastingly vivid in his perception of the impalpable. So one gathers from a letter by their mutual friend, Clara Potter Davidge.

62 Washington Square
April 26

MY DARLING FANNY:

I was in the drawing room just now, just after some friends had gone, when out of the Lord's open, in walks Mr. Henry James. He came to see Mrs. Elliott in the top of the house, and was shown into my drawing room, while he sent up a message. So I just told him I was not a bit of harm, and offered him tea, and told him of my thread-like feeling of a tie to his brother, and we began right in the middle. Of course I said at once that I had been so glad for you, who I so loved, to have had the pleasure of that stay this year at Mrs. Wister's. He disclaimed at once all power of giving pleasure to you, but he began instantly to talk about you. I must have given him some sense of confidence, or else of love for you, for he said you were the "most elusive" of all creatures, and that while you made it so impossible for any exact touch to be laid upon you, you yourself were not a participant in this elusiveness.

These are not the exact words — am not used to his rush of words of course. I said yes, but you were utterly unconscious, and then he said practically that that was what he had already just said of you. Of course then I had to tell him what you were to me, and why, and really we only had seven minutes, but when Mrs. Elliott sent for him he said, "Goodbye for the present" and I did not really love him a bit; only I *adored* that he had so loved you, and I write you this because you would hate me to be a discredit to you, and I so hope I was not.

He wanted to know about the boys and I told him how they were Heaven's own imps, and how wonderful; and he said he could not think of commonplace boys with you at all. I wonder he could even think the words. I never thanked you for your note about Uncle's death. Such a life as now! I will try and write of it.

C. S. D.

Clara Davidge was a born friend, missionary, zealot and re-former. Her father was Bishop of New York State. She once bought an old farm on Staten Island. It had a pirate's chest in it, she told me. Here she collected, fed, clothed, and supported over a period of years a heterogeneous lot of reconstructed alco-holics, artists and poets. One of them was Edwin Arlington Robinson. Another was a future husband of hers, who swore off hard liquor to take up painting where he had left it many years before. She and he later had much to do with the organization of the Armory Show of 1913. It is a pity she spent so little time in correspondence.

My mother drew much comfort and approbation from the affection of these two or three older women who idolized her. But for forty-five years in every great undertaking, upon every slightest contingency, through *sturm und drang,* when the weather was ominous with electric tension, or on those rare days when the sky was serene, she depended absolutely on the firm-ness, the tact and the loyalty of Annie Deane, her lean and diminutive Sancho Panza. Annie became her nursery-governess, housekeeper, general advisor, the spillway of her gusts and eddies, her moral comforter and confessor, her chief of staff, her official spokesman and her Colonel House. She was accepted before Father's death as one of the family, and her social and political stature grew throughout the years. Not only did she become an authority among our aunts, uncles and relatives upon matters of pedagogy and education, but she grew to be the arbiter of many questions of social taste or moral standards.

(37)

Scotch-Irish, raised in Canada, she inherited certain conservative old-world traditions. Staunchly Church of England, she was soaked with religious hypocrisy; and of all the human beings I have ever known, she was the stoutest, the most brazen and incorruptible snob. Religion with her was not so much a solace or even a threat as a splendid ritual of social stability. She was never really shocked by our own militant agnosticism or by the occasional robustness of our language. On the contrary these qualities in us became, antiphonally, as it were, the confirmation of her own grace. Human and understanding as any Jesuit, she took much solid comfort in eavesdropping on the other side of the bathroom partition, late at night, as we exchanged confidences. Such droppings as she gleaned she would store away in the recesses of her memory, not for any idle or prurient end, but to be used for godly purpose, brought forth at the ordained time in the long and arduous task of rearing us. She was seldom exposed for she had a tread as padded as a jungle beast, and when we occasionally caught her spying a proper show of anger and burning cheeks always set her up in the light of her own standards.

Her snobbism was in part a national inheritance and was therefore complicated in its old-world ritual. She insisted from the beginning that her position was that of a "nursery-governess." She realized that without a knowledge of languages and music, and shorn of the tag of "*Fraulein*" or "Miss," she could not rate strictly as governess; yet she was firm in her insistence that she was not a nurse. She used the front stairs although she had access to the back. Much of her day was spent in the kitchen, but she took her frugal meals alone on the edge of her bedroom sewing machine. She called the servants by their first name but below the nursery she was Miss Deane. To my mother and to us boys and indeed to all our relatives she was Annie, but this intimacy implied the familiarity of a social tie rather than any social condescension. She was not accordingly driven to the church on Ardmore Avenue at an early hour with the rest of the domestics. Dressed in resounding lavender silk and with the expression of a Roman cardinal, she walked abreast of my mother through the College woods to service at the Haverford Church. As we neared the worshipers chatting in groups on the church lawn, she would draw somewhat apart, eyes on the ground, and wait until we had entered. Then she would slowly glide in, like a ship to its mooring; and come to anchor among the rear pews, where she followed loudly in the responses. With an eagle eye for any petticoat that trailed half an inch below a dress, she would garner up any succulent bit she felt worthy to retrieve for my mother's inspection. When the service was over she would mingle easily with those domestics she had met from other houses. Although she had few intimates she possessed a vast acquaintance which she adroitly tapped when in need of information.

Annie Deane, or Miss Deane — in whichever role one chooses to evoke her — was Victorian to the very marrow of her whalebones. On the one or two occasions in her life when she was confronted in me with what she felt was the spirit of evil, she was not so much angered or sorrowed as, literally, almost choked to death. She was aware of evil, and wallowed, good Calvinist that she was, in its acceptance; but when she actually faced it, it just would not go down, and stuck in her throat until she nearly strangled. She was singularly human — too much so for our own comfort — for her suspicion was boundless and she had a nose keener than any setter's.

The following confidence, which seems even more of an explosion today, may serve as a partial explanation or hint of her Calvinistic suppressions. She was living in a world of sin and must flee from it in her frailty where she could not face it in her strength. Of what the occasion was I have only the dimmest memory.

"George," she said in answer to, or in mitigation of, some murmuring wail of self-pity in the darkness of my bedroom, and bending over me, herself too dry for any tear to glisten, "George, I too have a husband."

She had married him years and years ago when she was an innocent child. I have forgotten what he did, beat her up, got lousy drunk, took a woman. But she realized — like that — that she was cohabiting with the spirit of evil. So she rose up and left him; and had never heard from him since, and knew not his whereabouts. I promised in the dark to keep her secret. It bound us closer. To this moment I have never divulged it.

One year I attended a small Quaker school. Richard Gummere, eldest son of the great scholar of medieval literature, was the star of the school, just as his father was the shining light of the College. I remember the awe with which I saw him spell out in large block letters and then read aloud to the class: "Mr. Sharpless [the College President] has a Fine White Horse." It was my initiation into the magic of Prose and Literature. From Richard's brother, Sam, I picked up words of humbler origin. On my return from school one day, when Annie Deane reproved me for urinating on the front-door steps and bade me come into the house, I told her the hell I would, she was a God damn dirty bugger. Years later during a course of criminal law at the Harvard Law School I learned that this latter "low term of disparagement" derives from the name of "a most heinous crime practised by the ancient Lombards; and tracing its source from the Latin *Bulgarus*, which means Bulgarian, and then later a heretic, from a sect of heretics in Bulgaria in the eleventh century, to whom abominable practices were imputed; Bulgaria, Buggaria, or buggery being coitus *per anum* or with an animal other than a swan or goose." Of all this my mother said nothing, but she took me on her knee and explained to me gently and reverently that when I "God damned" Annie Deane I was asking the Almighty for her eternal and everlasting condemnation and punishment through hell's fires.

As we grew older and were shunted off to boarding-school or

college Annie Deane could feel her absolutely delegated authority diminish. She maintained, however, and at times even increased her sense of power through devious channels and acts of espionage. She was aware of my mother's suppressed jealousy of any young debutante who rivaled her in her sons' affection. And so on the none too frequent occasions when the candles were lighted, the sherry decanted and the invited guests had left the bedroom where they had laid their wraps and galoshes, she would slowly go through the articles of clothing with her long setter's nose; and could afterwards tell to a nicety just what garment needed repair, had been done over or had an unpleasant body odor. Of all the guests that entered our house over a period of fifteen years or so, there were but two that Annie Deane conceded to be young ladies. Miss Anna Ingersoll was one. I have forgotten the other.

Her scouting trips and covert information did occasionally more than fix my mother's prejudices. That winter a certain one of the four boys had supposedly become engaged to a lady, who, from the point of view of my mother and Annie Deane, might, if the match were consummated, not so much wreck that brother's happiness as retard his development. But this time my mother could not be roused to any action. She simply refused to envisage the possibility of such a development and double-locked herself in her bedroom, deaf to Annie's importunities. Annie, seeing that proof was needed, proceeded swiftly and deftly through the trunks, bureau drawers, valises, pockets and receptacles of the brother in question, and emerged therefrom with every sort of condemning evidence. With these various papers and tokens she returned to my mother's bedroom, knocked deferentially at the door and imparted to her the findings. My mother was very indignant, and shouted back that this underhand espionage was shocking and dishonorable; and that she would have nothing to do with it. She said: "Go away." Her back hurt her.

Annie Deane got down on her knees and shoved the evidence, letter by letter, underneath the bedroom door and then retired to her own quarters. The result was that an hour later a family conclave was summoned to my mother's side; certain of us were told that something had to be done immediately for the happiness not only of this brother but of the poor girl in question. It was suggested that they should take the first train to New York, hunt up the lady in her hotel, or there wait for her; and persuade her by every means possible that this young man was not fit either to support her, to marry her or to bring her happiness.

Such tactical triumphs Annie Deane accepted with deference, never alluding to any participation she might have had, retiring with bowed head to the depths of her humility, yet ever thereby increasing in the sure knowledge of her power.

Our friendship, which had grown so strong through mutual respect and affection, was shattered some twenty years later on what I believe was to each of us a moral principle. Annie would concede no compromise in me with the spirit of Satan and Adultery. I, having lived for years away from home, insisted on a strict convention of noninterference with my freedom. I had engaged that summer a lovely model, who of necessity frequented our summer rented cottage, although, for propriety's sake, she was lodged in a nearby boardinghouse. Annie Deane had immediately wormed herself into the intimacy of this charming but babbling young person, and at the end of a fortnight knew everything of her that one lady is apt to tell to another. If the model and I had many strong drinks together in my studio late of a Saturday night, Annie Deane would be the first to know it the next morning, for she always drove the young person to Sunday worship. This really sweet-dispositioned and generous child had a certain propensity, a psychic twist, a weakness for all sorts of harmless exaggerations. From various cronies and gossips of Annie Deane's rumors began to drift in that my young collaborator was affianced to me, that she could not quite make up her mind, that she refused to say yes until my divorce was definitely granted. All this gossip stirred Annie's sleuthlike instincts. Like a bloodhound she was on the scent, and would dog our steps, pry open confidences and follow us at night from the studio to the rustling gloom of the garden shrubbery. Here, one all too moonlight evening, she witnessed what made her choke and strangle.

Next day she repaired to my mother and did then and thereafter during the length of the summer months menace, cajole, blackmail and browbeat that poor, harassed woman to take some punitive action. She threatened to write to my brother Moncure, as the head of the family; to write to my wife or to my father-in-law; to report me to the owner of our rented cottage. She was living under a roof of sin and cried shame on my mother who by her silence became an accessory in the collusion.

A fortnight before our return to New York my peace of mind was flooded with a burst of tears from my mother who told me with sobs that as a last threat Annie was to confront the model openly with our corruption, God knows in what public place.

That night I faced Annie, mad enough to have shaken her, and, I am sure, threatened her physically. She stood up to me, however, the champion of the Lord's right, shaming me for the evil I had brought into my mother's home, thanking the God she prayed to that he had gathered my father to him before he might witness the depravity which had sprung from his loins, calling loudly that my years would be shortened in liquor and sin. She stood manfully to her guns, cursing me to the end. But my threats had some effect, for the model returned a fortnight later to New York, innocent of the passions which her gentle presence had engendered around her.

Once the danger was removed, I was only too anxious to be on peaceful terms again with Annie. She would have none of me, and always thereafter treated me as something unregenerate and a little vile. Several years later I came close to dying of a fever in the tropics. My mother wrote me that Annie Deane, having brooded over the news, had set to, as of old, to sew me a pair of flannel pyjamas. I knew then that at least I had been partially forgiven.

As a child I was shy and often shrank in real agony from the shame of a situation which existed largely in my own imagination, but which none the less to me was the cause of the deepest humiliation.

Once I swallowed thirteen prune stones with no physical after-effects — I have a perfect colon — but accompanied by acute moral suffering. I was visiting Mrs. E. Walter Clark at Chestnut Hill round Christmas time. The children of my age were out; but I sat and made conversation with Mrs. Clark, who in return plied me with a box of prunes. I was very partial to them and accepted them each time with a bow, swallowing the stones one by one, as I was too timid to ask for something in which to deposit them and I was convinced that voiding things from my mouth was not done in society.

"Just put your stones in this ashtray," she said at length.

I didn't say anything.

"George, what have you done with your prune stones?"

I didn't say anything.

She looked at me intently for a long time. I stared back at her, swelling with shame. At length I gathered the courage to say:

"My prunes didn't have any stones, Mrs. Clark."

She looked at me for a split second without any expression and we resumed our conversation.

Mrs. E. Walter Clark was a lady.

Mrs. Owen Jones Wister, a daughter of Fanny Kemble, was a great lady in her own right as well as by tradition, but, despite

HELENE

MICHAEL JOHN

the profusion of her gifts and the energy of her will to please, I never felt quite relaxed in her presence. She possessed a gracious dignity, a way of being always in the right, a smooth Athena-like brow which challenged my self-possession and at moments crushed me.

The day we first met remains in my memory a golden one. Dressed in some lovely flowing print gown, ribboned and bonneted, she had led us by the hand up the long avenue at Butler Place. A gate and a high brick wall shut out the lawn and shrubbery, the buildings, the stables and greenhouses, from the traffic and movement of the Old York Road. There was moss under the chestnuts and wistaria festooned the coachhouse. The lawn was broken with patches of periwinkle and starred with Quaker ladies. She had taken us to the gardens and given us our first smell of rose geranium and lemon verbena. There in the hothouses were real little orange and lemon trees, and grapevines and figs. Later her son Owen — Dan she called him, telling us over and over all the terrible, naughty things he had done at school and at college — took us to the stables where they were grooming a dapple-gray; and the cement floor was running from the hose; and the smell of ammonia mingled with the acrid smell of sweat and the rich musty odor of the horse stalls. Owen had asked us both if we liked music. We nodded back yes. And which was our favorite tune, he had asked us. Francis looked at me and I looked at Francis. There was a hurriedly whispered consultation. "Yankee Doodle" we both shouted together. He had pitched Francis into the air and caught him on his shoulders; and we had proceeded to the house, Francis clutching at his ears and wreathed in happiness. We drank raspberry vinegar with a sprig of mint and then Owen sat down at the piano and played and played to our hearts' content. And did we recognize the music, he smiled back to us. We certainly did not, but might one hazard a guess? I looked at Francis and Francis looked at me. By the other's expression each knew that consultation was hopeless. No we didn't recognize the tune, we said; what was it?

"Yankee Doodle"!

I had been given a new sixteen-bore shotgun. I was already at boarding-school in New England but the summers we still spent at Ardmore, and so this memory lingers with the Wister-Ardmore days rather than with the eleven years' death in New England. Mostly I shot English sparrows on the wing. They blackened the sky in flocks of hundreds, drumming like partridges in their short wheeling flights among the early stacked horse corn on Farmer Grimes's acres. Once I brought down a dozen at one shot. The fat from their corn diet spoiled their feathers when I tried to skin and mount them. But they were as tender as reed birds — New England bobolinks. I spitted them in the woods below the house and feasted on them. One day I shot a sparrow hawk and a little green heron — a shite-poke — on the wing. I was terribly proud and presented them to my mother. The next day was a Sunday. She suggested that I should take them over to show to Gammar at Butler Place on the Old York Road. Francis and I were scrubbed and curried and gotten up in a way that would have put little Lord Fauntleroy to shame. White sneakers, short white trousers, white shirts; red, white and black Groton belts, red, white and black Groton neckties, straw hats with red, white and black hatbands, and black leather kneecaps. How we ever ran the gauntlet of the Market Street muckers, from Broad Street station to the Reading Depot on Twelfth Street, God only knows. The whole day is one panic-stricken blur. Carefully wrapped in a basket I carried the disemboweled sparrow hawk and the shite-poke to lay at Gammar's feet. The great lady met us at the foot of her avenue. She would drive us to a restaurant in the neighborhood and there we should select our own menu, everything we never ate at home. She smiled at us graciously and we felt not at ease, but eager. At the restaurant all went well at first. We began with cantaloupe and raspberry vinegar. Then I said: "Broiled live lobster." Mrs. Owen Jones Wister raised her eyebrows. No, she couldn't do that. Did we know how they were prepared? They were kept for days and days on ice and then broiled alive over a slow flame. She belonged to the Society for the Prevention of Cruelty to Animals. She said it with the manner in which today she would have said: "I belong to the Society for the Preservation of Spanish Democracy." I felt then as I should feel now if I were to say in her presence: "I should like to eat a little Spanish baby." This is not irreverence. It was the way I felt. After that I would as soon have shown her the disemboweled sparrow hawk and the shite-poke as a little disemboweled baby. Everything — even the Philadelphia White Mountain cake — was lead within me. God knows I was grateful for her reticence when she put us on the train without any questions as to the contents of the straw basket.

I never really intended to be a naturalist. There was little purpose or direction back of my scientific excursions, but apart from stimulating an intimacy with nature, which still grows with the years, natural history had its lessons to teach, some burlesque and others cruel or beautiful to a degree fantastic. Nothing could ever quite rival the breath-taking miracle of the greater moths, the luna, the polyphemus and the Atticus cecropia, as they split through the chrysalis and emerged from the cocoon, weak and quivering in the rainbow shimmer of their radiance. I had many of them in boxes covered with gauze about my room. I could guess the hour of parturition to a nicety by the quivering of the chrysalis, the infinitely delicate cracking, ripping and tearing of the cocoon, the throbbing and convulsions of this resurrection into life of a thing long dead. It was as if the womb gave birth to the life of which it was a part; it was the living bird rising from dead ashes.

(47)

Once I hovered over a caterpillar, which had started to spin its cocoon. As the larva flung its head from side to side, as if manipulating a shuttle of fine silk, its back was suddenly alive with infinitesimal threadlike worms that jerked their way about, digging, wriggling, plunging from the living flesh of the caterpillar. The latter seemed sick unto death and swayed and curled up and hung, unable to shake off these tiny parasites. They in their turn were weaving their minute baskets, settling down to their long sleep, oblivious in their egotistic rapacity of the rent flesh which they had devoured. The ichneumon-fly had deposited its eggs by the score on the back of the caterpillar and the larvæ had emerged, fattened on their prey, ready to fulfill their destiny of sleep, concupiscence, procreation and death. Nothing hereafter in the struggle of life, on the battlefields of France, in the sadistic diabolism of Europe's petty monsters, filled me with as much horror as this little encounter with the ichneumon.

These and many other petty adventures — adventures with fire and water, with gun and knife, with horse, with dog, with bird or butterfly, with great lady, nursery-governess or witch — are the scattered and unrelated incidents, mishaps and hazards, insignificant and without pattern or principle, which, woven together in glowing tapestry of *mille fleurs*, form the saga, the background, the matrix of a growing child. It is not my purpose to draw from this tapestry of a thousand flowers — which to me are bright but which to another may lack odor and sparkle — some design or moral, or even some point of comparison. It is merely to present the not unusual background of a fairly normal boy of our generation.

Groton School
1898-1904

In any and all its forms, the boy detested school, and the prejudice became deeper with years. He always reckoned his school days, from ten to sixteen years old, as time thrown away.

The Education of Henry Adams [1]

I HAD had four happy years at Haverford School when it was decided, upon due consultation, that my education could be improved — intellectually, morally, physically, socially — by the benefits of a New England boarding-school. I had actually been withdrawn on account of delicate health from Haverford the previous spring, and was studying painting in Philadelphia with a young graduate of the Pennsylvania Academy. I rode in each morning to Overbrook, where I left Manners at a livery stable and did the rest of the trip by train. My mother felt that thus she was killing two birds with one stone. I got my daily stint of exercise, and my enforced vacation from school might be used to explore a possibly hidden talent. Father had apparently regretted at times not being an artist. My mother played with the thought that, if a serious profession would prove too much for my physique — which was always showing signs of cracking up — the career of a landscape painter was a thoroughly healthy one and an admittedly reputable calling.

Under this treatment my health improved and the following

[1] Houghton Mifflin Company.

autumn I was yanked away from my oil paints and lead soldiers, my shotgun, cricket bats, birds' eggs, butterflies, bicycles, fishing tackle, white mice, Belgian hares, stuffed birds, dogs and ponies, and sent up to the Reverend Endicott Peabody's school at Groton, Massachusetts, where my elder brother had already preceded me. Here I stayed for five years and another six at Harvard and the Harvard Law School. During those eleven years in New England I tried hard to conform to type, but always felt myself something of a stranger. I was ambitious and wanted to measure up to standard. Certainly from my own point of view I never succeeded. I might have been a failure anywhere and perhaps the chill of the New England temperament was a useful discipline.

Endicott Peabody was possibly as radical an influence on secondary education in 1890 as City and Country and the Walden Schools of the succeeding generation. There is, however, this difference: They had their roots in the thought-mechanism of Freud and in Dewey's pragmatic psychology. He modeled his school on an educational system stemming from the Middle Ages. Probably Mr. Peabody's most radical innovation was the attempt to break down on various fronts the wall which since the days of Pierre Abelard had separated boys and masters. He changed this relation by grafting on to the American school system certain traditions of the English public schools, modified in the light of New England idealism and of his own spiritual purity. The second great innovation of the Rector — as we called him — was the introduction of the honor system, which might be thus defined: In a few instances, conceded by all as essential to the welfare of the school and to the boy's own happiness — such for instance as not smoking, or drinking during the holidays, telling the truth, not going out of bounds at night — the boy undertook his own self-discipline; and if he broke such a pledge would probably be considered not a fit subject to continue at the school. A code is never rational, but religious; in that it is based upon faith and blind acceptance. Mr. Peabody was a generation ahead of his times in making the honor system between boy and master — as likewise between master and boy — part of the boy's own code of honor.

The third innovation which Mr. Peabody grafted on to the New England school system was a modification and combination of the English fag and hazing traditions. At Groton there was no straight fagging by a younger for an older boy. The Rector probably realized the incitement to homosexuality in such a relation. A boys' boarding-school, as such, is homosexual in tendency. This tendency can be promoted by the English fag system or reduced to a minimum as it was at Groton. Neither was there group hazing, and there was little individual bullying — the ferocious and junglelike joy of the older and stronger in humiliating and torturing the younger and weaker. Hazing and fagging were in a sense combined in a certain regimented hierarchic disciplining of the younger by the older boys.

Off the athletic field one never associated with the members of an upper or lower form, even in the case of a brother or close friend. Such an association at any rate was ground for the deepest suspicion. If one associated by habit with older or younger boys, it was ground for disciplinary action. If a younger boy met an older boy on the narrow boardwalk between Brooks and Hundred House, the younger stepped off into the snow. If younger boys failed to attend the football games of a Saturday afternoon, or to participate with sufficient enthusiasm in the regimented cheering, there was ground for very severe disciplining. An older boy might pull the cap off a new "kid," or trip him up in the mud if he showed underwear beneath his football trousers. There were in fact numberless small tokens, each in itself most insignificant, but which in the aggregate very sharply defined a "Grotty," and marked him off from all other American schoolboys to the outsider, but more especially in his own self-esteem. To others we might seem a little different. We knew

(51)

that we moved in a world apart — and always, of course, in a world above.

Here are some of these subtle, almost Masonic marks of distinction. We always dressed for supper, that is put on a white shirt and black pumps; and the younger boys wore Eton collars in the evening and on Sundays. We spoke of Mr. Peabody as the Rector — which to me has a distinctly British ring. In the winter we played the English game of "fives," rather than squash rackets or the more plebeian hand ball. So in cheer-leading, instead of sounding off with a "one, two, three — hurrah, etc.," it was always "hip, hip — hurrah," and this as far as I know is unique in America. The school was divided not into "classes" but into "forms"; and we never greeted each other with "Hello," if we met on the campus, but always with "Hi." "Hello" marked a boy at once as being a little city-schoolish. It was bad form — though not forbidden — to wear a cap; not to take a cold shower before breakfast; to swear or talk smut. A younger boy might easily have been disciplined by the older forms for dirty talk. I actually forgot the meanings, before I left school, of most of the one-syllabled words that Phil had taught me. Of course it was forbidden — not only by the upper-formers but by the Rector — to substitute tennis or golf for the major sports. We had to play football and baseball, no matter how thoroughly we disliked them and how indifferently we played, unless the doctor actually forbade it.

This Groton code, snobbish rather than military, precise rather than regimented, socially conservative rather than actually hostile to scholarship, was based on the mutuality of respect for the rights of the younger as well as of the older; and it was seldom necessary to resort to physical discipline. Two or three times a year there was a pumping. The sixth form met in the Senior Prefect's study and discussed the offense *in camera*. The Rector was informed of the Form's decision. He had, I suppose, some veto prerogative and in a measure he entered into the ritual. Usually after evening prayers in the Hundred House School

Room the Rector would dismiss the school. But on these occasions the Senior Prefect stepped to the desk and rang the gong to keep the boys seated, while Mr. Peabody walked out with his Bible and prayer book. The fourth form, big strapping fellows, one or two of whom played on the football team, ran out into the hall and closed the large double doors. The Senior Prefect said in measured tones, no less terrifying than would be those of the Grand Inquisitor to a condemned heretic: "I want to see so-and-so in my study."

In the ensuing stillness time seemed suspended. If anyone took his eyes from his desk lid he did it covertly. The offender, most likely a new boy who failed to respond to the niceties of the school code, had to walk through that silence and out to meet, as best he could, what he knew was coming to him. The school remained seated. The heaviest of the fourth-formers — perhaps a dozen of them — grabbed the offender, jerked him off the ground and ran him down the cellar stairway to the lavatories in approved football rush. Certain others stood at strategic positions to hold open a door or to deflect an oncoming rush. Over the lavatory faucet a fourth-former sat with a stop watch. A first offender was only given about ten seconds. The water came from the open spigot with tremendous force and the stream could be concentrated in violence by thumb and forefinger. Besides the culprit was winded and frightened and held upside down during the pumping. He was being forcibly drowned for eight or ten seconds. Then he was jerked to his feet, coughing, choking, retching. He was asked if he understood why he was being pumped. It wasn't hazing, remember, it was discipline. If he hadn't had enough the first time he was put under again for ten seconds. When it was all over he was allowed to go up to his cubicle and change his clothes before returning to the schoolroom.

No one asked questions. One felt it prudent to mind one's own business.

While I was in the fourth form we pumped little Teddy

Roosevelt, then in the second. It was not that he had committed any specific breach of the school code. He was selected, after a rather vehement debate and several consultations with the Senior Prefect, as the most typical of the form, the general tone of which we disapproved. He was held under twice for eight seconds. One of the form leaders then explained to him that he was fresh and swell-headed. To our amazement he denied everything, answered back, even started asking all sorts of questions. Little Teddy was quite voluble and our fourth-form leader was not so quick on the trigger under cross-examination.

"He was very plucky and began answering back. Shouts arose: 'Shut up! Under again. Shut him up! Under with him!' Most were for pumping him a third time but he was let off. It will do him and the whole form, whose tone is very fresh, a lot of good. Others are likely to follow his example. There was much loud talking in Brooks House schoolroom afterwards." So I recorded my feelings at the time, obviously upset that the third-formers should talk loudly about such a matter. I fancy, however, that the tone of the second form improved, for I cannot recall any subsequent pumpings that season. Little Teddy would have been about fourteen years old. This was on February 11, 1901. His father was inaugurated as vice-president some three weeks later.

Another season we pumped the Rector's son, Malcolm, recently elected Bishop Coadjutor of New York. Nor had he committed any specific breach of school code. We just didn't like his "tone," either; and it was definitely important to keep the tone of the lower forms up to Groton standard. The Rector was splendid about it. He certainly could take it on the chin.

During my first few weeks at school I was harassed by two continued obsessions: the fear of bed-wetting, and the fear that the boys or masters would discover a small box of lead soldiers that Francis had persuaded me to smuggle up to school, as a further toughening experience for them.

My first meeting with the Rector was a purely formal one but I have occasion to remember it. That week I was given twenty-two blackmarks. A usual allowance for a healthy-spirited boy would be three or four a week. Six was the maximum number that could be given for an offense. The record up to that moment had been perhaps a dozen.

The Rector read off the list of blackmarks Saturday noon after lunch. I was already somewhat nervous but when he reached my name on the school list and paused a long minute, scowling, without pronouncing it, I was really jittery. At length he looked up slowly, searching me out, and said:

"Biddle, go to my study."

As I worked my way clumsily forward between the rows of desks, I could not in sheer nervousness take my eyes off his angry stare. What had at first been a smile of frightened deprecation grew into a yawning rictus of despair. As I approached his desk, my eyes still on his, I was grinning, in sheer horror, from ear to ear.

When he came into his study a little later, he looked down at me not unkindly.

"George," he said, "if I had not known you were such a good boy, I should have sent you home long ago."

From then on I have never lost my respect for the Rector, and if I have understood him as little, I suppose, as he has understood me, I have always coveted his approbation. It was little Averell Harriman who once said of him to his father:

"You know he would be an awful bully if he weren't such a terrible Christian."

There you have the man in all his grandeur!

Years later he told me how at the very start Moncure also had vanquished him. Moncure's knife previously had been confiscated for playing with it in Sacred Studies. Subsequently in one week he had committed so many breaches of school regulations that the Rector felt it opportune to "take him on" alone for a talk. He there administered — he assured me — the most completely devastating and angry lecture he was capable of; and Mr. Peabody was a master in the art of exhortation and invective. Having shouted at Moncure for ten minutes, his eyes flashing, his lip flecked with indignation, he leaned back for a moment to catch his breath; and Moncure, patiently waiting for this split second in which to wedge into the conversation and get going on another topic, leaned forward and pointing to the Rector's desk said:

"Oh, look, Mr. Peabody, there's my knife!"

It is true that I usually headed my form, but I frequently headed the lists of latenesses and blackmarks as well. The Rector's hopes of me seemed doomed to disappointment.

In a letter to my mother, dating I should suppose from the same troubled period, I find this somewhat ambiguous passage:

I had a rather serious time this afternoon with Mr. Abbott [the same choleric, broad-shouldered, thick-set, one-hundred-eighty-pounds-stripped Mr. Abbott who had played on the Christ's College, Cambridge, soccer eleven, and who later became headmaster of Lawrenceville]. He gave me six blackmarks [the limit] because I told him in front of the entire school that I thought him very unfair. The Rector, with whom I later discussed the matter, explained to me that obedience comes before all else; and that one must not call masters names unless they ask one's opinion. I have been getting too many blackmarks lately. I must do better.

The Rector was always patient with me. Never really angry. And he seems to have made his points very clearly: — "First of all obedience . . . Wait until they ask one's opinion." Very military advice and it stood me in good stead subsequently in the army.

Mr. Abbott, too, who had shouted so loudly at me before the whole school: "Biddle, I am not accustomed to being called unfair and dishonest!" turned out perhaps my warmest friend among the faculty. He tried for several years to convert me to Christian Science; and only lost his temper once again when I broke his nose — quite inadvertently — trying indeed to escape his bull-like rushes as we sparred together one rainy afternoon in the gymnasium.

These years at school I was hungry for success. It may not have been ambition at all, merely a desperate, shielding effort to conform to type. To succeed at Groton, as later at Harvard, three paths lay open: athletics, social success and administrative ability. At sixteen years I weighed ninety-six pounds, was the smallest boy in my form and had no unusual aptitude for games. I was socially undeveloped, though never strictly unpopular. It took me about twelve years of failure to convince myself that I did not possess outstanding administrative ability. About the only thing left was scholarship. Mr. Peabody is not a scholar himself. He is a great administrator and a militant Christian. I should define his Christianity as an unshaken faith in his particular God and a fervent wish to keep physically fit, sexually clean, morally honest and — in every sense of the word — a gentleman. I fancy he dislikes a dirty collar as violently as a dirty word; and is shocked by an East Side accent as well as by outspoken Atheism.

It is true that the Rector wanted his boys to excel in scholarship — as in athletics, moral purity, clean living and manliness — and the school got a half holiday every time that Bayard Cutting was awarded a John Harvard Scholarship. So I pinned my ambition on the hopes of being head of my class. When he read out the marks at the end of the month I was always afraid that the tears might come to my eyes if I were unsuccessful. I would lift up my desk lid at the approach of my name, as if in search of something or other. I had not yet learned that one cannot get through life without a mask. It is just as important — more so perhaps — than a face.

In my third-form year I used to walk over from the School House to the Hundred House at morning recess to get fattened up on an egg-milk-shake and crackers. Daily for several months I met there one of the sixth-formers. Sometimes we walked together back to the School House. He was gray-eyed, cool, self-possessed, intelligent; and had the warmest, most friendly and understanding smile. Years later he told me he had been ill with scarlet fever. He had lost weight and the doctors seemed to think he should fatten up a bit. Though he was not athletic — perhaps because he was not an outstanding athlete — he seemed from my point of view all the more successful. He was — as I remember — manager of the school football team, head editor of the *Grotonian* and a prefect. I was rather surprised, then, to hear quite recently from a close friend of his that Franklin Roosevelt had always felt at Groton that he was unsuccessful and had not attained the prestige that he would have liked.

It was my fortune to get an occasional glimpse of another boy two forms below me, who was to become — in my estimation at least — the only other pre-eminent Groton graduate, also, curiously enough, a politician and a statesman. Bronson Cutting's reputation at Groton had in a way preceded him. His elder brother Bayard, shortly thereafter to die of consumption in Florence, had been such a brilliant scholar that much was expected of Bronson. When, then, the Rector, after one of his studied and dramatic pauses, early in November read out Cutting's first month's mark — which was so close to absolute perfection, so immeasurably above what we ordinary bright boys had been reaching after — there was an intaking of breath and whispered exclamations ran about the school. All eyes turned on the new boy, who huddled among the first-formers, gray-faced, spotted, sparrow-boned, a mere breath or shell of a human being. I used to come across him often in the school library. It was once discovered that his name only was on the index card of an eight-volumed history, entitled *The Lives of the Saints*. I wonder indeed if any other name was ever spelled out below his own threadlike, angular, delicate and scrawling handwriting. He, too, was head editor of the *Grotonian*.

A few months ago at a gathering at the Whitney Museum, being told that Mrs. W. Bayard Cutting was present, I introduced myself to her, telling her how little I had known her son but what a vast admiration I had for his liberal-mindedness, his valiant fight against reaction and his deep intelligence. She told me that Bronson had also felt himself a failure at school, unable to compete in athletics, so delicate that he gave the impression of a cripple; but that when he was elected head editor of the *Grotonian* he had written her: "You may not know it, but I believe today that I am the happiest human being in all America."

I am always skeptical about offering advice on any subject to anyone; because the advice may be wrong and I know it will not be heeded. If I ever should offer advice, however, it would be predicated on this general experience. As I look back on life I find that I have done a few things of which I am proud and a good many more of which I am heartily ashamed, but do not regret, however. My only regrets are the failures to act on impulse. It is the things one could have done and didn't which are the lost opportunities. Sometimes, however, genuine shame lingers.

My first year at school my brother Moncure was in the fourth form and had a study in the Hundred House. At that time he was a particularly lonely boy and yearned for companionship and affection. At moments I was homesick, myself. Rainy afternoons he would have me to his study, prepare me a cup of hot chocolate, make me comfortable on the couch with Mallory's *Morte d'Arthur* or T. W. Arnold's translation of the *Fioretti* of St.

Francis. He busied himself making a fair copy of a "Life of Oliver Cromwell," which he was preparing as his English prize essay. Mellow Indian summer afternoons he would walk me down to the village, buying fresh cider or apples along the way. At the close of the football season we paddled up the green windings of the Dead River on the Nashua or knocked balls about the golf course. We were closer together that autumn than at any time since. One day I noticed, meeting a group of fourth-formers on the way up from the boathouse, that they nudged one another and snickered as we passed. It was the same with my own form. They felt that we were "queer." One doesn't associate with an older brother. After that I kept away from him.

This isn't a pretty thing to tell. It's the ugliest indictment I have against Groton; this and the school's intellectual dishonesty.

One summer years later at Bermuda I had been reading Renan's *Life of Christ* and Tom Paine's *Age of Reason*. I said to William Norman Guthrie:

"Paine shows inconsistencies and contradictions, not through extradocumentary testimony but through the very words of Moses or of Christ and his Apostles. If the Old or the New Testament is the supreme evidence, then it only proves that one cannot believe it."

He answered: "The amazing thing is not that the testimony, taken by word of mouth over a period of centuries, is conflicting and contradictory. That one assumes. It is a miracle that in so many instances it corroborates the most trivial events."

I said to him: "I studied Sacred Studies for six years at Groton. I never heard of Renan or of Tom Paine; and I was never told that the Old and the New Testament are full of the most patent contradictions."

These are my indictments against Groton. Its effect was to stifle the creative impulse. Its code could tolerate a feeling of shame for associating with one's brother; and by and large, in

HELENE WITH MASK

PORTRAIT OF WILLIAM GROPPER   *Photo by Peter A. Juley & Son*

many small ways, it was intellectually dishonest. In other respects
the school was admirable.

I was on the edge of a nervous breakdown. I was about to be
confirmed, and in an ecstasy of religious emotion attended the
Rector's confirmation talks and made synopses of his exhortations.

February 5, 1901 — Mr. Peabody spoke about renunciation. There
are three kinds. First, renounce things which are absolutely wrong;
then things which harm yourself; lastly things which harm others.
He then spoke of the devil as a subtle spirit. His temptations are
pride, irreverence, swearing, telling religious funny stories, and praying only with the lips. The text for the week is: "Make me a clean
heart, O God, and renew a right spirit within me."

The reading is: St. John, First Epistle, Second chapter; and
Ephesians, Chapter IV, line 17, to Chapter V, line 21.

February 14. The Rector spoke about Gambling, Drinking and
Impurity. There are two ways of legitimately spending one's money.
First, spending it and getting something for it. Then giving it away.
Never tell an unclean story or allow one to be told in your presence.
The reading for the week is . . .

I was never particularly religious, but during these pitiful years
of adolescence, when my hopes, my convictions, the world itself,
seemed shattering about me, I wanted something to which I
could cling or drown myself in absolute faith and exaltation.

At sixteen I was still sexually undeveloped and completely
innocent. I doubt very much if I had ever heard of self-abuse.
The boys' habits were very intelligently — at any rate methodically — dealt with. Several of the masters worked through the
prefects and older boys. These in turn would select one of the
maturer members of an adolescent group, talk with him very
sanely and honestly, and ask his advice about contacting other
younger boys in his group. Howard Cary, who was a prefect and

sixth-former, had been told that I was probably ripe material for such friendly admonition and advice.

One May evening he asked if he might walk with me back to Brooks House after evening prayers. I was wallowing in a state of gloom and self-criticism. Such a request from an upper-former was most unusual, and I wondered darkly what was in store for me. He showed me the greatest warmth and affection, however, put his arm about my shoulder, spoke of my studies and asked me what books I had been reading. As we wandered up and down together through the apple orchard, the silver blossoms crepuscular in the rising darkness, my heart beat fast, so brimming over in happiness that I thought it would burst. Finally in parting he held my hand and said:

"If ever you want a friend, if ever you have need of unburdening yourself, if ever you are ashamed of something, so ashamed that you cannot face it in your own thoughts, then come to me. Perhaps I can help. Perhaps I can be that older friend to you."

Tears hung in my eyes and throat. That such an important and successful boy should care that way about me! For the following term or so I was literally in love with him, and did not for several years suspect the nature of his mission.

In the autumn of 1901 I was taken away from school for a year and sent to California. In eight months I grew nearly the same number of inches and put on twenty pounds' weight. I minded terribly being dropped a class. I felt disgrace in it. On my return to school my old form was now the sixth and I never quite knew to what extent to associate with my former classmates or to identify myself with the new form. I was not kept long in uncertainty as to the correct social attitude.

The Senior Prefect asked me one evening to come to his study. The whole sixth form was there. I was told by him that I should have known better than to associate with an upper form. Did I think myself too good for the fifth? Did I think the sixth-formers needed me or took any pleasure in my company? They would tell me frankly how much they appreciated my importunities. They then proceeded to rough me up. I fought as long as I could. I am ashamed of myself for not trying to kill someone. I was one against twenty and saw two friendly faces. My clothes were ripped off. I was thrown out of the window and my effects bundled after me.

Next day after chapel I stepped up to the sixth-form leader, whom I considered most responsible, and told him I wanted a word with him. We walked down toward the river. At the end of a few moments I was choking with anger and humiliation. I told him what I felt about the lot of them.

"I thought my old form were my friends. I see I was mistaken. I can get along without you all as easily as you without me. If you didn't like my society you need only have told me so. That would have been fair play. You didn't have to take me on, one against twenty."

He was not at all impressed by my vehemence and looked very bored and severe. After all it was a question of school code and discipline. He was evidently shocked by all this show of emotion. He was quite right. I should have taken him aside and tried to kill him; or else taken it on the chin and said nothing about it. Later this boy, who was very popular at school and at Harvard, committed suicide.

I got through the next two years all right. Off and on I headed my form. I was an editor of the *Grotonian*. I rowed on a school four. I knew I was a failure. I was liked well enough. I was never entirely defeated. I knew Groton was the finest school in America; I knew that being a failure was my own fault. I knew that I was a happy fellow to be there. I was that low. Life had compensations. Here are random extracts from my diary.

April 4, 1901 — Learn to play "Marching through Georgia" on a fife I bought for 75 cents from Louis Chapin.

May 2 — I now know all nine of the fife marches, three hymns and "Clementine." Vice-President Roosevelt came up today and our drum and fife corps gave him a reception. At half past five he gave us a bully talk about . . . shooting panthers in the Rockies. Among other episodes were the stories of the fellow who shot the editor and got off for thirty days; the man who missed his wife and shot the lady . . . the man who was accused by his mother-in-law of polygamy.

May 19 — Sit beside an old farmer at the May Services in Groton. He told me he was in the Civil War; and his father in the War of 1812, and saw Washington.

September 27, 1903 — According to Franklin Roosevelt [down from Harvard for a talk to the editors of the *Grotonian*] it must be beastly hard trying for the *Crimson*. Two days a week from 4 P.M. 'til 2 A.M.

March 9, 1904 — I preach a sermon at the Boston Road [social service work among the outlying villages], as none of the masters are able to. I interpolate into the First Book of Samuel a text of my own. I also make use of quotations from Cicero, the Greek, and the "Fioretti" of St. Francis. There were about sixteen present. Good fun but dreadfully cold.

March 29 — . . . I have decided to do several things this term. To get "A" every month. I cannot, alas! beat G. Howe, as there are but two months before Prize-Day. I am also going to try to broaden and expand my chest, sit up straight, and keep my digestion in order. These are minor things but they all help to broaden my character.

April 4 — I preach a second sermon, at Rocky Hill this time. There are thirty-two present, but they are more condescending than last time. One fat girl in particular drove me nearly crazy. I had to repeat the same sermon as I had only ten minutes in which to prepare it.

. . . The Rector never seems interested in me or anything I am saying. I am afraid I shall have to give him up.

May 7 — Stokes is annoying. [He was subsequently to become Herbert Hoover's private secretary and an editor of the *Herald Tribune*.] He started on the Latin prize — over which I must have spent forty hours — three days before the time limit. I have a haunting certainty that he will get it, too. Of the Greek prize and of one of the debating and form prizes I feel pretty certain.

May 14 — I am again moved up — I am sorry to say — to Mr. Peabody's table.

Tonight I asked Mr. Peabody if I might sit at a lower table for another month. He looked at me without cracking a smile and then said slowly: "You mean that you prefer THOSE tables to OURS?" I had never looked at it in this light, and he quite flabbergasted me. So I only said "Yes." I gained my point for the next month, however.

May 23 — . . . Then came the races. Our crew raced first against a graduate boat of F. D. Roosevelt, stroke; H. Peabody, three; Cross, two; and Hollister, bow. As there was some fear of George Howe's fainting, the race was started at the boat-house. The grads were given half a length. Though our stroke was short and choppy, we pulled right away from them and kept three lengths' lead all the way. George came off his seat four times; Stokes and I did once.

May 24 — Prize Day. President Roosevelt spoke after the Rector. As usual he spoke on the strenuous life; snobbishness at college, etc. He emphasizes his *ands* and *ifs* too much and gesticulates rather freely. He was a come-down after the Rector's straightforward speaking.

Then the prizes were given out. I got the prize for the best debate, the second form prize, and the Greek prize. Schenck got the essay prize; B. Cutting, the Latin. George Howe got the first form prize and Stokes the English prize. What pleased me most was that Francis got the prize for the best two-minute speech. When the President shook hands he said: "It isn't fair, you Biddle boys are getting all the prizes." . . . I drove down with Stokes, Kissel and Derby to the Rocky Hill Service. I preached a sermon on: "If ye have faith ye can move mountains," and "That which ye sow, ye reap."

After evening service I lay in the shadow of the chapel and thought over my school career. . . . I may not have made a success of my school life, but I would not have missed Groton for anything.

I cannot feel that Groton had much to teach me. One can suppose that its effect would be to smother — for a time at least —

the creative spirit in the growing boy. Can one even be sure that it was of much positive educational value in the careers and the flowering of B. M. Cutting or of F. D. Roosevelt? But I am far from sure that education elsewhere would have been of more value. For I learned this thing in Groton and in the subsequent five or six years at Harvard: that I heartily loathed not necessarily the standard which the Rector with all his fire and purity held out to his boys but the standard which through some sort of social preoccupation the great majority of his boys had elected to follow.

Ninety-five percent of these boys came from what they considered the aristocracy of America. Their fathers belonged to the Somerset, the Knickerbocker, the Philadelphia or the Baltimore Clubs. Among them was a goodly slice of the wealth of the nation, little Morgans, Harrimans, Whitneys, Webbs, McCormicks, Crockers, Stillmans. On the whole the equipment and the teaching were more admirable than at any other school in America.

Generally speaking, this aristocracy, this wealth, this admirable educational training was destined to flow into one channel: Wall Street or its equivalent. There were of course exceptions. Of the fifty-six members of my two Groton forms the names of seven have even been listed in *Who's Who in America*. A greater number, however, could, in terms purely of manhood, be listed as absolute failures: parasites on the community, cheats, drunkards, lechers, panhandlers, suicides. This is not entirely — considering the investment in money, in zeal, in single-mindedness, in purity — a successful experiment. Is it the educational system or the material — the social and financial aristocracy of America — that is responsible?

Not so long ago I attended at the Union Club on Park Avenue and 69th Street a dinner given by the graduates to commemorate the happy and complete recovery of Mr. Peabody from a long and serious illness. He was approaching his eighty-first birthday. I had not seen him for twenty-seven years. He had changed singularly little. His hair grayer; his face less pink and white. But he had the same vitality, the same clear eye, the same indestructible dominance and untiring energy. He looked more than ever like some splendid eleventh or twelfth-century Crusader; the militant Christian, half warrior, half priest. He spoke for an hour, with the occasional use of a note, and during that hour held all of us in the hollow of his hand. He was the father; we, his boys. There was much easy wise-cracking — as of old — and much reassuring statistical proof of the high standing of recent classes at Harvard, at Yale and at Princeton. He spoke about purity in the home and said that home life and purity were at the basis of our civilization. The audience responded with laughter or applause. Then the Rector spoke to this effect:

"Something has troubled me a good deal lately. Personally I don't pretend to know much about politics or economics. [A little ripple of gaiety spread among us.] But in national crises like the present one, we get pretty excited and perhaps we give vent to expressions that later on we are sorry for. I believe Franklin Roosevelt to be a gallant and courageous gentleman. I am happy to count him as my friend."

There was complete silence.

Now the dramatic meaning of this incident was *not* that the school was completely hostile to Mr. Peabody in his loyalty to perhaps the most popular president since Washington, to one of the half-dozen admittedly most important people in the world today, and to the only pre-eminent living Grotonian. It was rather — if I analyzed the Groton mind correctly — that they were silenced for a moment in admiration at his courage in thus daring, at a completely friendly, family meeting, to step into the breach and alone undertake to defend the President. I take it that what ran through their minds was something like this: "Good old Rector! By Jove he has nerve. And perhaps — after all — he may be partly right. Perhaps we should not *talk* the way we do. Not in public. Not of a fellow Grotonian."

Mr. Peabody is a somewhat great man, whom I find incompatible with my own conception of the adequate. It was Delacroix who said to his students, as they filed by Ingres's Odalisque in the Louvre:

"*Messieurs, le chapeau dans la main mais les yeux fixés à terre* — gentlemen, it has my admiration, but don't let it get you."

Our last serious correspondence was based on an episode bordering upon pure fantasy. One summer during the law school, cruising with my friend Harold Wilcox from Dark Harbor to Northeast, in an old Friendship lobster boat, we passed through the twinkling islands, the overhanging firs and the red and blue granite ledges of Fox Island Thoroughfare; and dropped anchor in North Haven, the Rector's summer home. That evening we invited on board my brother Francis and other younger college friends. As the night air was chilly we closed down the hatches and sat about a ship's lantern well into the night, yodeling, singing, shouting and plying our guests alternately with semi-fermented beer and straight whiskey.

At two in the morning we shook hands all around, swallowed a half tumbler of scratch-gut, and waved a lantern to them as they zigzagged their way through the lobster pots and North Haven dinghies to the dock. In ten minutes we were fast asleep. Two of our guests, less sober than we had realized, felt the need of extending their whimsies to the threshold of the Rector's home. There, under his window and up and down the silent, Sabbath streets, they impersonated in a two-hour dialogue, and well into the dawn, Mr. Peabody himself, and his lifelong collaborator Amory Gardner, shrieking, arguing, swearing, cursing at each other in language that echoed from one end of the village to the other.

Harold and I had the anchor up by dawn and were tacking close to the wind and well out of the harbor. We were unaware that warrants were sworn out for our arrest and that actions for disorderly conduct, public nuisance, etc., were pending against our guests. By the following mail, however, I got a letter from Mr. Peabody. It began by asking why I had singled out his summer home and Sunday evening as the site and occasion of drunkenness, bawdy language and blasphemy; and ended with a regret that my younger brother should be subjected to the influence of my company the summer before his last school year. I explained things a little — little by little — and Mr. Peabody forgave. On September twenty-second he wrote again:

". . . Francis and I went over the ground very thoroughly and, if he reported to you the conversation which we had, there would be little more to add. It was unfortunate all around, but we must now leave it behind."

Pierre de Chaignon LaRose tells this story of him. One evening when he had business in Boston he telephoned or wrote to one of "his boys" suggesting that he visit him that evening in his college club, the Gas House. When Mr. Peabody arrived the undergraduates were sitting about drinking orange juice and tea, and talking about Professors Royce and Münsterberg and James and Santayana. They asked Mr. Peabody about life in English universities and ordered more orange juice, and talked about Professors Palmer and Copeland and Kittredge. Mr. Peabody went home and felt that the influence of his boys had done something to change the tone in Harvard University. About midnight the Owl Club telephoned over to the Gas and said: "What the hell was all the noise about?" and the Gas said: "Hell, nothing. Dr. Peabody has been spending the evening with us. Come on over and celebrate, too. Later on others joined in. About three o'clock, the Gold Coast Clubs were still snake-dancing up and down Mt. Auburn Street and pulling up signposts and shooting siphons of club soda at the street-car conductors. Pierre laughed his rich, saturnine chuckle:

"Yes, that's the influence the Grotties have on Harvard!"

California

1901-1902

Here was the spot where that grand old Franciscan, Padre
Junipero Serra, began his work, full of the devout and
ardent purpose to reclaim the wilderness and its people to
his country and his Church; on this very beach he bap-
tized his first Indian converts, and founded his first Mission. And the only traces now remaining of his heroic
labors and hard-won successes were a pile of crumbling
ruins, a few old olive trees and palms; and in less than
another century even these would be gone; returned into
the keeping of that mother, the earth, who puts no head-
stones at the sacredness of her graves.

HELEN HUNT JACKSON: *Ramona*

IF SOME proper evaluation of the benefit to one's growth
and character were possible — as I believe it never is — or
if we could measure the degree to which we have found life
ripely blooming and sucked it dry — as I believe we always
can in the bright satisfaction of our memory — then the eleven
years' schooling in New England and at Harvard seem in retrospect eleven years of retardation of growth. The memories which
throb with the quickened pulse of life's adventure are of those
two years away from schooling and New England for reasons of ill
health. Later in Tahiti I learned — or rather I severely drilled
and compelled myself to observe — the absolute necessity for an
artist to keep life at arm's length, to see it objectively. One could
only savor its beauty — the beauty was there — if one were not
crushed by the ugliness of its little unimportant impacts; if it
were not on top of one like a thousand fleas and cockroaches. A

sunset is always seen more glowingly upside down. One must strive to live in contrasts, in order to get the full appetite and flavor of life, to dwell largely in country solitude, partly because it is the good life, partly because it makes one ravenous for city crowds; always to drink a glass or so too deeply, because with proper drinking life is more rosy, and also because otherwise water before breakfast would never taste so sweet. Perhaps, then, the sojourn in California — and subsequently that in Mexico — seem such a gaily colored and vivid pattern because the years before and after were by comparison so gray, so flat, so lacking in resonance or sparkle.

That summer at Penllyn and in the neighborhood there had been a plague of basket worms and tent caterpillars. The trees were stripped completely bare of all their foliage. There followed early in October a long and mellow period of warmth and sun. The trees, as if bewildered, put on fresh leaves and many of the wild cherries burst into bloom.

My mother and I left Penllyn in October. Three days later the train ran westward through the flat and then the rolling prairies of Kansas. I saw prairie dogs standing stiff and intently curious before their holes. Motionless they blinked at us gliding by; and then, courtesying, dived below as if into a bomb-proof shelter. A coyote watched us, standing off in the long grass, one paw raised and crooked. We ran by the parched sand and zigzag bluffs of Colorado; Pike's Peak, Spanish Peaks and Raton Range. In Arizona and New Mexico the crazy red orange purple mountains were the right background for the lean long-horned steer, staring moodily under gray silver sycamores. Sometimes the cattle towns were nothing more than printed names on signposts, empty loading pens and many parallel tracks in the dust, vanishing toward the horizon. Roads would not come to that part of the West for another decade. Through the Mojave Desert I saw my first Indians and bargained with them for their pottery as the train pulled to a stop to take in water. In the Ojai Valley in California we paused from the long trip. I tasted guavas, soaked overnight in sugar. Down in Little Mexico I talked with the greasers. For six bits I bought a loaded quirt from one of them; and from another — a fat, one-legged cripple and stench of a man — an eight-strand, six-length, rawhide reata for a dollar and a half. The roads lay four or five inches deep in dust. The rains would not fall until Christmas. One day I caught a tarantula under my sombrero among some rotting oranges by the side of the road.

It is difficult to find words to express the sharpness of these impressions. They still have that immediacy which one associates with a dream a second or two before awakening. It seems trivial to say that I fell in love with California, yet this is the accurate way to describe my feelings. They clothed acts and situations in a mellow light and mood of intoxication, which one associates with calf love.

From this time on and for many years I had vivid, recurrent — almost serial — dreams about certain places. These existed only in my dreams; but I associated them with California — and subsequently with the Paris Latin Quarter, Tahiti, Croton. That is, in these recurrent dreams I did not exactly revisit my beloved California, but I would immediately recognize this fairy country — which I had known in a previous dream — and would feel for it the same bittersweet yearning which only California had evoked.

My mother finally settled me at San Ysidro above Montecito, south of Santa Barbara. It was a small orange ranch and Mr. Johnson, the proprietor, took in boarders. My best friend there was Carmen, a former Mexican vaquero and handy man about the ranch. He taught me how to throw a lariat — from the Spanish *la reata*, the rope. Sundays we went quail hunting up the cañon, to the forks and beyond to the falls. Once we drove in a dilapidated buggy to Carpinteria after kildeer and ringneck plover, divers and spoonbills.

California

In the evenings I played my piccolo and read Helen Hunt Jackson's *Ramona*. Ramona was still alive, old and fat. Her colored postcard photographs were sold at the Harvey lunchcounters up and down the Sante Fe Railroad. When years later I learned from my friend Gardner Jackson in Washington that the author of my *Ramona* was not only his aunt but his father's first wife, I could only throw my arms about him and kiss his cheeks. Ramona and Fra Junipero Serra and Bret Harte's California lie buried deep, but they will never entirely be forgotten.

Carmen had a friend, Adolfo. He sold me for a couple of bits a flint spearhead which he had grubbed up in the Digger Indian mound at Montecito. It had been lodged in the neck bone of an Indian. Opposite the fine old tile-roofed Delaguerra mansion in Santa Barbara was a small curio store. In the very center of the shop window was the skull of a Digger Indian and in the skull was embedded an arrowhead. But it was priced at five dollars and although I drove my mother on several occasions to admire it she seemed curiously uninterested. My appetite was now, however, whetted. I asked Adolfo if he would go gravedigging with me. He was very much alarmed but I pestered him until he consented. We rode down to the beach one night and fastened our ponies to the branch of a pepper tree. He led me along the railroad track to the mound and there we waited until the moon was up. We dug for about an hour. I found a number of broken pestles and mortars and some babies' bones. I treasured them for months wrapped in cotton wool in an old pasteboard shoebox. My mother discovered them and explained to me the criminal nature of my act, and what might be the consequences. I somewhat reluctantly agreed to give the bones a second burial — in the shoebox — below Mr. Johnson's vegetable garden. I refused to part with the mortars and pestles.

Carmen had a face like a weasel, long, upflaring, mobile nose, close-set brown eyes, never at rest but flickering uneasily like tired butterflies; walrus mustache, receding chin. He wore dark inconspicuous clothes, a soft black felt hat, a heavy gold watch chain and unpolished red leather shoes. He was the trickiest man with a rope I had ever seen. He taught me how to throw it eight different ways. Forehand or backhand; circling or at rest from the ground; the neck, the hind-leg and the three foreleg throws; loveliest and most difficult of all the throws, popularized by Will Rogers but known to every *jinete* — cavalier — south of the Rio Grande, where the noose is kept open after the cast by a circular motion of the wrist and then guided at will, not from the hand, but by the undulation imparted to the rope itself. He taught me how to mount a plunging horse by the left-hand cheek-strap hold, grabbing the left stirrup with the right hand, and not catching the pummel until the foot was safely in the stirrup and the body flung into the saddle by the jerked-sideways plunge of the horse. He showed me how to pick a cigarette from the ground at a full run, hooking the left spur behind the cantle and holding the pummel by the left hand; or, even if it were a sixteen-hand horse, clutching a loop of the reata well below the pummel, to which it was half-hitched. He showed me how to vault into the saddle with a grip on the stirrup leather; and how to shoot or rope in safety from the saddle. No wonder I loved Carmen. He was *muy amigo* — my good friend.

Carmen introduced me in Santa Barbara to Old Ortega and his nephew, El Piton — the Sprig. Ortega was old school Mexican. He trimmed his white beard short and parted it in the middle. He rode a small white cow pony with flowing mane and tail. He rode at a reined-in gallop with his gelding's ears almost over the withers, pawing the air in front. When he came to a stop he jerked on the spade bit, sat his horse on his hocks, and slid twenty feet in a cloud of dust. He used a split-ear bridle without any nosepiece, brow band or throat latch, eight-strand rawhide reins fastened with chains to the spade bit, and carried sixty feet of twelve-strand reata. Old Ortega wore a broad black felt sombrero. He understood English but spoke only Spanish. His skin continually burned as if by fever. He was very scornful and abusive of Americans — *los Gringos* — but accepted me on El Piton's recommendation — and because I was in the market for a cow pony.

El Piton belonged to a different generation. He spoke English pretty well and was a tough guy. He punched cattle out at the Catalina Islands or up at Gaviota. He traded horses and broke them in on the stretch of beach at the foot of Main Street in Santa Barbara. He dressed tough and talked tough and was free with his money; but he knew how to ride. Old Ortega saw to that.

I bought my cow pony, Chapo, from Old Ortega. He was a black *mesteño* — mustang — from Idaho, broken to shoot from the saddle and to rope. He was a cutter, that is he was trained to follow and cut out a marked steer from the herd, and was quick as a polo pony on his pivots. But he was a real loco, went crazy mad and bucked like a circus if anything unexpected happened. If you started to mount him from the wrong side, or double-cinched him, he bucked, squealing and snorting, with his ears back. If you entered his stall from behind he tried to kick the stall to pieces. I entered it over the manger and was in other matters circumspect. Chapo was the only animal I ever really loved. I fed him and groomed him every day. He, too, galloped pawing the air, with his ears well back over the withers. He maimed, temporarily, two or three stable boys while I owned him. Bob Miller, the Ojai Valley ranger, offered me ten dollars more than I paid for him and when I left California El Piton bought him back for twenty-five dollars. In subsequent years when I had my recurrent California dreams, Chapo was ever there. When I came to California I had a very small frame and was abnormally light. That year I grew about seven inches. But what was more important, securely seated on Chapo's back in the broad Mexican saddle, embellished with the hand-carved saddlebags, the gun case, lariat, the silver-studded martingale and horsehair hackamore, the leather-thonged tapaderas and other trappings, I grew tall and acquired weight in my own estimation.

One morning before daybreak Carmen and I joined Old Ortega, El Piton and the boys on the strip of beach below Santa Barbara, where they broke in the *potros* and *potrancas* — the colts and the three-year-old fillies. They had a mean time saddling a young sorrel. El Piton had roped him round the belly to get him used to the feel of the cinch. He was blindfolded and jerked about in a circle on the hackamore to take the buck out of him. The muscles played like ripples over his barreled flanks. He plunged about in the sand, reared, fell over backward, squealed, struck out with his forelegs. El Piton roped his right foreleg. Passing the rope over his withers, he drew it taut, hobbling the sorrel's foot fast under his belly. They finally got the double-cinched saddle squarely girthed. The sorrel — three-legged — lashed about and flung himself in the sand. When he was up again Old Ortega — to draw his attention — buffeted him noisily on the cheeks, standing well off from the forelegs. The rider climbed — very gently — into the saddle. The blinders were ripped off. The men shouted, jumped aside, and slapped their legs with their sombreros to get him to a run. There's no danger in a running buck, especially if the rider can keep the horse's head from between its legs. But the sorrel wouldn't play ball. He walked round on his hind legs for a minute or two and then fell over backwards and snapped the pummel clean. The rider got away.

I begged to mount him. Carmen had told me to watch how the mane would lead to left or right. One cannot gage the direction of the next plunge by the head, buried between the fore feet. While the boys got the sorrel freshly saddled, Old Ortega cautioned me to jump clean, if the horse somersaulted.

It wasn't so difficult after all. The sorrel reared a bit, bucked a couple of times and then somersaulted. I jumped clean, somer-

saulted and rolled half a dozen lengths before I came to a stop.
When I got on him again the fight was out of him. He bucked
all right, but it was a loose, running buck. Old Ortega had the
martingale rope wound round his own pummel, and kept jerking up on the chin. The boys galloped along behind, belaboring
his flanks with their lariats. Two or three runs up and down
the beach in the soft sand and even the gallop was beaten out of
him.

One lives in such moments.

That spring, before I left California, I took part in a big rodeo
on the Dibblee Ranch near Gaviota, north of Santa Barbara.
I left San Ysidro at five o'clock in the morning and covered about
forty-five miles in ten hours. We slept at the Mac Kneily ranchhouse. It was a low clapboard affair, the porch high off the ground,
inset and roofed over. It nestled under sycamores; and a white-
washed picket fence straggled about the outbuildings. The ranch
had fifty or sixty thousand acres of rolling grassland, with ideal
bajíos — flats — for the herding and branding. The grassy hillocks
were spotted with clumps of live oak. Mesquite and chaparral
grew along the dry cañon beds. There were a couple of dozen
vaqueros in the outfit and we herded four or five thousand head
of cattle and branded and cut 550 in the three-day round-up.
Old Ortega, Carmen and El Piton; Bascus, Vicento Gaverra, Del
Vaya, Vacaro; and the three Americans, Johnny and Billy Beggs
and Ed Mac Kneily are the names that stand out as heroes in my
memory. At night, tired and dusty after twelve and fourteen
hours in the saddle, we rode back to the Mac Kneily ranchhouse
and supped on mountain oysters — calves' fries — scrambled eggs
and black coffee. I rode Chapo fifty miles back to San Ysidro the
day after the rodeo was ended. In addition to the actual roping
and herding he had traveled upwards of 180 miles in five days.
I gave him an extra measure of oats and a three-day rest. When I
took him out again he started to buck on me. Was I proud of
him! They don't breed them any more like my little Idaho loco.

$\mathscr{H}$arvard $\mathscr{C}$ollege

1904-1908

Socially or intellectually, the college was for him negative and in some ways mischievous. The most tolerant man of the world could not see good in the lower habits of the students, but the vices were less harmful than the virtues. The habit of drinking — though the mere recollection of it made him doubt his own veracity, so fantastic it seemed in later life — may have done no great or permanent harm; but the habit of looking at life as a social relation — an affair of society — did no good. It cultivated a weakness which needed no cultivation . . .

Luckily the old social standard of the college, as President Walker or James Russell Lowell still showed it, was admirable, and if it had little practical value or personal influence on the mass of students, at least it preserved the tradition for those who liked it. The Harvard graduate was neither American nor European, nor even wholly Yankee; his admirers were few, and his critics many; perhaps his worst weakness was his self-criticism and self-consciousness; but his ambitions, social or intellectual, were not necessarily cheap even though they might be negative.

Education of Henry Adams

IF IN retrospect Groton and the northern landscape of Massachusetts seem chilly and uncongenial, then the three years at Harvard College seem rather the challenge of a self-indictment. A New England boarding-school was emotionally thinner than a modern kindergarten, since it straitjacketed play and human feelings; and intellectually it was six hundred years behind the times, since it was avowedly medieval. But emotionally Harvard University in 1904 offered as wide a scope as the world outside it; with — one would suppose — the tremendous advantage that there was an implied guaranty of peace and happiness, or at least an implied insurance against war, starvation, sickness and death. Certainly in intellectual wealth the world's average made a sorry showing in comparison with the galaxy of brilliant men that were teaching then at Harvard. In philosophy, James, Santayana, Royce, Münsterberg and Palmer; in English, Kittredge, Barrett Wendell, Neilson, Perry and Copeland; in economics, Carver and Piatt Andrew, all lectured in the general undergraduate courses. Even in Fine Arts there was the white-haired and atrabilious Charles Moore, who so peevishly carried on the learning of Viollet-le-Duc and the scholarly aura of Charles Eliot Norton, who had been a friend of the great John Ruskin, who put, had he not, Joseph Mallord William Turner on the map, who was born in 1775 — even The Fine Arts Department carried on a tradition, though hardly one spelt in letters of contemporary painting.

The fault, then, was not with Harvard. There was plenty there if one had the intelligence to pick. It is true there was little compulsion from Dean Briggs's Office. One could stay out and drink all night, at one's club or at the dances for Boston debutantes at the Somerset, if one appeared, not too obviously drunk, in the next morning's classrooms. One must not cut too many lectures; but by a judicious selection of snap courses, by an avoidance of those that fell on Saturdays, and by the discreet and well-paid tutoring of the "Widow," one could have a really splendid time with a minimum of effort and many weekends in New York and on the North Shore. Virtue at Harvard was noticed not at all by the faculty, and was rewarded by undergraduates in the most casual fashion. At Yale, if one made the football team, or the *News*, or achieved the presidency of the Y.M.C.A., one might hope, as a reward, for *Skull and Bones*, and so at Yale there was the temptation to excel in scholarship, journalism, drama, athletics or religion. At Harvard the social reward for such excellence was meager and fortuitous, but one might look, on the other hand, for a deeper sincerity in the pursuit of literature or religion.

(79)

Such being the opportunities, one would expect from an average class of six or seven hundred men perhaps a dozen who might in their professions achieve some fame; and as many as fifty who later on in life would write their own unread epitaphs in the dreary cemetery of *Who's Who in America*. My class has a number of pre-eminent names: Van Wyck Brooks, Samuel Eliot Morison, George Richards Minot, George Howe, Edward Brewster Sheldon, John Hall Wheelock, Alfred Vincent Kidder, Joseph Pulitzer, Charles Louis Seeger and Warren Delano Robbins, who died in 1935. Here are a group of men outstanding in their several professions, in literary criticism, history, medicine, architecture, drama, poetry, archæology, music, journalism and diplomacy.

With such opportunities and with this accomplishment — modest in numbers indeed — must not one impute any undergraduate failure to the student rather than to Harvard College? Yes. But *failure according to what standard* one is immediately provoked to inquire. There can of course be only one legitimate standard of success in university education. It is that *which best fits one, according to one's aptitudes, for one's chosen career in after life, in maturity*. Now herein lies my criticism of Harvard College — indeed of all American colleges — at the time of which I speak. This only legitimate standard of success was never the actual standard, accepted either by the undergraduate, the graduate or the parent body. We were judged by the general American — as slightly modified by the Harvard — standard of the day; and by this standard I should say that one half of the only important men, which the class subsequently matriculated, considered themselves college failures; and two or three of them at the most at that time were considered highly successful. I may seem to indict myself of much worse than failure, that is of snobbism. Possibly; but I don't think I am that any more. I happened to know all of these men fairly intimately as undergraduates. They then showed every promise of brilliance. Two or three of them told me during those years that they felt their college life a failure because they had not been elected into certain of the purely social final clubs. They felt their fathers or uncles were ashamed of them. Some doubted whether in after life they could ever live down the fact that they had made fairly good — but not the best — social clubs in college. Remember, I am not speaking of average undergraduates. I am speaking of the men who as undergraduates excelled in their own chosen fields of scholarship, writing, drama or music.

Thirty years ago the standard at Harvard was established by the socially well born; and those who were not socially well born sensed this standard. There was no insistence on wealth; but a moderate income was for most a necessary end to happiness. Many who were really poor overcame their poverty; and earned — along with success — their livelihood through college. Others supplemented their income. There were many opportunities offered. My brother Francis and I earned a good deal of money, tutoring and on the papers. We could have squeezed through without it — and pinched. There were a few men who achieved undergraduate success with neither a social background nor money. It was unusual. There were many with both social background and money who achieved no success whatsoever. That also was not uncommon. The undergraduates had their own rigid standard of — let us call it — manliness and manners, but there were too many successful and snobbish nonentities who were completely devoid of anything except their family's trust funds and a social rating. Harvard, then, was less sophomoric in its sophistication than other American colleges; and also a little less democratic in its ideals and standards than the world we live in.

At Harvard — by the measure of undergraduate and graduate prestige — college activities far outweighed scholarship; athletics outweighed undergraduate activities; social standing — the importance of club life — outweighed them all. On the other hand, since clubs were an end in themselves rather than a reward for virtue, there was far more genuine participation in a wide variety of interests — including scholarship — than at any other university in America.

At Harvard, then, the New England boarding-school boy went in for clubs — social success. If that were not one's line, one opted for major athletics — although even in the field of major athletics there were social overtones. Football and rowing were of course the *ne plus ultra*. About the baseball squad there was something a little — well you know. Very few Grotties went in for baseball at Harvard. The track team was quite all right and of course tennis, golf and soccer; but one hardly knew the fellows who played lacrosse or basketball; or for that matter the members of the Pierian Sodality; and never, never, never, the members of the wrestling or debating teams. They were probably Jews and one might just as well go to Columbia University.

After athletics in undergraduate prestige came the various papers. There was a certain solidarity among them but there were also nuances. The *Lampoon* crowd would be awfully hale-fellow-well-met, and a little sarcastic and conversationally very quick on the trigger with just the trifle of a drawl. The editors of the *Crimson* had more solidity and would probably attend the Law School and subsequently emerge from life's scrimmage as vice-presidents of New York insurance companies. The *Advocate* and *Monthly* were heavily dedicated to poetry and the higher criticism — a little long-haired, spiritual and baggy in the knee; but mingling with the best sort for that matter.

From a social point of view one never went in for scholarship. One carried one's honors lightly, with just a note of deprecation. High honors did not actually leave one in bad odor, so much as under a cloud of suspicion. My friend, George Minot, confided to me once that he, too, had collected lepidoptera; that he had discovered a new species, which, as I remember, was named after him. In his class history, written a quarter of a century later, when he had achieved the Nobel Prize in Medicine, he even re-corded the fact that "My interest in science was formed in youth when I ardently collected butterflies. Apparently I was the first to note the larval stage of the butterfly Melitæa gabbi."

But he too occasionally found it necessary to compensate in the eyes of his clubmates for these youthful escapades in ento-mology. I remember a bet — made also perhaps in the pursuit of science — as to whether one could drink more champagne by imbibing a teaspoonful every four seconds or by swallowing half a pint at a gulp and then resting with closed eyes for a quarter of an hour before the succeeding swallow. I remember, too — it may well have been the same evening — when another clubmate was carried in an automobile, quite lifeless, and buried under a mound of stones, wrenched from the crumbling wall which circled Mount Auburn Cemetery.

Perhaps I am wrong in interpreting such charming memories as compensations. Perhaps I am too hard on my Alma Mater. Perhaps we were just young.

I myself had the most completely colorless and drab career, which means of course that I was not entirely unsuccessful. I was still very ambitious. I watched my neighbors. I stood in line and waited. I squeezed myself into many uncongenial molds. My Maker had not cut me out in the figure of an athlete and I found after three years of further effort that I could not much improve on his original pattern. I went out for the crew and rowed indeed all through college, but being some forty pounds underweight I only lingered a few weeks on the Freshman squad. I took a try at hockey, played on my dormitory squash-rackets team, flirted with trapshooting and finally settled down to cricket and soccer. In cricket I had a short-lived success. With the exception of a few Oxford or Cambridge postgraduates there were hardly a dozen men who knew how to play the game. To my rage the team was disbanded a week before the match with Haverford on account of lack of funds for traveling expenses. I had so counted on a white sweater with a red cHt! But my Junior year I did play on the soccer team, even scored a goal against Columbia; and got a red sweater with brass buttons and a black aHf. That was my final bid for the wreath of bay leaves.

I went in for every type of undergraduate activity; my second barrage to achieve a career. I was dropped from the managership of the football team and of the hockey squad. I finally made the *Crimson*. I was not to be defeated. I was in the chorus of the annual play of the *Cercle Français*. I got elected to the *Deutsche Verein*. I was provisional president of the Freshman debating society but never made the team. I was kicked off the cross-country team and made a few unsuccessful drawings for the *Lampoon*. I carried on. My torch was never extinguished; but the light it cast was pale, diffuse and wavering.

Scholarship remained as a final resource, a substitute for a more legitimate undergraduate career. I was interested in my work in a playful, superficial way. I did pretty so-so; never was brilliant. I graduated in three years with a degree *cum laude*. One year I got a Harvard College Scholarship and received in acknowledgment the usual letter of felicitation from Mr. Peabody. But what of it? I had no direction or passion in my studies. I wanted a smattering of polite learning in art, literature and languages. My own real desire was to prepare for the subsequent enjoyment of life, during vacations from law practice, with as much intelligence and culture as could be picked up without effort between soccer games, *Crimson* editorials, club dinners and "Boston" waltzes. I took one course motivated by a clear, hard intent. I had determined before I died — somehow or other — to spend three months cowpunching in Texas and riding through Mexico. Elementary Spanish was, then, in terms of realistic purpose, the most solid achievement of my three college years. I learned, actually, less Spanish than subsequently in six weeks from an outfit of semi-illiterate Mexican and Texan vaqueros.

And lastly of course I made my clubs — really a great many of them but not the best by a long shot. One or two literary clubs — where incidentally I met almost all those of my classmates who later on amounted to anything; a couple of waiting clubs, a final club; and so on. I was elected my Junior year to a club called the O.K. The initiation fee was twenty dollars. There were two qualifications for membership. One had to be a club man and one was supposedly a convivial trencherman and drinker. The only function of the O.K. was to give one dinner a year for its sixteen members, which cost — as there were eight new neophites and no further obligations — 160 dollars. The O.K. had many great ones inscribed on its roster, my satanic friend, Pierre de Chaignon LaRose, and Theodore Roosevelt among others. During my Senior year it was disbanded; the accredited rumor being that the ex-president had by mistake packed among his luggage its only possession — a silver tea set of debased, and heavily voluted and embossed, Victorian design — and had disappeared therewith somewhere in the Orient.

If I think, then, of my college years in terms of preparation for creative art they are a complete blank. Never would the chances of my becoming an artist seem so negligible. But even thinking of these years in terms of preparation for life, they seem irrelevant. At Groton I had been in my own eyes something of a failure and I was consequently miserable. I could not conform sufficiently — though God knows I tried — and so I remained, against my will, a rebel. But I was neither miserable nor a rebel at Harvard. I was learning to conform; and consequently life was no longer of much educational value.

Two events occurred at the end of my Sophomore year, which in retrospect outweigh the importance of all the clubs, athletics, undergraduate activities and college courses. I traveled through Europe on a bicycle and I fell in love. That trip opened up to my anæmic and conventional outlook such visions of clear happiness, such floodgates of sunshine, such stirring experience with life as I had not encountered since my year in California.

The trip was conventional enough. On the steamer I talked art with Joe Breck and read Alphonse Daudet's *Sappho*. In my diary I recorded its closing words, which to me seemed a little less than immortal: "*Adieu, un baiser, le dernier, dans le cou . . . m'ami.*"

In Holland and Belgium, in Switzerland and then in Paris, for the first time I saw the works of the great seventeenth-century *maestri*, Rembrandt, Franz Hals, Rubens, Velasquez, el Greco; and the suave virtuosity of their forerunners, the Venetians, Titian, Tintoretto, Veronese and Giorgione. Perhaps it was not the best beginning in art. As Mary Cassatt said to me in later years, "*C'est le dernier mot.*" I think it would have been wiser to feed a while first on the primitives — the great schools of primitive design from fifth-century Greek, Coptic and Gothic to Navajo, Hopi, Mayan and Congo; and the great primitive sources of European sculpture and painting, early Greek and the Quatrocento. Perhaps, who knows? It was the seventeenth century that opened my eyes to the sensuous glory and rich tonal orchestration of oil painting.

In the Maurithuis, in The Hague, I saw Paul Potter's Bull, Rembrandt's Anatomy Lesson and Van Weyden's Crucifixion. I sketched in the market at Scheveningen and bought old prints of Ada, Queen of Holland, Dirk V and Louise de Coligny. I saw more Rembrandts in the Ryks Museum at Amsterdam; and bicycled and sketched through Monnickendammen, Maarken, Enkhuizen, Appeldoorn and along the edge of the Zuyder Zee. At Heidelberg in Frau Professor Scherrer's pension we spent a fortnight studying German and exchanging amenities at mealtime with the one Russian, one Japanese, two Americans, three East Indians, seven French and eight German students, who constituted Frau Professor Scherrer's family and partook of her sliced sausages, boiled meat and pickled red cabbage.

Harvard College

In the Black Forest it rained for a week, mist drifted lazily in the valleys and broken shreds of cloud hurried by the hilltops. There I met her; and looking at her once, felt that I was bewitched for always. She had soft brown hair that curled in crisp ringlets on her nape. Her skin was ivory white and sometimes wine-flushed. Her nose had enough mockery in its upward tilt to goad one to any extreme — to drive one crazy. Her eyes were warm and dark and a little slanted; and rippled rather than sparkled. She would glance smiling, sidewise, hovering low, "through mysterious loopholes, brilliant between the fringed lids." Her mouth was ever parted, half-smiling like her eyes, faintly upcurling at the edges with the wanton savor of some fifth-century Etruscan goddess. I associated her face immediately with the lovely profile in the Brera at Milan, supposedly of Bianca Sforza and attributed to Leonardo.

I spent ten days there in the mystery of her presence, at Schönwald, bei Triberg, in the Black Forest. We took long walks together over carpeted paths and under dripping pines and hemlocks; up to Martinskapelle and to the tower at Brend, from which we could see in the distance the blue line of the Vosges and the Rhine Valley. In the evenings we danced the "Boston" together in the empty dreariness of the hotel dining-room. She had among her dresses an old plaid walking skirt. I felt it should have been enclosed in a shrine and presented as a reliquary to some church or museum. A week or two after I left Schönwald I received a postcard from her. On it she had scrawled in her unformed schoolgirl penmanship: "Lest we foget." I was as enraptured by her gentle humor as I was enslaved by the wholly alluring aroma of her presence.

For two years I dreamed of her two or three times a week. I saw what I could of her during my holidays and she flirted with me gently and evasively by correspondence. I loved thus to be flirted with and I suffered accordingly. Whenever I thought of her, I felt a small pain in the pit of my stomach, something akin to heartburn. When someone mentioned her name in my presence, it was as if I had received a blow in the diaphragm.

During these two years I never tried to kiss her — although I was under the sorest temptation — or to hold her hand. I never told her that I loved her. I suppose I felt, with my somewhat Victorian upbringing, that until I had first made some sort of an overt declaration, any physical advance was a blemish on the perfection of our relation. Subconsciously, I realized that I was not ready for marriage. Yet I could ask for nothing less; for I was so romantically disposed that I could only envisage her in terms of absolute eternity. Consequently some two years later she married someone else — a *coup de foudre* on his part, too, I suppose. She could hardly continue — even in terms of eternity — to flirt with me in gentle and evasive correspondence. She must often have been puzzled by the temperance of my ardor. Even as sweet and gentle a soul must at times have been irritated by my complete abstemiousness. I felt terribly when, at the end of a long buggy ride together, she announced to me her engagement. The world was quite heavy with rain clouds. And yet I must have known — in the bottom of my heart — that I had already begun to flirt with another. But I did love her distractedly — in my own strange way — for a year or two; and — lest we forget — she was my first true love and my sweetheart.

The fusion then of these two events — my trip abroad and the first explosive eruption of romantic feeling — had a most happy effect on my development. It kept alive in me — indeed from then on there constantly grew and expanded — whatever small desire to paint lay buried in me at the time, and it made me realize how riotously happy life can be, quite apart from one's hard-earned successes as managing editor of the *Crimson*, as forward on the soccer team or as the recipient of an A.B. *cum laude*. Here was knowledge to shake to its foundations one's eleven years' education in New England.

(88)

Texas and Mexico

1908-1909

The cowboys and the longhorns, who partnered in '84,
Have gone to their last round-up over on the other shore.
They answered well their purpose, but their glory must fade and go;
Because men say there's a better thing at the Chicago Live Stock Show.

Texas Cowboy Ballad

I GRADUATED from Harvard by the end of my Junior year and my Senior year entered the Harvard Law School. For a variety of reasons — partly from a badly infected hand, which required several operations and probably had the effect of weakening my general physical condition, partly no doubt from some emotional maladjustment with life, from the feeling that I was a failure and would continue to be a failure in maturity, I became, at the end of a year, something of a physical and mental wreck. I had heart palpitations, spasms of fear, blinding headaches and the other symptoms of a major climacteric. Doctors advised a year's rest; and what better than a year on a ranch? I had so longed for just this occasion; ever since the rides on the beaches of the Pacific, over the West Coast sierras and among the live oaks at Gaviota. Consequently I took a year out, most of which I spent cowpunching in Texas and riding through Mexico. My mother seemed doubtful as to its permanent value. "It will be fun," she argued, "but hardly profitable later on in life." Frankly I was equally dubious as to the eventual profit to be extracted from cowpunching, but I was successful in my determination to spend a winter in the Southwest.

(89)

I booked steerage passage from New York to New Orleans on the *Comus*, of the Southern Pacific S.S. Co. We were quartered six in a cabin and there were no sheets or mattresses on the wooden bunks. A fellow passenger, who lay immediately above me, slept in his trousers and neither washed nor shaved. Before breakfast he rolled many Bull Durham cigarettes with stiff, damp, yellowed fingers. The pouches under his oily, low-lidded eyes looked like black, rotting fruit. He had a small wet mouth like a garden slug; and his cut-away chin receded to his collarless Adam's apple. At mealtime in a low voice, throaty with hatred, he cursed the maggoty ham, rancid butter and bitter tea dregs which were served us. He told me that he was the champion Singlehand Pinochle Player of Chicago. He had had a lucrative season but thought it advisable to try his luck somewhere else for a time.

I traveled by train from New Orleans to San Antonio, through the cane brakes and wooded swamps of Louisiana. Miles and miles of tropical wilderness. Here and there a clearing, a crazy Negro hut, blue-shuttered on supporting joists; patch quilts hanging from clothes lines; African Negresses, sucking short white clay pipes; starved dogs; sleeping mules; hang-jaw Negroes. By night the country had opened and we were riding over the gently rolling, moon-flooded hills of East Texas.

For about a month I worked with the C. P. Taft outfit on the Gulf, north of Gregory. Here in Texas they single-cinched their saddles and used short manila grass ropes instead of the long rawhide California reatas. The *remuda* — the outfit — was predominantly Mexican. The whites held apart. Your Texan cowboy had all the weaknesses of the South, from which he had largely migrated; of the West, that had molded him; and of Old Mexico, which had also left its impress. He had the white supremacy cult of a Southerner and could brag about "taking a bead on a lousy, yellow greaser just to see him jump like a jack-rabbit from a cactus plant." He combined the Southerner's dislike of the Northerner with the cowboy's scorn of the tenderfoot. He was doubly suspicious and had a twofold inferiority. He had achieved the independence of the Westerner and had lost none of the braggadocio of the pioneer. He had deep reserves of pluck and endurance but none of the good nature of a Wyoming rancher or the manual skill and sensuous charm of a Mexican vaquero. He was largely illiterate and had sometimes a shooting record. He spoke Spanish as fluently as English and was excessively proud and loyal — in a deprecatory, lacrimose sort of way — to the Lone Star State. All too frequently he would refer to "us Texaners and you Americans."

It was the good life. We breakfasted at four o'clock in the morning on goat ribs, mutton steaks, hominy or meal cakes, and tins of black coffee. The Mexicans would add a handful of chile peppers to give it tang. The men crouched about the mesquite coals, sitting on one heel, smoking corn-shuck cigarettes; or stood with their backs to the fire, their fingers stretched out to the warmth of the flames. Sometimes we were ten or twelve or fourteen hours in the saddle. It would be darkening as we reached the chuck-wagon. At that hour the jack-rabbits, curious, would approach the camp. They stood up, tall on the flat horizon; their ears perpendicular above some cactus plant, their noses in the wind. I found them good eating but the cowboys would not touch them. They said their loins were full of worms. The coyotes sang out their evening wail. At night they would smell their way into the camp and filch a quarter of goat, if it hung too low from a branch of mesquite.

The round-ups — branding, cutting, separating, herding and driving — were over in November. I was offered a job at eighteen dollars a month on Las Catarinas ranch at Encinal, about three hundred miles north of Gregory. I made the trip in easy stages, packing my blankets, slicker and few belongings behind the cantle of my saddle; and making about forty miles a day.

(91)

Texan ranchmen were hospitable. If there were no spare bed, I was given a shake-down in the barn. I paid for my mare's oats but never for my own board or lodging. There were no roads and the ranches were far apart. It was all cow country then. Cotton had not come to the Rio Grande. Occasionally near the railroads or on the outskirts of the cattle towns one ran across the tin-can, soap-box huts of the squatters down from Missouri or Kansas, with their covered wagons, dogs, babies and potato patches, but elsewhere no plow had ever turned a furrow. There were wire fences, but sometimes one might herd cattle for a week in one pasture and never see a fence. The beautiful scissor-birds with their long forked tails and salmon-colored breasts flickered in and out of the bushes, and the silly chaparral cocks with their great crests and long sweep of tail ran along the trail in front of me, sputtering and scolding. Quail drummed through the low nopal cactus and the cardinal birds looked never so bright as against the dust gray-green of the mesquite. An armadillo waddled into the bushes before I could pull my Winchester from the scabbard.

One night I spent at Jim Murray's ranch which lay a few miles out of Oakville. We supped and breakfasted on shoulder of pig, cold biscuits and unsweetened black coffee. Jim lived alone with a pet deer and was glad to talk to someone. He had come out from Ireland in '55. His father and mother had died in New Orleans; and he was "given to a man called King," who brought him to Texas. He had fought the Comanches and his wrist had been broken by a Comanche arrow. "They come down after ponies on the full moon," said Jim, pouring out a panful of coffee for his deer. "They ride abreast of one another, not in file. On the long drives up to Oklahoma they will slip into the herds and stampede the steer. They carry their quivers over the left shoulder and shoot well at a hundred yards. Their arrows will cut flesh at a hundred fifty. On wet days the bowstrings stretch and their shooting is less effective. Inside a house

BULLDOGGING

DETAIL FROM
CENTURY OF PROGRESS MURAL

Photo by Robert Imand

you can face fifty of them. They're like coyotes. They're only dangerous if you lose your head. I've killed Comanches; plenty of 'em." He continued to speak throughout the evening in the present tense but admitted that the last he'd "seed on 'em was in '73."

Next night I stopped at Tilden, the county seat of McMullen. It was fifty miles to the nearest railroad, had five hundred inhabitants, a courthouse, a jail, four stores, eight saloons, six churches and a cemetery. In Texas a cemetery was a sign of age rather than of respectability. Like all Texan towns Tilden had been planned much as if its hundred wooden shacks, sheds, lean-tos, outhouses, churches, bars, privies, stores and cemetery had been dropped from the sky and left facing just as they landed. There was a great stir in Tilden that night. A preacher was over from Pearsall, preaching all day and in the evenings, converting the heathen. Upon inquiry I found that dancing was heathen, rather than drinking, cursing or shooting. I slept in the "dollar hotel." The price of a room and of each meal was two bits. Towels were extra.

One night I spent with a family called Ratcliffe at San Roque. Mrs. Ratcliffe had gentle brown eyes, a soft Southern drawl, and kept up an endless and rambling monologue as she pattered about the one-roomed cabin in stockingless, slippered feet. She fed me on the hindquarter of a wild *jabalí* boar, fresh bread, rice, honey and coffee and cream. I had not eaten all day.

The Ratcliffe children, Jesse, Louis, Jode and little Tom, sat on a bench against the wall, staring at me in silence. The elder boy, Jesse, was eighteen but had the shrunken face of a man of thirty. His eyes were close, watery and without luster. His white skin was almost blotted out with gray freckles. His cheeks were flat and his lips were pale and cracked. There were dark, moist passages under his pink lids. His red hair was parted on one side and fell almost to his shoulders. He stared at me furtively for some time and then asked me in a creaky voice whether

(93)

Oklahoma were on the other side of California. When I had satisfied his curiosity he lapsed into an opaque silence.

Mrs. Ratcliffe wandered about the room urging me to eat. Ten-year-old Jode asked me for some Bull Durham. They all smoked, said Mrs. Ratcliffe, even three-year-old Tom. Once he had chewed a quid for an hour "just like a li'le ol' man." Her father wanted her to chew, too, as it preserved the teeth. She had tried, indeed, but it always made her ill. Jesse spoke up and said chewing was unhealthy as it made you spit up a lot of what ought to stay inside you; but smoking was all right as you only spat up what ought to come out.

I asked Mrs. Ratcliffe if she had borne other children. Yes; three of them had died on her. "But you caint expect to raise 'em all," she added apologetically.

Mr. Ratcliffe came in. He had been out all day fence-riding. He was a whale of a man with gentle, resigned eyes under his black brows. Over his blue flannel shirt he wore the short brown cowboy jacket with corduroy collar and sleevebands; and cured leather chaparejos over his blue overalls. He nodded to me silently, laid his hammer, wire-clippers and fringed gauntlets on the table, and removed his Cheyenne spurs from his short, high-heeled boots. His wife addressed him as "Mr. Ratcliffe" and the boys called him "Sir." Jesse brought him a basin of soap and water. One felt that the Ratcliffes were Southern gentry.

That was the end of my journey. Next day I rode into Las Catarinas. It took me six days to make the trip from Gregory, on the Gulf, through Sinton, Beeville, Oakville, Tilden and Cotulla to Catarina. Today there are roads and I fancy one could do it in as many hours. But it's thin country and it probably has not changed much. Tilden, the county seat of McMullen, on the Rio Frio, still has a population of five hundred. Perhaps the cattle country hasn't gone over yet to cotton and truck farming. I hope not. It could never be as beautiful as the flat, waterless desert that I knew, that waste of sand and parched arroyos; of gray mesquite and twisting chaparral; of dust-covered nopal, cocanopal and towering cardón cactus; of lonely ranches; and groups of moody longhorn, knee-deep in the mud of some dried-out water hole, or sleeping under the shadow of the dusty silver gray-green Texas sycamores.

I worked for a couple of months with the Catarina outfit. We slept in the open and the chuck-wagon carried our bedding. The nights were cold and the men doubled up, two in a blanket. We wrapped our boots in our canvas jackets and used them as pillows. We were up early and as we rarely had a noonday meal we supped at four o'clock when we got back from the round-ups. Morning and evening we ate goat's meat, potatoes, frijoles and black coffee. Sometimes we had as a dessert fried flour, sweetened with sugar and raisins — poor man's pudding, the boys called it. After supper and before night settled down we played games, jumping, running and wrestling. I got the boys to sing their ballads in English or Spanish, "Hell in Texas," "The Passing of the Longhorn," "The Midnight Stampede," "La Recién Casada" and others. I achieved a certain success myself by translating into doggerel Spanish a song which in my time had had its day of popularity among the Harvard undergraduates: "No balls at all" rang the challenge of the provocative, though somewhat repetitious, chorus.

The autumn round-ups were over on the Rio Grande. I said good-by to my friends at Las Catarinas, rode down to Laredo, where I sold my horse for forty dollars, and crossed the border into Mexico. Seventeenth-century Spain and frontier America mingled. Neither had left too strong an imprint on the Mexican. He remained what he had always been — an Indian. In the store windows were Siegel-Cooper overcoats at ten dollars, advertisements of Singer sewing machines, Winchester rifles and Stetson hats. At street corners, in front of iron-grilled windows, silent eyes looked out from the encircling sarape. Old women heated tamales over coals and sold warm tortillas, wrapped in dirty rags.

The next day the train rattled through the cactus-covered flats of Nuevo Leon and Coahuila. At the stations girls were offering *carne de chivo, queso de vaca* and *enchiladas*. About their heads and faces they wrapped the black Spanish mantilla, or the brown, or blue-black, narrow Indian *rebozo*. The sombreros of the vaqueros were wide and heavy; they carried machetes, slung below the knee; their saddle leather was of uncured buff rawhide; the cantles high; and the pummels, the girth of a man's leg. We left the dusty gray-green yellow flats and ran straight into the mountains, that had trembled all morning on the horizon. They were cut out of blue, blue-black, green-brown cardboard. It was a wonder world of fantasy.

Monterrey was a hollow between two mountains, the Cerro de Mitres and the Cerro de Silla. I had not had a bath for two months and was tired from thirty-six hours spent on the wooden bench of a third-class Mexican coach. I dropped my saddle and blankets at a *fonda* and took a trolley for the municipal baths.

On the way out I picked up a friendly little American, a Mr. Stuart. He could hardly believe it when I told him I had lived at Ardmore. "Bless your soul, what school did you attend? The High?" And when I told him it was Haverford: "Why I can't believe it. I was there two years myself. It would have been before your day. Who did you know there? We must have friends in common." It turned out we had many friends in common; and before we got to the baths I had told him about my trip and just how much money I had with me, saved up from college for the great adventure. He was a charming little fellow, somewhat vulgar, just a trifle voluble; but very friendly in a strange land. After the baths we had a beer together. At the table next us sat an old man, playing solitaire. He had gray hair, a mouth like a crack in a cement wall and long, flickering, blue-veined hands. He wore loose, black clothes; a black sombrero; and had green spectacles on his long narrow beak.

"Why, bless my soul," said Mr. Stuart, "if that isn't the first American deck I've laid eyes on in four months' time! You don't see honest-to-God cards often in Monterrey; or honest-to-God Americans, for that matter." He hailed the stranger to our table and we had another beer together. Mr. Stuart suggested we all three join in a game of Colorado poker and the winner to pay another round. I said: "No thanks; I don't play but I'd like to sit and watch." They played a while; Mr. Stuart was winning. He shoved me a handful of chips and said: "You play, too; it's just for beer anyway." I played for about twenty minutes and there was nothing to it and I won about six bits myself. I didn't bet high because I was cautious and there were no cards to bet on. The highest I had was a pair of Jacks.

Then my luck turned for the better. Mr. Burns, the green-spectacled stranger, was dealing. The first card he dealt me — face down — was an ace. I drew another ace and Mr. Burns a king. He bet fifteen dollars. I thought he must have two kings but I had two aces. I wasn't going to drop out for fifteen dollars. On the third round Mr. Burns dealt me a Jack and himself an eight. Stuart had fallen out by this time. Mr. Burns bet fifty dollars. I knew, now, that he was tough; but I knew that I could beat the best he had on the three cards dealt. I put my money on the table. Mr. Burns dealt me a Jack and himself a five spot. He bet a hundred dollars. I had aces over Jacks. Mr. Burns's strongest cards would have been a pair of kings. He didn't know I had two aces. There was three hundred and thirty-six dollars on the table. I had never played cards in my life, but I knew something about the mathematical law of chance. I kept my head on my shoulders and did some quick thinking. I wouldn't let the old bastard string me for a sucker and bluff me out of three hundred dollars. I put my money on the table. Mr. Burns dealt us each a five spot.

All along I figured he had the other king covered. He would have kings over fives to my aces over Jacks. There was one chance in fifty-two that he had three fives. But would any damn fool have bet seventy-five dollars — on his third hand — on a five, an eight and a king? Mr. Burns bet five hundred.

I was pretty mad. I got up and said I thought things looked crooked. I didn't have that much money with me. They had started playing for a round of beer and now there was over eight hundred on the table. I said I didn't like it and put my hand on my pistol holster.

Mr. Burns didn't say anything through his green spectacles. My friend Mr. Stuart became very angry and excited. He said he didn't like the looks of things a bit. He wasn't playing that hand but he thought things looked crooked. He said he didn't know anything about Mr. Burns. He was going to stick by me. He said:

"Have you got the cards?"

I said: "Sure I've got the cards. But I haven't got seven hundred dollars. It looks to me crooked." I eyed the green spectacles with my hand on my pistol holster.

My friend Mr. Stuart said: "I'll stake you half. Have you got the cards? Will you do it?"

"Sure I have the cards," I said. "But I don't like the way he's playing." I knew I had the cards and I was getting pretty mad.

Mr. Burns got up. He said: "Gentlemen, we started out in a friendly game. The betting's got a bit high. I propose we call the whole thing off for a magnum of champagne."

I hesitated a split second. My friend Mr. Stuart had worked himself into a fury. He was frothing at the mouth. He roared:

"No, damn it! It's your bet. You stay by it." He reached over and whipped Mr. Burns's card face up. It was the fourth five spot.

We paid up. I put 418 dollars on the green baize table. Mr. Burns offered us an *aguardiente* and shook hands before we left.

Outside Mr. Stuart said he felt ill and went round the corner to vomit. On the way back to Monterrey he asked me if he could loan me some money, "just to tide things over." I said: "Never mind." I had about ten dollars left and my ticket to Durango. He gave me his hotel address and pumped my hand when we parted. Next day I went to his hotel. No; there had never been a Mr. Stuart stopping there; or anyone answering his description!

I lingered almost a month at Durango, trying to explain by correspondence to my mother in the most dignified way what had happened. I had no money to stop at a hotel and I put up with a photographer, Jerry O'Shea — on credit. My host was then a man of sixty. At thirteen he had run away from home in Philadelphia and had roamed the world ever since. He had been for two years in the Transvaal in the mounted police, had traded in Ecuador, prospected for gold in Peru, sold real estate in Florida. He had reached Torreon, beaten; an old man with a dollar, Mex, in his pocket. His first night there he won the hand of Guadalupe Duhalde, the rich widow of a Sonora ranchero. Together they set up a photographer's studio in Durango, where they prospered. I slept in the patio, back of the studio, with four white rabbits, a dove, three hens, a Mexican hairless, two lovebirds and an ancient and splenetic parrot, Augustin de Iturbide.

All day long I wandered through the streets of Durango. The buildings were gay with color, pink, blue or white; and the various stores had the most fanciful of names painted in bright letters: *Flor de Amor, Playa de Palestina, Montaña de la Suiza, Fuente de Araba.* I went to a bull fight and saw the great Spanish *espada*, Relampaguito, kill four bulls. It was pretty bad with the horses. Their ears were laced up and their off eye blindfolded so they could not see the bull. The picadors jerked the horses up and lifted them on to the bull's horns. Again and again they were dragged to their feet and thrown against the maddened bulls. Sometimes they caught their feet in their own entrails. If they were too weak to get up they lay in their blood until the fun was over, when they were dragged out by the feet at a gallop by four cream-colored, caparisoned mules. The crowds shrieked, whistled and cheered. It was a good fight. Relampaguito had seldom demonstrated a greater suavity of sword play.

All the time I was in Durango I never met a soul except Jerry O'Shea and Guadalupe. In the evenings I strolled about the Plaza. The caballeros walked in one direction and the girls and their duennas in the other. The band played "*De Terreon á Lerdo.*" I felt terribly lonely. Moody and exotic desires prayed on me. I dreamed of settling down in this lovely mountain town. I would raise cattle; and marry a Durangonese, proud of carriage, with low forehead and slant Mongolian eyes.

Jerry O'Shea, seeing that I was lonely, asked me why I never went to a *casa pública*. He said: "Once in a while it does a fellow good to get a bellyful of hot guts." Throughout his adventures Jerry had remained a realist; devoid of sentiment and poetic feeling.

Sometimes in the evenings Doña Lupe sang to the accompaniment of her guitar. Her voice was thin but it pulled my heartstrings. She would say: "Ay! Ay! Ay! Don Jorge, life was beautiful when I was young. Life was better in Sonora, on the cattle ranchos. The *cardón* cacti were forty feet high and the Yaqui carried bows and arrows and wore their hair long, with a red fillet fastened about their foreheads. You should have seen the *jinetes,* riding in from the flat *llanos* with silver spurs and silver bits and gold braid on their sombreros. We watched the vaqueros rope the yearlings at the spring round-ups. We danced all night in the patio of the ranchhouse. *Ay! Válgame Dios!* Don Jorge, it was beautiful."

Her eyes were watery but they had been blue. Her hair was nearly white; it had strands of gold in it. She seemed more French than Mexican with all the delicate raillery, the sweetness and gentleness of French women. When she picked up her guitar and sang, she was far away in the golden heat and youth of Sonora and Baja California:

> "Adiós! Adiós!
> Quien sabe si en la vida
> Ya nunca mas
> A verte volveré?"

There was another pretty little song of hers, a dialogue between a boy and a schoolgirl. He tells her how sad he will be if she will not sing and dance for him, and she refuses because it will put her to shame. At length he threatens her that he will leave her and go to Cosalá; and she, almost consenting, asks whether he will not consider her too bold.

"But wherein lay the sting, Doña Lupe, of his threatened journey to Cosalá?"

"Ay! Don Jorge," she smiled at me. "All the prettiest girls in Mexico come from Cosalá. No wonder we others were jealous. You know the adage:

> Cosalá es cosa linda
> Con sus lindas Cosalindas.
>
> Cosalá's a pretty findin'
> With a comely Cosalinden."

She took up her guitar and sang:

> "Cantame, niña, 'sta danza!
> Cantala por carida'!
> Mira! si no me la cantas,
> Me voy pará Cosalá."

HE: By the schoolhouse door, child,
           Sunday morn, a week ago,
           I watched you dance and sing, child.
           Don't wag your head. It's so, you know.

The verses were so quaint, child;
The steps so light and fair;
They are graven in my heart, child;
The dance, your voice, the air.

Sing me those verses, Panchita,
Dance to me for charity!
You have no idea, if you don't, dear,
How desperate I shall be.

SHE: I know you're mistaken, sir.
I never could dance; I could never sing.
And if I should, you would take me, sir,
For a bold-faced little thing.

HE: Dance me those steps, fair Panchita.
Sing for me, *por carida'!*
Look you, next Monday, I'm going
Up yonder to Cosalá.

SHE: I believe you're mistaken, sir.
I never could dance, I rarely sing.
And — if I should — would you take me, sir,
For a shame-faced little thing?

Doña Guadalupe's parrot was named after the great Mexican patriot, liberator, soldier and emperor who was miserably shot in 1824. He had a black tongue, evil red eyes, an irascible temper and, generally speaking, a very military disposition. He chewed tobacco and swallowed the quid. At five o'clock every morning he would clear his throat — it sounded like distant artillery practice — and shout:

"Doña Lupe, Doña Lupe!"

"*Mande usted?*" screamed back Mrs. O'Shea. [What do you want?]

"*Toque la corneta*" [Play us the cornet], bellowed Iturbide.

"*Tocala tu*" [Play it yourself], shrilled Guadalupe.

Iturbide would once more clear his throat and then proceed to play every tap and reveille in his repertoire. *Toc Toc Toc Tocala tu. Toc Toc Toc Tocala tu.* It went on until, hours later, she brought him his breakfast.

Whenever I went by Iturbide's post, to which he was fastened by a silver chain, he would open his black mouth and roll his eyes at me in a concentration of hatred. I would fill my cheeks with tobacco smoke and blow a full cloud into his evil face. He would open and close his mouth and eyes several times and glare at me in apoplectic silence. A few days before I left Durango, I blew a final puff of smoke into the General's face. Whether it was old age, high blood pressure or acute indigestion I cannot tell. He slowly rolled up the whites of his eyes, opened and closed his black mouth, loosened the grip on his perch and slid — quite dead — the length of his silver chain.

Doña Guadalupe was at first disconsolate. To mitigate her sorrow I suggested to her that no dish was as savory as a ragout of parrot. She winced a little at the thought of eating the General. Curiosity, rather than thrift, got the better of her; she served him up next evening *à la cacciatore*, with many olives, tomatoes, green peppers and hot chile sauce. His muscles were hard and tasteless and had the consistency of an automobile tire. Poor Iturbide! I am told that parrots live to a great age. I have often speculated whether he actually saw military service with the Emperor, during his campaigns with the Yaqui Indians through the hot plains of Sonora.

A few weeks later I set out over the sierras with Juan Santana, an ex-*arriero* — muleteer — and Indian from the high tablelands of Chihuahua. He wore tight-fitting green corduroys, pleated down the sides and spreading at the instep; a short Mexican jacket, trimmed with brown lace, and a straw sombrero, fashioned for six reales by the convicts of San Luis Potosí. He was shod in leather sandals — *huaraches* — and carried a three-foot machete under his stirrup-leather. Both of us rode armed, as there were bandits in the sierras. We packed flour, dried fruit, rice, tea, coffee and wolf traps on a mule. We traveled light and hunted along the way.

Juan was a storyteller. At night, over the fire of *jocote* logs, he would narrate adventures which he had experienced with lion, mountain wolf, bandit or other pest: —

"It was at Duraznito that the *malditos* [the cursed ones, the bandits] killed my father in bed with me. My father was *caporal* [overseer] at the Pino Blanco Rancho, two days' ride from Duraznito. He was a heavy man with a square gray beard, a *trigueño* [dark-skinned] like my poor brother Adeleido. Monthly he rode to Duraznito to collect his pay. Well, good now. It is Ash Wednesday and the inns are crowded. You have not seen Ash Wednesday, Don Jorge — la *Fiesta de Ceniza?* The old women and the girls will paint a cross on their forehead and in the evening the girls walk to the *Plaza de Armas* with flowers; and the men throw confetti. There are bulls and music in the Plaza, although it is not Sunday. It is very gay and there are many young rancheros in from the country. In the evening they drink pulque. In the marketplace the old women sell *enchiladas* and *chile con carne*. And what dancing! Ay! Válgame Dios! I was quite drunk — *crudito* — with mescal and pulque. My father and I slept together in the same bed in a small inn in the suburbs. The inns and the stables were all full. My father came back late and hammered on the door a long while before I heard him. It was icy cold, February. I let him in and he slipped off his sandals and flung his sarape over the bed. He climbed into bed. We lay back to back, I next the wall; and for a while I slept heavily."

Juan Santana stooped. He picked a coal with his thumb and forefinger from the embers and lit his *changa*. His small red eyes were shining. He straightened himself, removed his sombrero and passed the back of his hand over his forehead. His hair was straight, long and black. It grew down low over his forehead. The crown of his head was high and flat. Juan Santana filled his lungs twice with a deep intake from his *changa*. He looked at me intently with his gray red eyes. He opened and spread the fingers of his left hand, palm down.

"When I woke up there were three men in the room. They had come for my father's money; but they had not noticed me, because I slept next the wall. One of them stabbed my father in the ribs with his knife. Well now, good. Another of the *malditos* carried a machete. I jumped from the bed right onto his back and the machete dropped from his hand. At the noise the other two were frightened and ran. I stopped and picked up the machete. Then I turned and recognized my attacker as the innkeeper. He seized me by the waist and we stumbled against the head of the cot together. I would have killed the innkeeper with his machete. Now his wife, who was a fat woman and strong, ran in; and while I wrestled with the innkeeper, she tore the machete from me and she cut me over the knuckle — so. They got away — the two *malditos*, the innkeeper and his wife. But they killed my father. He was no louse of a man like me. He was as big as a Texan. When I was little he would take me riding with him, to visit the bear traps which he set about the ranch. He made me ride the yearling calves, sitting on their rump, holding the tail over my thigh. He wanted to make a *jinete* [a horseman] out of me. But I wanted to be an *arriero* [a muleteer]."

Ay! It was a gay life, that of the *arriero*. I tell you it was something to live for to hear a caravan of burros and muleteers coming down a mountain trail. High up among the pines one could hear the "Hay, haya, burro! vamonos, hombre! v-a-m-o-n-o-s!" of the drivers. In a twist of the path out would swing the leader, his long ears nodding in time to each step, his body swaying rhythmically from side to side. Little mouse-colored burros with black stripes down their backs and shoulders; tiny burritos, trotting by their mothers' tails; long-haired mountain mules, white, dun and sorrel; and shiny, smooth-skinned mules from the coast; and the *arrieros*, their shoulders and faces swathed in red and white and blue sarapes, their black Mongolian eyes peering out under wide sombreros.

"*Adiós, amigo!*" sings the *arriero* as he stumbles by.

"*De donde vienes?* [Whence do you hail?]" Juan calls.

"From Guadalupe de los Reyes with oranges," in a rising crescendo.

"And Trinity, the mother of Sorrow? Is she better?"

"Dead," screams the *arriero*, now hidden in the pines. "She slept with a hairless dog to cure her rheumatism, but it ran away in the night and she was dead a week later. *Ora! Ora! Burro! Busquela, maldito!* [Make haste you brigand]"

"Ay! Pity me God!" soliloquizes Juan Santana. "It is that which is bound to be! [*Es lo que ha de ser*]"

We made the coast in three weeks in easy stages, hunting and trapping a bit along the way. In the high sierras it was pine timberland. The burro trails were bitten deep into the rock, where for hundreds of years thousands of precise little feet had deftly picked their way. We camped under crisp, metallic stars, our feet to the *jocote* embers. From the arroyos the lobos howled like derailed locomotives. In the morning we broke the ice from the necks of our canteens. At an adobe ranchhouse at El Salto, the watershed between the Gulf and the Pacific, we bought a round of goat's cheese, a dozen cold tortillas and jerked pork cured with chile — *carne adobada*. From El Banco at daybreak we could see range upon range of multicolored mountains; orange, red-ochre, gray-green, gray-brown and black. In the distance over the blue foothills shimmered the plains, melting and merging still further into the mirror of the sea. And from this shimmering transparency, that was either sea or sky, rose two faint blue clouds or islands — Los Lobos — that watched the

Harbor of Mazatlan, 130 miles away in the Gulf of California.

We dropped like a plummet from the timberland and tall pine forests into the dry river beds of Rio Chico and the *tierra caliente*. Until very recently Rio Chico had paid its tribute to six bandits who infested the mountain passes. Their leader was a boy named Julio. He was a *mestizo* — half Yaqui on his mother's side. He was a good boy and a hard worker, but he lost his job; he was hungry and he stole a chicken. He was caught in the act; hot words were used. The owner of the chicken drew a knife and Julio shot him. Then he fled to the mountains; he was an outlaw. Others joined him; highwaymen from Zacatecas and an escaped convict from Tepic. There were six of them in all. They held up travelers in the mountain passes and took their toll in slaughtered steer from the rancheros. A troop of *rurales* — the mountain police — had been sent by the federal Government to mop them up. In a month of skirmishing and sharpshooting about the steep escarpments of the valley, three of the bandits had been killed and six of the *rurales*. Ay! Julio was *hombre valoroso*, a real bandit!

Then three Indians from Rio Chico volunteered to get him. They took with them rifles, tortillas and a jug of mescal. They came upon the *malditos* high up in a cleft of the mountains, feasting on a slaughtered steer. The Indians told a story of an altercation and the shooting of a muleteer at a coast-town *mesón*. They sat with the bandits all night, drinking mescal and eating meat with them. Two of the bandits drank heavily and slept; and the Indians, too, feigned a drunken slumber. Julio, the *mestizo*, sat and watched the others from the corner of his small shoe-button eyes, his rifle across his knees. All night he watched them, sullen and suspicious. Toward morning his chin nodded on his white sarape. A bullet whipped his chest and he fell forward on his face coughing blood. His back was broken and he was paralyzed. But he retained consciousness and watched them shoot his two friends in their drunken slumber. Then they cut his throat from ear to ear. They dragged the three bodies down to Rio Chico and strung them up by the heels, Julio in the middle.

"I saw his head," said Juan Santana. "His hair was bushy and a foot long. His lips were wide and thick and his eyes small. His tongue was hanging out and he was slit from ear to ear. *Chinga'o!* What a man! But our Indians did by cunning what the Governor of Durango could not do with all his *rurales*. Pum! Pum! Pum! And after that there were no brigands in the mountains of Rio Chico."

We stopped off and rested for a day or two at Mazatlan. It was a coastal town with its black and white chequered cathedral, a chop-house, a theater, an adobe jail and many gaily colored bars. The Mexican Central Railroad had not yet been extended through to Mazatlan, but engineers were busy in the neighboring hills, surveying and mapping out the gradings. The town was overrun with the flotsam and jetsam of humanity, drunken, fighting, shooting miners and construction men. In the bars and brothels sailors, surveyors and pick-and-shovel boys fought over their mescal or panhandled a *real* from strangers for a half tumbler of *aguardiente*.

Juan Santana was visiting a cousin and I wandered, a little lonely, about the cobbled streets. The *cantinas* were gay with color and their names provocative: *La Parisiense, La Esmeralda, Puerta del Sol*. One — perhaps in irony, perhaps in a gesture of atonement was called *Al Pie de La Cruz* — At the Foot of the Cross. I entered, ordered a drink and fell into conversation with a pretty little barefooted Indian girl. Her breasts were high and firm under her clean white dress. Her long oiled hair was tightly bound in a blue ribbon about her forehead. Her eyes were lustrous and dark; her full lips like two lovely unfolding petals.

"And how is it here in Mazatlan? It is a fine pueblo? It is gay [*muy alegre*]?"

CRIPPLE CREEK

PORTRAIT OF MARGUERITE ZORACH   *Photo by Peter A. Juley & Son*

Painting owned by Metropolitan Museum, New York City

"Ay, ay, ay! señorito, it's a sad town, Mazatlan. Here only money counts. All one sees are Americans. Poor, drunken, abandoned creatures. Here the mothers will not permit their daughters to go to dances unless they are affianced. All is for money. No one holds a girl in respect. And the Americans are lost to all decency."

I said: "Might I take the señorita to the theater? They are playing 'El Angel del Cielo.' "

"Ay! Ay! Ay! De veras! Truly in Mazatlan the theater is dreary beyond tears." She looked at me with her soft brown eyes and lowered the velvet fringe of her lashes. "And what will the señorito be," she asked, "a Frenchman?"

I said: "Soy americano."

"Ah!" she said with an intake of finality.

"So you don't like Gringos?"

She said, "Pues, no [Well, no.]"

"And how many have you met?"

"Pues, dos [Well, two]."

"And where do you come from?" I said. Her whole face lit up with a through-shine glow of pride and love.

"Ay, señorito, I come from Cosalá."

At Mazatlan I put up at a typical coastal *mesón*, or inn. The horses were corralled in an open patio. About the patio ran a covered portico, on which opened narrow cubicles. Iron-grilled slits of windows gave from these cubicles to the street; heavy, iron-studded doors opened to the patio and inner court. We locked our saddles and belongings in the rooms and slept on trestle tables under the portico with the horses. I asked the *mesonero* what was of interest in Mazatlan. He told me by all means to visit the jail, one of the finest on the Gulf of California.

I was admitted to the jail without having to show credentials. The guards wore *huaraches* — sandals; their white cotton trousers were drawn with a string tight about the ankles; and their shirts were looped low about their hips. They had double bandeliers of cartridges and carried fixed bayonets in their rifles. When I came in they were playing cards with some prisoners but got up and saluted me. The prison had a wide, clay-floored patio. Wistaria drooped from the high adobe walls. There were pots of yellow and black croton, purple poinsettia and white oleander about the yard. Dripping water jars stood in the cool shadow of a patch of bamboos. A royal poinciana hung its scarlet clusters over the prison wall.

The lieutenant asked me if I should care to visit the *americano*. He was *muy bravo y feo* — tough and ugly — and confined to close quarters. He beckoned a couple of guards to accompany me with fixed bayonets. There was much rattling of chains and unbolting of heavy, iron-studded doors. When I stepped into the cell I could not see. The light trickled down from a high and narrow crevice. The floor was of clay with a bundle of straw in one corner. The American lay on the straw; a chain was fastened to a ring about his ankle. His skin was neither white nor yellow; yet it was a transparent parchment of a sort, lit up by some pale inner glow of unhealthy vermilion. His forehead was wet. No doubt he had fever. There was a look of poised, calculated and inhuman evil that emanated from his pale blue-green eyes from under the heavy red eyebrows and red shock of hair. He gazed at me steadily in the twilight of the narrow cell, with eyes that were the eyes of a cat or a serpent or a turtle. I asked if there were anything I could do for him. He said in a very measured, lifeless voice, "Yes. Speak to the *jefe político*. Better speak to the Governor at Culiacan. I have been here for two years. I haven't long to live. I'm dying — dying of the bloody flux."

I promised him. Later I kept my promise. But I wanted to get out into the air. I asked if there were anything else I could do. He looked at me, taking my measure, with his blue-green serpent's eyes, and said: "Yes, get them to bring me some water." I knew he was dying — of the bloody flux.

Beyond San Pedro de Guanaceví in the tableland of Chihuahua the crooked *manzanillos* of the coastal ridges gave way to scrub oaks and cedars. Eroded gullies twisted down the barren hillsides and snarled piñon roots scratched a holding among the sand and gray boulders. Off on a mound some twenty raw-headed vultures flapped awkwardly about a dead steer.

On this winding and tortuous path, worn deep between two banks of sand and rubble, we passed a Tarahumara Indian. He was long-legged, flat in the chest and high-shouldered. His head was passed through the native *talma* or poncho. A strip of red rag, bound round his forehead, held back from his face the shaggy black mane. Underneath the bulging forehead peered tiny bloodshot eyes. He carried a rifle and a dozen tortillas in a red handkerchief. We walked along beside him and exchanged the amenities of the road.

The Tarahumara had recently married a girl from Atascaderas. They got along well enough together, it would appear. Then the mines at Santa María del Oro shut down and he was without a job. He had almost starved, and he could give her no money. Last Sunday she had left him, jilted him; fled into the mountains with another man. It was several days before he could pick up their movements. He was close behind them now. They had left Guanaceví that morning. He was following their footsteps in the sand of the tortuous mountain path.

At high noon we pulled off the trail to rest the horses in the shade of an oak tree. We called a *"Buena suerte* [good luck]*"* to the Tarahumara; and he nodded an *"Adiós, señores."*

We came upon all three of them the following morning — the Tarahumara, the girl from Atascaderas and the other man. They must have been eating breakfast when he overtook them. The woman crouched on her haunches, her back to the trail, so that we could not see her face. The Tarahumara stood there, cursing her over and over in foul, brutal words. He was too angry or stupid to argue or ask her questions. He cursed her again and again in the same low, vile, monotonous tone. She never moved, but lowered her head a little as we approached. Once in a while in a tired, toneless voice she broke in with explanatory words, while he cursed her. Then the Tarahumara stooped and deliberately struck the woman in the mouth and she fell forward sobbing. Quite as deliberately the other man unsheathed his *daga*; and told the Tarahumara in the same blasphemous language that he had gone far enough and might get a knife blade in his belly. The two glared at each other with bloodshot eyes. Then the Tarahumara turned to the woman, who had ceased sobbing, and began cursing her again with the same filthy monotonous words. He of the *daga* watched them both for a moment. Apparently making up his mind that no further harm was intended, he returned to warming his *tortas* over the *jocote* cinders. We stood there for a few moments, and then, shaking the lead rein of our pack mule, we wished them Godspeed and stumbled up the path. The woman kept her back to us and did not return our "*Adiós señores.*"

In the sierras of Chihuahua I met various members of the de la Rocha family. They were clannish and feudal; Spanish rather than Mexican; cruel, arrogant, lavish in their hospitality; sometimes illiterate, decadent and poor white; sometimes with the fire and energy of the conquistadors.

The widow of Remedio de la Rocha, the miser, lived at Molle Viejo in the foothills above Culiacan. When he died a half-witted peon showed her where lay hidden a buried box, heavy with gold coin. Between them they could not lift it. All her life, childless, she had slaved for Don Remedio. Sallow, devout, embittered, she had spent her days crooked over washing vats; in the cooking shed, the vegetable loft or the counting-house. I met her once on the trail above San Coyotano. She was dressed in black, and wore a long black veil. She rode by on a white mule, sitting the heavy sixteenth-century Mexican side-saddle with regal air. She did not return our salute as she trotted by, followed by her retainers and laden pack mules.

"That," said Juan Santana, "will be the widow of Don Remedio. She is leaving the foothills of Culiacan and riding over the sierras to the Capital, to spend the gold of Don Remedio, the miser."

I had formed the habit, while cowpunching in Texas and on my lonely eight-hundred-mile riding trip through the sierras and the coastal plains of the Pacific, of jotting down a diary in my somewhat rickety Spanish; as subsequently, on other journeyings, in French, German or Tahitian.

In Durango, on the twenty-second of February, 1909, I recorded in my journal — in language which, translated into English, would lose all its rhetorical flavor, romantic glow and spiritual significance — the fact that I was no longer virginal.

"*Esta noche fué a una casa publica. Hablé, como media hora, con una muchacha bonita — Helena. Su nombre de familia sera Esperanza. Estaba de buena figura y cara, pero sin verguenza. Tomaba mucha cerveza; comió con sus dedos, me dando tambien arroz y pollo en un cuchillo. Despues, en el salon de baillar, gritaba mucho, se peleando en chiste con el tocador de piano.*

"*Yo salí muy temprano, pocito emborachado, pocito disgustado — no con lo que habia hecho, el designo de meses — pero con la vida de esas pobres — tan bonitas, unas; pero tan sin verguenza. En no mas que una hora, me habia como enamorado de esa pobrecilla descarada.*

"*Que solitario se siente unas veces en esta bonita pais! Como quiero hablar con muchachas iguales, unas veces, para perseguir de mi mente los malos pensamientos — frutos de soledad continuel y de esos rostros y figuras sensuales de las Mexicanas. Unas veces casi se huien todas mis principias, mis ideales; y esta no mas que costumbre de años que me tienen en el camino derecho!*"

It was quite impossible for me in after years to explain to others the wealth of experience, the warmth of the emotions, the bright colors which I had drawn from this short six months' adventure. What Melville's cruises in a deep-bottomed whaler among the palm-fringed atolls of the Pacific were to him, what that short summer's camping trip among the Indians of the Northwest was to Parkman, what it meant to Samuel Clemens to pilot a broad paddle-wheeler through the snags and currents of the Mississippi — all that to me were these months of pan-handling, riding, roping and shooting, north and south of the Rio Grande.

Harvard Law School

1909–1911

The life of the Law has not been logic; it has been experience.

OLIVER WENDELL HOLMES: *The Common Law*

IT SEEMS strange in retrospect that, having experienced life in the full color and closely woven design of the tropics — and on top of that, having spent three months studying art and architecture in Paris in a loose, purposeless manner, yet with absolute moral contentment — I should still have kept my eye bent on a legal career, and spent two more gray and wintry years wandering through the tasteless, colorless and to me patternless corridors of Langdell Hall at the Harvard Law School. Yet merely to assume that I was too little the artist, contained not enough warmth, was composed of too cottony a substance, is perhaps an over-simplification of the filaments which constitute the organism of growth, the more proper explanation being that there is always in us a certain amount of dynamic energy, of combustive power, which is exactly countered by the one billion facts of life which impinge upon us in terms of present, past and future. And it is this exact balance of inner and outer forces which does indeed prevent us exploding forth to Russia, to Spain, to China or to other seemingly remote adventures of life. Only indeed when this exact thrust and counter-thrust of life's desires and emotions is disturbed do we make momentous decisions — effortlessly, even subsconsciously, if the disbalance is sufficiently extreme.

(115)

As a preparation for creative art, no one could well imagine, at that spring solstice of life, a period of more absolute waste and inconsequence than three years at a law school; and yet of the eleven New England years I should rather by far sacrifice the five years at Groton or the three in college. Perhaps this is merely a recognition of the bankruptcy up to this point of so expensive and methodically planned an education. Where the Law School stands out so uniquely in my experience, amazing as the admission may seem, is this: Here there was but one standard of success, the study of law. At the Law School the most arrogant Porcellian snob, or successful college drunkard, or publicized all-American football star, or supercilious North Shore socialite, or eager East Side Jew might now compete and achieve success on the presumed basis of his enrollment in the school — on his honor rating. Here for the first time in my schooling I could judge myself — and was judged by others — by a criterion not hypocritical. The fault, I repeat, had not been altogether that of Harvard College. The fault was rather that without knowing it I belonged to a future generation which would demand of Harvard College something which it had never been. Harvard in 1904 remained pretty well faithful to its best — or at any rate its safest — tradition. Although for fifty years under President Eliot it had advanced in *educational opportunities* with seven-league boots, yet in terms of *traditional standards* it had hardly moved at all.

Henry Adams records that in 1854 "no one took Harvard College seriously. All went there because their friends went there, and the College was their ideal of social self-respect. . . . Leaders of men it never tried to make. . . . Its ideals were altogether different. The Unitarian clergy had given to the College a character of moderation, balance, judgment, restraint, what the French call *mesure*; excellent traits, which the College attained with singular success, so that its graduates could commonly be recognized by the stamp, but such a type of character rarely lent itself to autobiography. In effect, the school created a type but not a will."

Perhaps I was subconsciously eager for something more than becoming a type — even with this commonly recognized stamp to vouch for "what the French call *mesure*." Perhaps succeeding generations would demand of education something a little less nebulous in preparing them for their role as "respectable citizens" and in furnishing them with "something of what they wanted to make useful ones."

Very quickly then at the Law School I achieved, as did also the other students, some idea as to the relation of mind and social manners; of mind and mental discipline; of the relation between the purity of the Harvard Law School mind and the crass vulgarity — so we were told — of the way law is commonly practised. I observed that a mind can be held in the highest esteem, although its owner never made the D.K.E. I also learned — and I confess it somewhat bothered me — that not all the great ones of the earth had graduated with honors from a law school. This indeed seems to me another weakness of our whole system of education, which is predicated on the idea that success, as well as excellence, can be measured by a fixed set of standards. We obtain *what we take out of life*; and this essence can rarely be graded by any one set of ratings. Lastly I learned that mental capacity is not a result of method and long hours, as much as it is of mental capacity.

I had hoped that, as a law student, I would shine with a certain luster. I was mistaken in judging my own brilliance, quite as much as in appraising that of others. One of those whom I thus underestimated, and who got a high A, while I with infinitely greater method achieved a very average C, was my brother Francis. I have often speculated how much the excellence of his marks had to do with my growing disillusion with law and the legal profession. Certainly during these three years my interest in painting grew steadily. I sketched somewhat during the summers, attended night classes in life drawing, read the Pennells' life of J. A. M. Whistler and the de Goncourts' biographies of Utamaro and Hokusai; and made occasional trips to study the Puvis and Sargent murals in the Boston Public Library.

I had long talks that last year with Bill James about my predilection for an art career. Why not try it, he said. You can't tell for several years yet, whether or not you have any creative talent. Aptitude is, after all, of the least consequence. Don't worry about starting late in life. Puvis was a lawyer and didn't begin painting until he was thirty. Van Gogh and Gauguin started as businessmen. Go to Paris and draw, draw, draw, draw. Julien's is still the best place in the world. It's not the teachers. It is the standard of the other students. Get your law degree. Pass you bar exams. Play safe. And then go for a year to Paris. And draw, draw, draw.

I took his advice. That's the way I started. Bill James never realized — how could he — what a hero he was to me. He was a clubmate of mine, several years older. He had been captain of the crew his Senior year but had resigned because, I believe, he disapproved of intercollegiate athletics. I felt this was a tremendous gesture of idealism although his clubmates thought he was a sap. He had spent a year or so in the Medical School and chucked it for art and Paris. He was tall and handsome and terribly serious. I worshiped him and hung on his words. He told me what quarter in Paris to live in; and to keep an eye on a chap called Matisse. People were talking about him. We had tea together with Mrs. Jack Gardner, who had bought a portrait which he was finishing of his Uncle Henry James. Bill invited me to his studio. I shook hands ecstatically with another young artist, who was told that I showed talent. He and Bill leaned in reverent concentration over the somewhat woolly profile of the great man of letters. They whispered together about turning edges — they had both studied under Tarbell — establishing passages, feeling the line, achieving paint quality and building in planes. I had no idea what it was all about, but felt like someone out of *Trilby*.

I got through the Law School, even got an honor rating that last year. During the summer I was admitted to the Pennsylvania Bar and I sailed early in September, 1911, for Paris.

Art Student
and the Latin Quarter
1911-1914

BILL JAMES had told me to draw at Julien's. Henry McCarter, with his admirable insight and poetic, though tortuous symbolism, had advised me not to work at all too insistently. No one's mind is as quick as Mac's; though his words are slow-motion imagery. All the Irish must have a little of James Joyce in them. "Julien's . . . perhaps . . . but always the unessentials . . . Japanese prints or old leather bindings . . . not to read . . . along the quays . . . of course Montmartre . . . one will resist; but try also to absorb . . . always in moderation . . . and good food . . . not necessarily at Larue's; but for two francs fifty . . . Miss Cassatt, you subsume . . . but why not Madrid, London; John Sargent, too, essentially by way of antidote. . . . Yes, Paris cannot actually harm you . . . although, of course, you will do nothing to equal these [he was loosely thumbing the leaves of a sketchbook, without — it

seemed to me — so much as glancing at my precious drawings]
. . . you will do nothing to equal these for . . . another ten
years."

I could hardly indeed know how right Mac was in divining
that by instinct and training I should attempt to possess art
through determination and method rather than through self-
surrender and self-scrutiny. Nor could I realize that my friend
was a supremely great teacher in that he was more interested in
his students as human beings than ever in art theories. Accordingly for three or four years — in Paris, at the Pennsylvania Academy of Fine Arts, in Munich — I doggedly set out to become a
proficient art student; thereby acquiring a certain volume of the
completely dead but none the less weighty and cumbersome
Beaux Arts tradition; which paraphernalia it would take me another decade to eliminate.

Years later I asked Mac, somewhat shamefacedly, remember-
ing my former stubborn and dogmatic convictions: "But, Mac,
how could you ever keep faith in me?"

And he, sly man, out-trading my humility in fulsome praise:
"I had, George, enough faith to keep my eyes generously fixed
on you, and resolutely closed to everything you painted."

Perhaps there is no other way to muddle through. Perhaps
since it takes three or four years to acquire a certain manual skill,
it is quite immaterial what tradition one follows or what is the
mental and artistic waste in the process of acquiring this physical
dexterity. Perhaps it may take ten years or so to mature one's
individual and creative personality, the only obviously necessary
thing being that one has matured; the conditions from which one
has matured having, then, no possible importance. There is no
way of isolating an educational experiment. But one can hazard
an opinion.

Most of our esthetic criticism is based on the concept that
beauty is a furtive imponderable, shimmering in and out — like
a Grecian psyche or an early Christian soul — from things called

works of art; and that the male hormone or genital which begat and brought to earth this flitting radiance from the matrix of material experience is of the Parnassian Superman, alias Genius. This lovely legend is of course a hangover from one of Plato's fantasies; and is therefore, as esthetic theory, not more than two thousand years outmoded.

We may flatter ourselves, then, that our generally accepted art education — as practised traditionally at Julien's, at the Beaux Arts and at the American Academy of Rome; intermittently, at the Pennsylvania and National Academies; at Harvard, modestly; and with a ferocious appetite at Yale — is not more than 250 years behind the times; involving seemingly the accepted faith that Raphael improved a little on fourth-century Greek, by infusing sentiment into cold perfection; and that David improved much on Raphael by adding French eighteenth-century moderation, morality, reason and Directoire furniture to Raphael's a little too uxorious and purely Italian point of view. The theory is something like that. Now here is the method to perpetuate this noble Beaux Arts tradition, which was completely dead at its parturition some 250 years ago.

For several years your student makes photographic copies of plaster casts and of the nude, the emphasis being on accurate values, as the camera would achieve them, and on understanding the movements or dynamics of anatomy — *la mise en place*. Such manual virtuosity is accompanied by an indiscriminate study of David, Poussin, Raphael and late Hellenic sculpture, with the view of subsequently incorporating their elements in a great contemporary masterpiece.

One thing perplexed me at the time and for years to come. While in art school the ultimate goal, rewarded always by the highest praise, was one's approximation to the standard of the most talented student; whereas, the moment one graduated, the meanest dig that one could thrust at a fellow artist was the suggestion that "perhaps he was slightly reminiscent of so-and-so." This absolute contradiction between what one had so laboriously achieved for so many years and what, as a mature artist, one aspired to, is an instance of the muddled, purposeless and dead-traditional aspects of all art schools, as I have known them. An artist's profession is highly technical; yet these needed techniques are not commonly taught at the academies. Practical chemistry for instance is necessary to the ceramist for his glazes, to the fresco painter for the proper knowledge of his colors and preparation of his wall or to the sculptor for his bronze patines. Yet practical chemistry is not taught in the academies. A comparison of the great schools of formal design — the Etruscan-Hellenic, the realistic-Egyptian-Pompeian-Victorian, the Gothic, Moorish, baroque and the various primitive — is certainly more important than a comparison of the great schools of painting. Yet neither is taught. One would surely suppose — any carpenter would advise as much — that, before painting, a student should be given some familiarity with the use or preparation of his brushes, colors, paper and canvas, but this is never done. The charcoal or oil painting in traditional manner of plaster casts, still lifes and nudes is considered a satisfactory preparation for the subsequent highly technical and creative business of painting pictures.

One might further suppose that there is no permanent loss in immediately teaching what one must subsequently learn. Drawing, as taught in the academies, is largely a stippled competition with photography; or, as taught in modern schools, a psycho-emotional vent. Why not teach it from the beginning as it is ultimately used, as a mode of language, expressed in personal symbols? Any child of four can tell his mother in word symbols that he has dreamed of an animal with six legs, a geranium growing out of its forehead, the face of an old horse and a permanent wave in its tail. But few mature painters, alas, have the fluency in their own professional media of a four-year-old child in his. Why not from the beginning, then, teach drawing as a personal language of thought and narrative? If this were once generally understood, it would not seem so completely unreasonable to the art student or layman, as often now it must, that the Chinese, the fifth-century Copts, the Trecento Florentines and the contemporary French do not necessarily speak in the same art idiom.

Fred Frieseke first taught me this difference between the sincere, individual and the Academic-Yale-Art-School approach to drawing. For several years my method of study, after carefully establishing my figures and composition in charcoal, was to draft them in hastily with a bold free wash in a few direct tones of color. I would then laboriously, bit by bit, with patient and uninspired integrity, patch my painting together, as if I were completing some enormous picture puzzle. Frieseke, on seeing a fresh, direct and living sketch, remarked that it was the best thing I had done all summer. I argued: "Yes, of course, but I am still a student. I must aim at more than a happy start. I must push it further, even though in the process I lose the charm. I must learn how to draw."

As is Fred's habit when laboring in emotional distress, he slowly swung his head from side to side, swallowing air as if in acute gastronomic pain. "Granted, George, that you must learn to draw. . . . But surely . . . it would seem to me . . . that, as you work further on a drawing or a painting, you should improve it — not make it worse!" I had never thought of it as simply as that. It was a gentle knockout blow to the pedantry of all carpenters and academicians.

I have suggested that the academies do not teach the many techniques of the craft; and that what they do teach — drawing, design and composition — they teach blindly and without purpose. Yet one can be a significant artist — though never truly great — with neither a knowledge of the crafts or a mastery of drawing or design — witness such one-sided personalities as Cézanne, Van Gogh, Marin or Soutine. But one can never be an

WRESTLING MATCH

WHOOPEE AT SLOPPY JOE'S   Photo by William McKillop

artist at all, of even microscopic shadow, unless one has some philosophy of life; some yearning, desire, love, or hatred; something to express in one's painting, which is beyond or different from what has already been felt or said. It is the blind disregard of this only ultimately important thing in an artist's growth which accounts for the sterility of our academies.

If it be argued that originality cannot be taught, I would answer that it is therefore the more important that the student in some manner plumb the depths of his own feelings. If it is true that one is born with a creative outlook, yet nevertheless in the beginning it is always latent. I would urge that in our schools we hasten its development. The problem to the student of creating a work of art is no whit different than later on in life to the mature artist; or, rather, the only difference is that the artist is mature through his experience, while the student has not yet faced enough experience to achieve maturity. I would propose, then, from the day that a student envisages an art career, that the ultimate problem of creation be placed foursquare before him, and that he immediately face it; by beginning, while studying at other things, to attempt personal, creative painting.

I wasted, then, my time by not wasting enough of it. I pursued my own obstinate, narrow, orthodox path. But, God knows, I was happy that year in the Latin Quarter!

I registered immediately at Julien's, in the rue du Dragon, off the rue des Saints Pères. The school was in an enormous hangar, a cold, filthy, uninviting firetrap. The walls were plastered from floor to ceiling with the prize-winning academies, in oil or charcoal, of the past thirty or forty years. The atmosphere of the place had changed little since the days of Delacroix, Ingres or David. Three nude girls were posing downstairs. The acrid smell of their bodies and the smell of the students mingled with that of turpentine and oil paint in the overheated, tobacco-laden air. The students grouped their stools and low easels close about the model's feet. While they worked there was a pandemonium of songs, catcalls, whistling and recitations, of a highly salacious and bawdy nature. The girls enjoyed the fun; but the work was rigorous, the studio was never aired, and frequently they fainted.

Among the students were two cousins, Bordelais, Ducos and Alaux. Ducos was suave of manner and punctiliously groomed. He wore spats and carried gray gloves and a gold-headed cane. He looked all of Valentino; and was invariably accompanied by a sable, wide-eyed, oriental mistress. Alaux was tall and emaciated. He coughed and had a damp, drooping handshake. He wore a flowing black tie and a black felt hat, and shaved every third day. Alaux had a fine tenor voice and sang the little Bordelais ballad:

> "Deyust' ma fenestro un aoselo
> Canta tout la neit; canta no per io."

The whole atelier would take up the chorus, singing in parts:

> "Se canta, que canta,
> Canta no per io;
> Canta per ma mio,
> Que sta lein de io."

He sang another little couplet that was always a great success:

> "La peinture à l'huile est très difficile,
> Mais la peinture à l'eau c'est beaucoup plus beau."

Then there was an interminable epic about the sexual adventures of a certain Père Dupanloup — a veritable stallion of a Frenchman — who started his amorous exploits in the cradle; and from then on pursued his prey relentlessly, right up to and through the gates of Heaven, sparing neither his old nurse, God, the Holy Ghost, or the many other victims of both sexes, which he encountered along his way. The tune is a very popular nursery melody, which adds of course to the zest. It starts out:

(126)

Art Student and the Latin Quarter

"Père Dupanloup dans son berceau"

From then on, even in French, it is unprintable.

Another of the students was a Breton sailor — le Mathurin, they called him. Having been left some small inheritance he quit the sea and drifted to Paris; where, ever in search of adventure, he discovered the Latin Quarter, which turned out to be far more colorful than codfishing. He fitted himself out in the customary corduroy trousers, black felt hat, broadcloth coat and flowing silk tie; and settled down to enjoy Bohemia. One day I found a pair of boxing mits and between poses was explaining to a group of French students the different hooks, leads and parries. Le Mathurin volunteered to have a lesson. I took him on but jokingly warned him to go easy with his punches. He was hard as nails, weighed half as much again as I did and had arms like a gorilla. He was good-natured but had a quick ugly temper and as the French boys said: *"C'est breton."* All went well for a couple of rounds. Then, through no fault of mine, he stuck his nose on a left lead. The students roared with laughter. Le Mathurin went white with rage. He lowered his head and charged, butting at my stomach, his arms flaying. I uppercut to defend myself and caught him on the chin. It took him off balance and he was going at such a pace that he somersaulted, upsetting three easels, and landed on his back. He and everyone else was convinced that I was a prizefighter. My reputation was made from that moment; and when I told them that I had cowpunched on the Rio Grande — and to prove it roped a milk-cart horse in the rue du Dragon — I was for the time a hero. I had not yet learned that the surest appeal to the French — the most intelligent but also the most conceited and parochial people in Europe — is the exotic. Had I properly understood the ground for my popularity at Julien's, it might have saved me subsequent loss of pride in my desire to compete with Paris reputations.

I worked hard that winter in the life classes; sketching in the evening at Colarossi's or at the Grande Chaumière. Sundays I lived in the Louvre, studying the French Schools, the Dutch, the Venetians and Velasquez. From the Louvre I wandered through the Trocadéro, the Cluny, the Luxembourg, the Place des Vosges, the Musée Guimet and the Musée de la Ville de Paris. At night I was blind with fatigue. But on a bottle of red wine the world was rosy. I would fall asleep over Delacroix' *Journal*, Meier-Graefe, Théodore Duret's *Peintres Impressionistes*, Albert Gleize's and J. Metzinger's *Du Cubisme* or Paul Signac's *d'Eugène Delacroix au Neo-Impressionisme.*

Modernism was launched that year in Paris. I went to the exhibitions of the cubists and the futurists and read their manifestoes. Someone took me to an evening at the Steins, where I saw the Matisses and Picassos. Fundamentally there is nothing difficult in the esthetic enjoyment of abstract art. In the designs of oriental carpets, wallpaper, neckties, dresses or streamlined automobiles, the public is perfectly accustomed to abstract pattern and frequently shows discrimination and taste. If one can enjoy an abstract design on the floor, one can presumably enjoy it hanging on the wall in a gold frame. I have indeed no fault to find with cubism as *style* or *design;* but when its protagonists designate an abstract pattern as a *picture,* they are twisting the usage of the English language. Nor do I object to their intention to widen the range of our esthetic vocabulary and our outlook on art, but their murky use of words and their half-baked metaphysics are the reason why they are so little understood by the general public. The proper function for abstract art is to enhance the meaning and form of a useful object — a utensil; and conversely in the enjoyment of pictures, where the work of art has no ulterior utilitarian purpose, the average human being gets the maximum of esthetic pleasure from representational art. In 1911 I had not thought this out. I responded sensuously and without effort to the new tonalities in minor keys, to the marked preference for asymmetry and to the many elements of primitive design — dots, dashes, angles; and the emphasis on horizontals, perpendiculars and diagonals, rather than on the reverse curve of late Roman and late Renaissance art — all of which was so stimulating to the jaded European eye after three centuries of decadent baroque. I read the manifestoes of the modernists, and their pompous and meretricious metaphysics. I was puzzled by it all. The next morning I would return to my academies at Julien's.

That winter I spent a month in Madrid, studying the Goyas and El Grecos, and copying Velasquez; and later in the spring made a short pilgrimage to London to see the fine Moronis, Piero and the Tintorettos. England seemed a far more foreign country than Bavaria, France or Mexico. I could talk at least to these, but one could hardly speak the same language as the British. London recalled Philadelphia. This was not entirely to London's credit. But English food was the final reminder that they were an alien race.

I had a letter of introduction from Mrs. Leverett Bradley to John Singer Sargent, and spent several evenings with the great man. Two things impressed me about him. He returned my visit the day after I called on him; leaving his card, bent down at the corner, at my rooming-house. This struck me as a very courtly and polished gesture. I sat with him the next evening over a whiskey and soda, which he bade me pour myself from his mahogany sideboard. He inquired after our mutual friend Mrs. Bradley, and asked if she were still doing water colors. He spoke of her as Susan Hinckley — her maiden name. This in a way affected me even more than the card dropped at my hotel. Not only did it bring this tremendous figure within the orbit and currents of my experience, but I could picture him — as I never otherwise should have — as thus intimately addressing by her Christian name a mere white-haired friend of my mother's.

Sargent asked me many polite questions about what was happening in Paris. He had rather lost track of things for ten years. Had I, then, seen the cubists and Matisse? He showed me many of his sketches for the Boston Public Library and admitted that in one of them he had "rather had El Greco in mind." After that a number of English friends and members of the British aristocracy drifted in — critics, Prince-Alberts and Ladies Thing-um-a-bob. They all said "Amazing" and "I say" and "Rather." One critic said: "He holds his brush like a foil." Another said: "He has the fencer's wrist, you know. I've seen him, late at night, with a flick of the palette-knife remove the paint, clean, from the canvas . . . Really . . . Amazing."

When John Singer Sargent was a little chap, he had evidenced some childish precocity at caricatures and had done, I am told, a whole series of the Newbolds and other Philadelphia cousins as barnyard animals. Years later, after he grew up to be a great man, these drawings came to light in some family attic. They showed little of the quality that gave him his pre-eminence; and, as they were held to be in bad taste, they were of course destroyed. As a youngster he had shown some sense of humor.

Back in Paris, when I was not working, I divided my time between certain elegant members of the Quartier St. Germain and the scum of the Quartier Latin, which possessed at least an equal integrity. I had a letter to my Grandfather Robinson's old friend Madame Michel Chevalier, the wife of the eminent free-trade economist, who had died in 1879, and to her nephew Paul LeRoy-Beaulieu, economist and member of the Institute. At his house I met the Contesse de Franqueville, who lived in the beautiful Château de la Muette, perhaps at that time the finest private residence in Paris. The old lady took a fancy to me and promised to visit me and see my work. She arrived one afternoon in a victoria and pair. Her equipage filled the narrow street. A footman stood at attention in front of the Bon La Fontaine, while she climbed the five flights of stairs to my small, unheated bedroom; where I had spread out on the red eiderdown quilt and pinned to the walls the fruits of my winter's work. I had told her that my grandfather had lunched with Lafayette and she vowed she would do the same for me by his descendants. She consequently had me meet the de Lasteyries; and drove me out to lunch with them at their country château. I remember an old man with a neatly-trimmed white beard, who talked much about English park landscaping and foxhounds; and his very shaven son, who raved about American railroads, Pullmans and grain elevators.

Life in the Latin Quarter was a carefree and a pleasant one; rich in enthusiasms, in ideals and in those lovely youthful loves that are so fragile because they carry with them none of the obligations of maturity. In the cold, descriptive words of final appraisal, after a quarter of a century's interval, it all seems nearer to the rather sordid adolescence of Greenwich Village than to the gentle and witty romanticism of Du Maurier's *Trilby* and Murger's *Vie de Bohème*. I was in my twenties and I was living in the Paris of before the War. I know — alas — that I shall never live there again.

Toward morning at the Bal des Quatz Arts we were still quite sober, although we had been drinking steadily all night. Some little model or other had helped me with my costume. The various ateliers at Julien's — downstairs, those of Professors Bachet, Royer, Pages and the tottering Hubert-Robert; upstairs, that of old Jean-Paul Laurens, with his meridional accent, his bearded, satyr's goat face and his seventy-four years of unimpeachable success and bad painting — had been working feverishly at their loges for the past fortnight. We had all dined together with our girls and drunk champagne. Some of us were on the entrance committee; and everyone in the atelier, after a few cursory questions, had been easily passed through the double row of police.

We had paraded, danced and drunk all night. It was essentially spectacular, a pageant, a work of art. The French students, with that curious mixture of licentiousness, critical appreciation, shamelessness, restraint and sensuality, grouped themselves, applauding, about the naked and quite drunken girls, urging them on to further excesses and exhibitionistic ritual. A few sought the comparative discretion of the heavy burlap curtains which draped the loges; and there, rolling on the dusty boards amid the pasteboard, tinsel and debris, they brought their evening to a climax. Only the Americans and other foreigners remained soddenly grouped about the bar, non-participating, outraged, heavy with the fumes of drink, their backs turned in stiff and resolute disgust to all this lovely bacchanalian excess that so fascinated me. A few lay in the sawdust sleeping in their own vomit. One splendid, naked giant swung a chair above his head as he defended himself for a moment from the police who closed in on him.

In search of a lavatory I had opened the wrong door and found myself in the makeshift infirmary or first-aid station. The air reeked of chloroform. Half a dozen efficient young doctors, in white uniforms, were sewing up cuts, bandaging heads or administering a shot in the arm to some more urgent case of delirium tremens. One girl squealed and bit, as they clapped the ether over her mouth. Three or four police stood by with stretchers.

By now it was daylight and the procession started home, down the winding, cobbled streets of Montmartre, past the baroque ostentation of the Opera, under the lowering gloom of the Louvre and through the narrow mysteries of the Left Bank. The students crowded the roofs of the taxis, rode the shafts of the ancient "sapins" or strode along the gutters, full of song. The girls, naked or half naked, enjoyed the luxury of plush seats. At the courtyard of the Ecole des Beaux Arts in the rue Bonaparte, the gateway was lined with early market shoppers.

Art Student and the Latin Quarter

We splashed about in the fountain, singing the refrain of the Quatz Arts song:

> "On dit quelquefois au village,
> Qu'un casque ça sert à rien du tout;
> Ça sert à donner du courage
> A ceux qui n'en ont pas du tout
>   pas du tout!"

That is my last impression of the Quarter: the cool June mist, billowing up gently from the Seine; the early green of the trees over the gray stone walls; the pink cheeks of the French house-wives, their baskets under their arms and their black woolen shawls drawn across their mouths; and the pale, disheveled ardor of the French youths in their cheese-cloth togas, with tinsel swords and pasteboard sandals, singing, dancing, gesticulating in this final, frenzied orgasm of undergraduate student life.

Next day I left for Berchtesgaden in the mountains of Bavaria, where Abram Poole had rented a three-roomed, sixteenth-century peasant cottage, a thousand feet up in the hills above the village, tinkling, pastoral and gay in the rain and sunshine at our feet.

One cannot in justice say farewell to student days without a word as to those hours of abstracted musing, spiritual elation and reverence spent in the private and public art galleries of Europe and America. It is the fashion today among certain economic critics of esthetic history to speak of museums as of dead archæol-ogy, having little relation to living art and contemporary life. My old friend Emile Bernard — a younger friend of Paul Gauguin and of Paul Cézanne — used to comfort me through the gray winter months at Tonnerre after the Armistice with his profound belief in the validity of art in life.

"Once," he said to me, "I met Ignacio Zuloaga in Munich. He was flushed from a visit to the *Alte Pinacothek*. He threw

(133)

both arms about my neck and embraced me. 'Come,' he said, 'I will show you the most beautiful painting in all of Munich.' And he led me in front of Titian's *Christ Crowned with Thorns*, which he had painted in his ninety-fouth year. And there we sat all day in front of this masterpiece, glorying in it. And I said to him, 'My friend, it is not the most beautiful painting in Munich; it is without any doubt the most beautiful painting in this wide world.' "

Although my visual memory is not always strong and clear, yet I can instantly, today, recall the different shades of emotion, of esthetic reaction, which were invoked in me twenty-five years ago by certain paintings: the Burial of Orgaz in Toledo, the Surrender of Breda or Las Meninas in Madrid, the Mosaics of Monreale at Palermo; or that wild intake of breath as I entered the Sale Carré of the Louvre, hesitating between the Correggio, the Titians, the Leonardos, and knowing not in my eagerness which way to turn. What is it, in the presence of a work of art, that gives us this feeling of physical and spiritual intoxication? I believe it is the intense and concentrated participation and awareness by the spectator of the absolute economy of means; the inevitability of line, color and design; the unity, or rhythm, or purpose, or beauty of the whole. And this response to art — this feeling of power, of elation, of experience — is never merely a negative participation but always an energizing impulse. I have rarely left a great painting without a conviction that I could and would do as much.

I have had the not unmixed pleasure of talking to great collectors, surrounded by their collections. Mrs. John Markoe once took me to have tea with the elder Pierpont Morgan in his library. Certainly nothing that he had to say about his art treasures was worth recording, but I remember two incidents of this meeting. In speaking to Mrs. Markoe from the depths of a leather armchair into which he had slumped — his trousers working somewhat up the leg, so as to expose the long jaeger underwear and garterless, woolen socks — he addressed her, still standing before him, as "Tilly." This I felt to be an outrageous familiarity, which not even that somewhat mythical Mr. John Markoe could ever thus have perpetrated. Second, the power, the vitality, the exuding bearlike ferocity and personality of the man was such that, later, I recalled that I had neither seen nor been aware of his nose.

Hearing that I was an artist, he begged Miss Belle Green, who was loquaciously flitting in the background, to bring out the portrait of himself — the only work of art in the library postdating, I suppose, the seventeenth century — by Baca-Flor, the Peruvian portraitist. I was anxious to see it, as rumor had it that the price was twenty-five thousand dollars and that there had been seventy-five sittings. The thing was built up with many timid brush strokes — like the encrusted Christmas cards which had a renewed vogue some years ago — until it had achieved an undulating papier-mâché vulgarity, the more incredible for its very life-like unreality. The great bear of a financier sat staring at his effigy, which stared back dully at the original.

"It is the finest portrait he has ever painted, and Baca-Flor is the most significant portrait painter since Romney."

Never did a great man open his guard more completely to an art student's scorn.

Mr. Edward T. Stotesbury in his galleries was in practical matters more intelligent. He grasped the significance of a painting with the same sharp, ruthless detachment with which he envisaged traction, steel or finance as part of an entire industrial picture. Small, electric, wiry, he hurried from canvas to canvas, snapping out the appraisal like a ticker tape.

"That Gainsborough in the corner, Mr. Biddle," and then bobbing forward "No, no — you know — what's his name — Reynolds. Oh! I guess I was right. Yes, it's a Gainsborough. Well, I was top-heavy with Dutch, two years ago, Terborch, David, Hals — you know, Dutch–Flemish. My wife, too, has very shrewd hunches. Mrs. Stotesbury had been advising me for some time to soft-pedal on the French. I got Duveen on the phone and made a deal. I traded in some early Italian — you know, primitives — and a couple of Bouchers and the Dutch. Market was plugged. Unloaded just in time. Concentrated on English. And by the way, Biddle, never buy the men. Not worth half the price. But this Raeburn is different." Again bobbing forward at the brass plaque: "No, no, bless my soul, Romney of course. Well you see his wife was the King's mistress. Got the letters from Rosenbach. Knoedler never even knew it. Fancy! And Duveen offered to take it back at just twice the price."

The amazing thing seemed to be that Mr. Stotesbury never did make a mistake — not in market values. As Adolphe Borie put it, his art commentaries were as vivid and exciting as when he explained why the price dropped out of the umbrella market the year he consolidated Philadelphia traction.

John G. Johnson was different still. Apart from his law practice he had three interests in life: eating, reading detective stories and collecting paintings. He had a prodigious memory and real scholarship. When he argued with Berenson about the authenticity of a Carlo Crivelli, backing his argument with the memory of a drawing of a forearm by Squarcione or Girolomo da Cremona in the Museum at Padua, sometimes Berenson was right and sometimes he was. He had eleven hundred masterpieces in a firetrap on South Broad Street. I had a ticket of admission to his house; and once when he was not at home, I poked my nose into various corners that were not commonly visited by the public. I found two Chardins in his boot closet, many examples of the Barbizon School in his bathroom; and Sargents, Manets and French impressionists in the corridors of the servants' stairway. Among the many portraits by Holbein which he possessed, was an exceptionally fine one — the gem, he averred, of his possessions. One year, not finding it in its accustomed place of honor, I asked him what had become of it.

"Biddle," he drawled in his slow, Philadelphian, nasal twang, "I venture to hope that some day my collection will have some breadth of educational purpose. You can pick up a Holbein anywhere. He's on the market. But I wanted a Correggio. There was no Correggio in America. So I swapped in the Holbein and now I have my Antonio Allegri."

I have known other famous collectors in New York, Boston, Baltimore or Merion; in Rome, in Paris. Some of them were acquisitive, arrogant, pathological; others, without sensitivity or understanding; while a rare few showed intelligence and sympathy, not only in their possessions but toward the occasional artists who came to enjoy them. Among these latter collectors was my friend the Baroness Elsa von Freytag-Loringhoven. I met her in my Philadelphia studio one gusty, rainswept morning in the spring of 1917, a few weeks before I enlisted in the Officers' Training Camp. Having asked me, in her harsh, high-pitched German stridency, whether I required a model, I told her that I should like to see her in the nude. With a royal gesture she swept apart the folds of a scarlet raincoat. She stood before me quite naked — or nearly so. Over the nipples of her breasts were two tin tomato cans, fastened with a green string about her back. Between the tomato cans hung a very small bird-cage and within it a crestfallen canary. One arm was covered from wrist to shoulder with celluloid curtain rings, which later she admitted to have pilfered from a furniture display in Wanamaker's. She removed her hat, which had been tastefully but inconspicuously trimmed with gilded carrots, beets and other vegetables. Her hair was close cropped and dyed vermilion.

The Baroness appeared to be about forty. She had the body of a Greek ephebe, with small firm breasts, narrow hips and long smooth shanks. Her face was lined. Her eyes were blue-white and frightening in their expression. Her smile was a frozen, devouring rictus. I bade her be seated and offered her a cigarette, while I continued working. We entered into conversation. She told me that she had fled her husband before the War, because he had the soul of a successful art dealer, rather than because he was a sexual pervert — not androgynous but something or other more sinister. Paris she found lacking in spirituality; and she had come to America in search of freedom and to establish her reputation with her colored poems. But she was disillusioned in her quest for liberty. Thrice that week she had been arrested for trying to bathe in the public pools; which, surrounded by borders of gladiolus, adorn the landscaping of the stations on the Main Line of the Pennsylvania Railroad. I asked her where she was staying. She replied somewhat wearily that she slept mostly with a sailor — on park benches. He was beautiful; but, it would appear, crassly American. She asked me in turn if I should care to look at one of her color poems. It was painted on a bit of celluloid and was at once a portrait of, and an apostrophe to, Marcel Duchamp. His face was indicated by an electric bulb shedding icicles, with large pendulous ears and other symbols.

"You see, he is so tremendously in love with me," she said.

I asked: "And the ears?"

She shuddered: "Genitals — the emblem of his frightful and creative potency."

"And the incandescent electric bulb?"

She curled her lip at me in scorn. "Because he is so frightfully cold. You see all his heat flows into his art. For that reason, although he loves me, he would never even touch the hem of my red oilskin slicker. Something of his dynamic warmth — electrically — would be dissipated through the contact."

From then on over a period of years I saw something of the Baroness. She was, perhaps, the first surrealist, although she would have scorned to be thus pigeonholed. While overseas during the War I received from her many letters; long poetic diatribes in Joycian vernacular against my very bourgeois art, and other lyrics of a more narcissistic and intimate nature. They were generally illustrated on celluloid, *par excellence* her medium. Some of them subsequently appeared in the *Little Review*. She scorned my art but something about me always gave her hopes of my spiritual regeneration. I found her, however, a shrewd and salty critic; and I would in later years occasionally pay her a dollar or two — she was invariably starving — to review some exhibition of mine on Fifth Avenue. I remember how she enraged Jerry Kelley, who was tolerance itself but who felt the need in strictly business affairs of some conventionality. She appeared the opening afternoon of a show of mine at Wildenstein's, where Jerry was in charge of the modern gallery. She had made a clean sweep of Schwartz's Toy Store that morning; and had sewed to her dress some sixty or eighty lead, tin or castiron toys: dolls, soldiers, automobiles, locomotives and music boxes. She wore a scrapbasket in lieu of a hat, with a simple but effective garnishing of parsley; and she led, tied on one string and fastened at different intervals, seven small, starved and terrified curs. The gallery was crowded. The Baroness had her say, remorselessly, in front of every painting. Luckily Monsieur Wildenstein did not put in an appearance.

Another time at my behest she was induced, although in a snobbish and skeptical mood, to visit a modern exhibition which Louis Bouché was arranging for Ruby Ross Goodenow at the Belmaison Gallery. Louis arriving one morning — he was always a little late — found the Baroness at the top of the stairway leading to the Gallery haranguing with unmeasured violence the sheeplike crowd below, who had come for their homeopathic dose of modernity. She had rehung the entire show, each picture at a different angle and one or two upside down, while others lay face down on the carpet, and she was now inveighing in the most truculent manner against the bourgeois spirit of a department store which, in hanging modern art, had achieved the un-inspired symmetry of a parking lot.

I have spoken of Elsa as an art collector. She was a marked example of what my psychoanalytic friends call the anal-aquisitive type. She induced me once to visit her collection. It was in an unheated loft near the river on 14th Street. It was crowded and reeking with the strange relics which she had purloined over a period of years from the New York gutters. Old bits of iron-ware, automobile tires, gilded vegetables, a dozen starved dogs, celluloid paintings, ash cans, every conceivable horror, which to her tortured, yet highly sensitized perception, became objects of formal beauty. And, except for the sinister and tragic setting, it had to me quite as much authenticity as, for instance, Brancusi's studio in Paris, that of Picabia, or the many exhibitions of children's work, lunatics' work, or dadaist or surrealist shows, which in their turn absorb the New York and Paris intellectuals. For the Baroness Elsa von Freytag-Loringhoven *had* validity. As I stood there, partly in admiration yet cold with horror, she stepped close to me so that I smelt her filthy body. An expression of cruelty, yet of fear, spread over her tortured face. She looked at me through her blue-white crazy eyes.

She said: "You are afraid to let me kiss you."

I knew she was suffering agony. I shrugged my shoulders and said: "Why not, Elsa?"

She smiled faintly, emerging from her nightmare. Enveloping me slowly, as a snake would its prey, she glued her wet lips on mine. I was shaking all over when I left the dark stairway and came out on 14th Street.

Before sailing for Germany in 1923, Elsa wrote me several blackmailing letters, threatening that if I did not fork up with ten thousand dollars she would divulge everything to the Phila-delphia newspapers. I sent her a reply, suggesting that all artists were in need of a press agent but could not afford one. I had no doubt that anything the papers printed would double my sales.

FOLLY BEACH PAVILION,
CHARLESTON, SOUTH CAROLINA

DRAWING: AT TWENTY-ONE WEST FIFTY-SECOND

Not only was I unprepared to buy her silence but I was ready to offer her a modest honorarium if she would make good on her threat. Seeing that she could get nothing out of me by blackmail, she turned up one morning with a gunny sack of her art objects and said she would sleep under Hunt Diederich's stairway, in whose house I had a studio, until I forked up. The matter dragged on. Hunt Diederich's nerves were more than usually frayed, but Elsa was hard up for cash. We compromised for five dollars. She shook hands and departed with a brace of dogs and her gunny sack.

That was the last I ever saw of the Baroness. Friends of hers gathered a small fund to help her back to Germany. Her spirit was withering in the sordid materialism of New York. She felt she had not long to live. In Berlin she enjoyed an Indian summer's vogue and was, I am told, the life and moving spirit of a homosexual circle of surrealist artists and poets. A year or two later she drifted to Paris, where she starved to death or was shut up in an asylum. Of all the art collectors I have known the Baroness Elsa von Freytag-Loringhoven was the most sensitive, critically understanding and emotionally generous.

By 1915 my student period, in the narrower sense, lay behind me. I could by now adequately construct exhibitable paintings, belonging to a definite tradition — and who does not — yet with some personal approach in design, color or treatment. I was still of course essentially interested in technique. I still breathed to myself: "Some day I shall paint as fine a picture as Cassatt or Degas." I still argued with the Philistines that "a fine passage of painting needs no moral or ulterior justification." This was the inheritance from the French. I consequently looked down my nose at the American rebels — Sloan, Henri, Luks and Bellows. They seemed to me a little out of date and never quite sterling. And much which was hailed in *The Masses* as the creative vigor of American youth struck me merely as a thin and meretricious distillation of what had been done ten or twenty years before in *L'Assiette au Beurre*, by such artists as Steinlen, Forain, Naudin, Picasso, Kees Van Dongen and others. It had not dawned on me that art is vision and that technique is artistry. But I was convinced that technique must be acquired first.

Then came the War to upset my nicely calculated theories in esthetics, the progress of my professional career and my normally happy development in the world we lived in.

A Soldier in the War of Liberation

I know not if I deserve that a laurel wreath should one day
be laid on my coffin. Poetry, dearly as I have loved it, has
always been to me but a divine plaything. I have never
attached any great value to poetical fame. . . . But lay on
my coffin a sword, for I was a brave soldier in the war of
liberation of humanity.

HEINRICH HEINE

AS A child one had garnered here and there impressions
— secondhand it is true — of the Civil War. My
mother could picture Grandmother Robinson out at
the Penllyn farm, tying up packages of lint, with old
Black Ben to help her — he had been freed years before by
Grandfather. The lint was for the Confederate wounded. One
remembered, too, the old muskets, some with bayonets fixed,
that the farmers on the Gulf Mill Road or out toward Doylestown, in Bucks County, painted with red lead and clamped to
the whitewashed masonry above their doors. On many a hot
Decoration Day one had marched through the dust, in column
of fours in the fife squad, piping to those strange, white-bearded,
hard-smelling and neolithic men — the Grand Army of the Republic. One knew not precisely what questions to put to this
debris of a Homeric past. Once, mustering courage, one inquired
if he had ever killed a Confederate. Likely as not Uncle Charley
Chauncey, or old Professor Higley at Groton, would answer in
aloof abstraction, in a tone at once colorless, courteous and low,
the gray eye unemotional and coldly watering. Yes, he believed

(143)

so; he had sabred an infantryman in the charge at Antietam. Yes, he had slept in the open and for three days had fed on chestnuts and on the grains that he had husked from the unhusbanded stacks of corn. Yes, he had bayoneted a Louisiana Zouave at the second Battle of Bull Run. Agnes Irwin, white-haired and splendid in her hard, cold wisdom, had once said, reminiscing over a cup of tea with Professor William James in her Cambridge drawing room: "Our generation lost much of its youth in the swamps of Virginia. Those who survived this schooling grew up to be MEN."

Before I die I shall most assuredly live through another War of Liberation, a second war to "make the world safe for Democracy." Let me speak a word, then, for our generation, which was brought up on the shining memories of one war and which has lived through another.

I would suggest this: War has its romance; war has its physical beauty — which at their best are not very different in esthetic quality from the romance and beauty of an automobile accident, of a slaughterhouse, of an earthquake, of a vessel pounding on a reef, of a prairie or forest fire, of starvation, drought, erosion and death. War has never the esthetic beauty, either in panache, trappings, color or parade, of a third-rate bull fight. I have seen both. The greatest panache of war is that of the flags, and the strips of torn newspapers floating down on the returning troops from Fifth Avenue office windows. War at the front is dust and mud.

After war was declared I lingered on in Munich. There was little else I could do. I had intended to spend that winter in Paris. To get there now seemed impractical. The German troops, though not actually in Paris, were at its gates. Count Hugo Lerchenfeld, back from the front with an Iron Cross — I had known him one summer when he was Bezirksamtmann at Berchtesgaden — assured me that it would be over by Christmas.

A Soldier in the War of Liberation

We climbed together the Zugspitze from Garmisch-Parten-kirchen on his first leave of absence. He said the French were fighting gallantly. The young officers, fresh from St. Cyr, stood in front of their troops in white gloves and were slaughtered. That was their *jour de revanche* for Sedan. But England was jealous of Germany. "They want to strangle us. They want to snatch away every commercial and industrial advantage that we won for ourselves in the past two generations." Tears stood in his eyes. "The dirty shopkeepers! Perfidious Albion! It has always been their policy. Let others do their fighting. We beat them fair and open in the markets of the world, while the graduates of their medieval public schools played cricket and sneered over their whiskeys and sodas at our thrift and honesty; our scholarship, our philosophy, our music. We have nothing against the French. But those shop-keepers want to strangle us."

I said: "You have nothing against the French. But perhaps the French hold something in their reckoning with you — since 1870."

He was tolerant and amiable as far as the French were con-cerned — as tolerant and amiable as a piece of rubber, a complete nonconductor to such suggestions. French art and literature were decadent, but the French were gallant soldiers. His wife, an American, was less amiable about the Belgians. Their women had mutilated the German wounded; three Prussian officers had been crucified outside of Lütich. My model, old Drezl, had a cousin at the Masurian Zee. The Cossacks were eleven feet high and eat the German children.

But one admired the rank and file. They were fighting for their country, for their own Bavaria — "*Unser' Heimat.*" Europe wanted to destroy them. Their backs were to the wall. The soldiers marched off to the front with stern faces through the silent lines of weeping women. Garlands of flowers festooned their helmets. They sang Lutheran hymns, "*Ein feste Burg ist unser Gott,*" "*Deutschland über Alles,*" "*Ich hatt' einen Kamer-*

(145)

aden, *Einen bessern giebt es nicht.*" Slow-moving, stolid, pink-faced, grim, the Bavarian peasant boys marched off to death like men.

All my sympathies went out to France. After France to Germany, at least to my Bavaria.

The pale Roman sun of April, 1915, was warmth after the chill fogs, the thin-lipped suspicion, the slowly smoldering HATE of Munich. The Germans had behaved like men. They tended strictly to their war business, and we few stray foreign artists, even a lone Englishman or two, could wander about unmolested, painting, climbing, ski-running, beer-drinking at the Vier Yahrzeiten. "They let one ply one's trade like a whore in a Western cattle town," as a friend remarked. "No one will interfere; and a policeman to escort one home if need should arise. But one might expect little sympathy in a street accident; and God help you if you start a row!" But this attitude was scarcely annoying. Anywhere in America it had always been much the same toward artists. Yes, the Germans had behaved like men, but they were beginning to HATE.

In Rome I had a studio in the Via Margutta. I floundered about without quite knowing what I was doing. I painted as nearly as I could in the manner of Cassatt and Degas. They were my lodestar. I studied the Venus Rising from the Sea, in the Terme, and fifth-century mosaics at Santa Maria Maggiore. Occasional lunches at the English or American Embassies quivered with politics and somewhat cloudy interpretations of the troop movements on the eastern fronts. One heard from unimpeachable sources the same atrocity stories which had impressed one in Munich — stories of rape, eye-gougings, castrations, crucifixions. There were variations on the usual themes. Out of vandalism the Huns were shelling the French cathedrals. I wrote to my friend, Hugo Lerchenfeld, repeating the accusations. Not that I believed them: The Germans were the most cultured, disciplined and sober-minded of nations. One long letter of his got through to me. "Yes, we shelled Rheims Cathedral, as little of course as possible. What else could we do? French artillery officers were directing the bracketing and charting out the *canevas de tir* from the towers. We could see them with our field-glasses." I repeated his explanation to English and Italian friends, citing my unimpeachable authority. They looked at me through closed windows. They knew which bed I slept in.

I picked up what I could of Italian politics. They seemed filthy enough. Things were coming to a boil. One heard at the embassies that Italy would have joined the Allies months ago, but for some Quartermaster-General scandal. No shoes, or blankets, or underwear. Count Lerchenfeld had given me a letter to the German chargé d'affaires, Fürst von Bülow. Their hopes were crumbling, his wife told me. Both sides were working on Italy. But now Giolitti was definitely out. One heard a lot about the War of Liberation, traditional Anglo-Saxon friendship, Latin culture, Garibaldi and *Irredentismo*. In other *saloni* other epithets were handled. Traitors, double-crossers, and pimps have in various languages somewhat similar connotations. During the last days of April the war fever was at the boiling point. A deal obviously had been concluded.

One morning the cavalry, with sabres drawn, filed down the Corso d'Italia and drew up in close formation in front of, and to protect, the Austrian Embassy. The crowds were massing. "*Abbasso i barbari! Fuori i Tedeschi! Fuori gli Austriaci!*" It was picturesque, *opéra bouffe*, very Latin. The Corso was packed, sweating and shouting with massed hatred. The students came on with a roar. They were after the Embassy. The cavalry charged, the dragoons beating right and left with flat sabres. A boy turned, screamed at the others to come on and dropped on his hands and knees in front of a charger. The horse trampled him. I flattened myself against a doorjamb. The cavalry pounded by.

It was very romantic but it was no place to paint. I had come abroad for a quiet year's apprenticeship; full of enthusiasm, full of energy; and I was sick of all this hysteria and HATE. I had a letter from Frieseke in Giverny-près-Vernon, in Normandy. At the *Banca Commerciale* I was told by a harrassed clerk to leave for Milan the next day. Any moment there might be a general mobilization and the railroads would be tied up for weeks. I got out of Rome in time and reached Milan the next night.

I remembered a small hotel, the Métropole; and climbed into the hotel's empty motorbus. While the bus was away at the station one of the crowd of patriots, milling about the Piazza to protect Italy from the Huns, saw a light in one of the hotel windows. It was a German hotel and the light was a German spy. The patriots in the Piazza wrecked the Métropole from cellar to roof. They smashed the windows and broke up the furniture. My bus came driving up the Corso. The crowd made a run at it. "*E un Tedesco! Fuori i barbari!*" The driver spun the bus round in time. He was pretty white and stepped on the pedal. Mounted cavalry with drawn sabres galloped along on either side. The crowd roared behind. At the *polizia* they were suspicious but my papers were in order. Later I returned on foot to the Piazza. The patriots were still milling round. Occasionally someone would shout: "*Austriaco! E un Austriaco!*" A crumpled form, squealing like a rabbit, scuttled for safety; his elbows above his head, his chin down. Once or twice the crowd beat their man to earth before the police could get to him.

"No place," I reflected, "for one whose accent after nine months in Bavaria is doubtless as German as it is Milanese." The next morning I got out of Italy. War had been declared. The HATE had been much the same in quality as in Munich. Rather the intelligence and the manhood of those who hated seemed to differ. Little nations should keep out of big wars. They might singe their reputations. They might even burn their fingers.

Caporetto and von Mackensen's drive through the wheat fields of Rumania would subsequently corroborate this early impression.

The two ensuing years were for me comparatively peaceful ones. Long summers I spent in Giverny near my friend Fred Frieseke, painting in the good plein air, impressionist tradition. Frieseke had a clear palette. I fell into it as a duck takes to water, after the mud of Munich, Julien's and the Pennsylvania Academy. He had an easy flowing sense of design that was at my finger tips. One watched old Claude Monet over his garden wall, as he tramped about among his fruit trees, or sat contentedly on a canvas stool in front of the little wooden bridge that spanned his water lilies, or superintended the new studio on the upper road, through the north windows of which in 1916 one saw with amazement high up on the wall the yards and yards — the acres — of blue water lilies which were the grand, but aged, artist's conception of a mural. I saw them again after the war, after his death, in all their sterility in the Camondo Collection in the Louvre.

I had started late and I developed late. At thirty-one I was still a student, but I was learning to paint and draw. If I had no direction of my own, I had a little more intelligence in the selection of those I wanted to follow. One day I said to Frieseke, joking:

"This nude of mine with the black stockings looks nearly as good as a Degas."

This upset him very much. I could see he was angry. He said: "No it does not. It looks — almost — like a Biddle." It was the first time I ever saw in my own work something which had not been contributed by others. Frieseke is a good critic as well as an artist. He, Henry McCarter, Adolphe Borie and Mary Cassatt were my friends, never actual teachers, but they were my only student influences.

For two years, in Philadelphia as in Giverny, I worked feverishly. In Paris, assembling an exhibition with Abram Poole for the benefit of the *Appui aux Artistes* and the *Appui Belge*, I met in their studios Steinlen, Forain, Naudin, Poulbot, Sem — my heroes of *L'Assiette au Beurre* — and Rodin. Forain had fought on the barricades during the Commune, but he was grown worldly and snobbish and had two Siamese kittens. Steinlen spoke with a Swiss accent. He was old and gentle and courtesied frequently during our conversation. Rodin's old peasant mistress clattered in wooden sabots in the background. The master eyed us slyly — especially the ladies — as he conducted us at Meudon through the galleries of his pornographic wash drawings. One Sunday I bicycled with Abram Poole to lunch with Mary Cassatt at her chateau at Beaufresne. It was the first week of the Somme offensive. We could hear the artillery gently booming to the north. Miss Cassatt opened a bottle of old Burgundy and served us Philadelphia White Mountain Cake — God knows where she got it.

I saw few of my French friends. They were at the front. The wives and mothers were all fighting mad. But the officers on leave seemed to think the Germans were good soldiers. They were anxious to get back to the trenches. They didn't know when the War would end. Oh! it might easily last a generation. Paris was gloomy at night but the French hadn't changed, thank God! They could still joke and enjoy a good bottle of wine; and their girls, too. No, the French were grand and behaved like men. Everything well within their stride and within their appetite. They'd lick the Germans yet!

I had exhibited two small paintings at the Pennsylvania Academy, had arranged an exhibition the coming fall at the Philadelphia Art Club and at the Milch Galleries in New York, and had secured a number of small portrait orders. It was a late start, but I could see some sort of recognition ahead of me. I hoped any day to announce my engagement. I was really in love — for the third or fourth time. Then came the German submarine campaign. I knew that this was WAR. I must face a decision.

I knew I should have to fight. But I didn't hate anyone. I loved the French and I liked the Germans. I knew these two people. Each had given me much. The English had given me nothing. I disliked their mentality; I avoided their women; I dreaded their cooking and I loathed their manners. I had read enough history to know that there was right and wrong on both sides. Of all the nations at war the closest similarity was that between a French and a German peasant. Yet these formed the sinews of those two opposing forces which in the long run were destined to build up if not the most savage, at least the most enduring HATE.

It is human nature to intervene in a dogfight. If your friends have been fighting all about you, two years on end, it becomes increasingly difficult to keep out of it. But for my particular generation there were conflicting emotions to adjudicate; there were moral qualms to satisfy. I had a career in front of me. I was passionately in love with my work. How sincere a career, you may ask; how passionate a love? Would Michelangelo have quit his work on the tomb of the Medici to join issue in a squabble written in mud? He who does not admit conflicting passions has not seen the face of war. That face is not serene. It is one of conflicting passion. Michelangelo's whole life, his entire art, were the expression of conflicting passions, the expression of the late Renaissance in Italy, and he did desert his work on the Medici's tomb to join the Republicans in Florence and fortify the city against the Medici. The question then became: How could one resolve the conflict? My career was at stake. So I thought. Those first exhibitions were arranged. I must prepare them and hold them in the autumn. Then I would join the French Foreign Legion. After all my sympathies were really in France. Wilson was re-elected for keeping us out of war. The average American had no possible interest in France or in Germany.

But would this satisfy one's moral doubts? My own generation was deeply serious; deeply moral, many of us. If I had been a college boy it would have been so easy. Instead of looking for a tutoring job to take me abroad I would have enlisted for a summer, or even for longer. Was a college degree so everlastingly necessary? But one had one's career, one's profession, one's art. If one sacrificed that, it must be for a purpose, "freeing the world for Democracy." I had no wife or child but I was in love and believed — off and on — that I was engaged. I knew that she thought I was a slacker. We were tortured, some of us, during those two years after the sinking of the *Lusitania*. Perhaps, morally, we were a squeamish, sentimental generation.

Then in February the German General Staff intervened with the submarine campaign to resolve our legalistic conflicts and to silence our moral scruples. I knew that I was fighting for Democracy — not against the German people — but against their *Hauptgeneralstab*. In May I enlisted at the first Reserve Officers' Training Camp at Fort Niagara.

I elected the infantry. As long as I was taking a chance with my career, with my love, with my life — no matter how remote — I wanted some compensating romance and adventure. An artillery officer's education was a longer one. I was in mortal dread the whole thing might be ended before I went overseas. I knew that I was a coward, but I knew that fear is imagination, and can always be overcome by imagining with sufficient concentration what is necessary to face it. For me the great lesson of the training camp was bayonet practice. We lunged at canvas dummies and fenced with one another. A Canadian top sergeant rationalized the stance, thrusts and parries from his own practical experience:

"Aim low for the belly, and you can draw your bayonet clean. If you strike a rib or the backbone, it may be hard to extricate the blade."

A Soldier in the War of Liberation

This kept me awake at night — I had just enough imagination — but with concentration and time one can face anything. That obstacle — the imagination — was the greatest fear I ever hurdled in war. Greater, I believe, than it ever would have been in fact. Not worse, I suppose, than that early dawn in the chaparral of Nueces County, Texas, when I had driven a three-inch blade into the jugular vein of a wounded deer. It was not cruelty — nor masochism either. For educational purposes I had elected to face that ritual. For educational purposes I had faced the disemboweling of some forty horses at a dozen bull fights in Madrid and Mexico. I had chosen perhaps the wrong curriculum, but having so chosen I would see it through.

In August I received my commission as first lieutenant in the infantry. Six officers, without command, were forthwith sent overseas from each regiment. I had worried my regimental commander into designating me as one of them. My troubles seemed now over. I was to sail in a fortnight. I telegraphed my good news to Nancy, to whom it would seem I definitely was not engaged. She wired back that we were getting married immediately. It was done somewhat in a hurry. The honeymoon was a rather disastrous affair. Here and there, mostly in New York hotels. I had to report now and then for sailing orders. Nancy wanted to say good-by at the hotel. She was badly broken up at not being able to get to France then and there. She had already done some sort of war work in Paris, had even gone junketing down to the trenches once or twice, and she had set her mind on getting back, but it was not easy for officers' wives to go across. They had clamped down the lid. We promised to see each other "over there" soon. We never did. It was a typical war marriage. I was very much in love, curdling with romance and tuned for the great adventure.

We sailed with the Second Regular and the Twenty-sixth (New England) National Guard Divisions. Only the First

Division had preceded us. We had the usual troop convoy. The men were kept below and only let up on deck for an hour or two daily. Then they were jammed on the decks like sardines. We had general orders always to carry side arms and to use them in maintaining order in case of emergency.

We landed at Saint-Nazaire. I was full of sunlight and happiness. I realized what a strain the past two years had been: legalistically sitting on the fence, splitting moral hairs, splitting emotional hairs. I loved the French. They had given me too much. I was glad to be in France now, fighting. I was brimming over as I ran down the gangplank.

The French did not seem glad to see us. They looked suspicious and unfriendly. General Edwards was disembarking the Twenty-sixth. They were disorderly and undisciplined. Most of them were drunk as coots as soon as they landed. The M.P.'s were putting in riot calls all night. By nine o'clock the soldiers were lousy, fighting mad, manhandling the French girls, beating each other up, rolling about the cobbled gutters, retching and bleeding. The storekeepers were terrified and pulled down their green iron shutters. The M.P.'s swung their night sticks. The Irish doughboys cursed and fought. It was a riot.

"Ah, *les saligauds, les saligauds!*" hissed the French shop wives. That was their impression of us. That was my first impression.

We unassigned officers on landing were immediately examined. Those who spoke French and German, as I did, were assigned to Enemy Intelligence and shunted to General Headquarters at Chaumont. The rest were dispatched to various technical schools, machine-gunning, bombing, trench-mortar practice, etc. I begged to be sent to an American line division or to be given a liaison job with the French. The regular officers looked at me rather cautiously. Just what did I mean? I realized I was in the army. The next nine months I spent at General Headquarters. I was sent, as a liasion officer or for training purposes, to the Thirty-second French Corps at Metz, to the crack French Ninth and Tenth Divisions in Alsace, to our own First Division, to an English Staff School in Flanders. All the romance was licked out of me. I despised our own regular army. I pretty well disliked the French. I was vastly educated; if not in war, at least in the architecture and psychology of the regular army.

Enemy Intelligence is the only and absolute source of information to the Chief of Staff about the enemy. The Section gets this information through trench raids, the examination of prisoners, airplane photographs, airplane and balloon observation, telescopic observation from ground posts. It analyzes troop movements behind the front, artillery and airplane activity, and the significance of the location of certain technical arms or units. The news is telephoned up from the trenches, sifted, co-ordinated and relayed back to the next higher command. It was telephoned to us from the French, English and American headquarters, and relayed from us to the trenches. The information, which the Chief of Staff requires from Enemy Intelligence and which the Section is at any moment prepared to give him, includes general enemy artillery objectives, the location of trenches, dugouts, artillery emplacements, company, regimental and divisional headquarters, wire entanglements, narrow- and broad-gauged lines leading to the front, communication roads and airplane hangars; the strength of the enemy, the quality of their soldiers, the dates the divisions came into line, the contours of the area back of the front. We had airplane photographs and maps of whatever of this material could be transcribed. We had in published book form an account of every division in the German and Austrian armies. We knew the names of the General Staffs, the regimental insignia, the training grounds and the military history of the divisions. We usually knew the movements of a German division three or four days before they occurred, and of course the German Intelligence was equally informed about the movements of our own troops. On July fifth a balloon went up behind the enemy lines carrying a long banner: "Hello Twenty-sixth; good-bye Second." Five days later the New England Division moved into the trenches.

After a few months at Headquarters I was ordered to join the divisional staff of one of our new units operating under a French brigade near the Swiss border. One of my superiors was a regular army type, a man with an opaque eye and a muddy complexion. His bald, greasy dome was pocked with blackheads. He wore a red mustache, and the quality of his black hair gave his face that slightly bluish tinge characteristic of angry monkeys. The feature which chiefly distinguished his countenance, and gave it its dramatic mobility, was his slightly moist, pendulous and highly expressive lower lip, uncontrolled, petulant and in a constant state of quivering excitement — the lip of a frightened old Jewish fruit peddler, or an exasperated Turkish Sultan, of an angry baby.

This man's character was compounded of four dominant traits: He was genuinely histrionic, he was always in a hurry, he was completely without any mind or mental process and he suffered from violent and chronic indigestion.

The war was to most soldiers an endless stretch of monotony. To one particular Staff officer it had all the dramatic actuality of a dime novel battlefield, of moving picture blood and death.

His office contained a monumental map — 1/250,000 scale — on which were pinned in four colors the units of the German and Austrian armies. The shock divisions were red; the weakest Erzats divisions yellow. White and blue were scattered in between. To impart a further touch of military realism to the Enemy Battle Line, he ordered through the Ordinance Department, and obtained from some toyshop in the Paris Latin Quarter, a box of all the flags of all the nations in the world. In front of these he spent one whole morning sorting out Russian,

Bulgarian, Austrian, Prussian, Bavarian, Saxon, and even Turkish pennants. It is true that he somewhat confused the symbols. The lunch hour had come and he still sat scowling in heated absorption at the dozens of little heaps of flags. Between a bulbous thumb and a heavy index was the unmistakable emblem of the Swiss Republic.

"Turkish ensign," he whispered in a tense, preoccupied growl. "Turkish ensign, unmistakably. You can tell it by the cross."

Having thus dressed up his Battle Map in the most warlike possible manner, so that it fairly bristled with insignia, he proceeded to impart to it that final touch of mystery which he felt to be the distinguishing mark between the Higher Staff and the common-line soldier. The lettering he designed himself, on a gigantic scale. It was a huge placard:

SECRET

BUSY

KEEP OUT

THIS MEANS

YOU

This placard, many times blue-penciled and underscored, he nailed himself, his officers and orderlies standing about him in awed silence, to his door. It contrasted, quite to our advantage, we felt, with a similar admonition penned on the back of an envelope and thumbtacked to the door of the Chief of Staff of the French corps under whose command was our division:

"*Entrez sans frapper.*"

We were now prepared for any eventuality on the part of the enemy. They attacked in force — as the whole world knows — on March 21, 1918, with fifty of their first-class (red-pin) divisions. On the afternoon of April first, when the German offensive achieved its maximum depth, every pin was in the proper position. There was a bellow.

"Officers, attention!"

We leapt to our feet. A general, down from Chaumont to inspect the divisional staffs, nodded us an "As you were," and was piloted, a little wearily, from the Masurian Lakes to Switzerland, from Flanders to Arabia. He finally alighted like some tired bird on the St. Mihiel salient, and stood watching a group of Ersatz divisions that were gathered in reserve behind the line. For the moment it was an exceedingly quiet front. The look of the map-making officer seemed to lift and brighten.

"General," he asked, "what do you suppose they are doing there, those old, tired, fourth-class divisions? General, do you suppose Ludendorff is using them, to haul cannon to the trenches for the next offensive?"

Toward the end of June I was called back to the First Corps, which was in line at La Ferté-sous-Jouarre on the Marne, about to participate in Foch's brilliant counter-attack of July eighteenth. Our Commanding General was Hunter Liggett, a gentleman of the old school, the finest product of the army post; courteous, slow-moving, gently wise in his control of human beings, as he was subsequently firm in his control of armies. Yet on occasion he could bark out an order with the asperity of an automatic. One evening in Alsace I had sat with him in his billet on the edge of his army duffel bag. He was visiting the Fortieth French Corps, quartered at Montreuil-le-Vieux, and I accompanied him as liaison officer. He had taken off his tunic, thrown back his suspenders, eased open the upper buttons of his pants and removed his riding boots. He was stiff in the joints and somewhat paunchy, but had a fine, dominant head and long, beautiful, rather incompetent-looking hands. He waved to the night table, where he kept his whiskey bottle, and motioned me to pour out a couple of tumblers. The General and I talked strategy long into the night. When it came to the Civil War, I did the listening; but I had spent not in vain two weeks with General Gamelin of the Ninth Division and knew something about the

French tactical defenses after the attack on the Vesle. After that General Liggett was my hero. It was with deep regret that I saw him subsequently leave the Corps to take command of the First Army on October thirteenth during the Meuse-Argonne offensive.

Brigadier General Malin Craig, his Chief of Staff, was a different sort. He seemed almost of a different generation. Squarely built, well-knit, quiet, aggressive, he was like a dynamo and had the reputation of being an able strategist and an informed tactician. He would hurry into our office, quiet, purposeful, intelligent; take a quick look at our maps, ask a few pithy questions — no side, no swank, no vanity.

One evening a few months later — it was during the St. Mihiel push — I found Craig pacing up and down in front of Operations Section. I asked him directly if he would recommend my transfer as G2 officer to a line division. I knew this was a breach of discipline. Any such petition should have gone through my own Chief of Section. General Craig paced up and down in silence for a few moments.

"It is customary to take a course at the Staff School before getting an assignment as G2 divisional or brigade officer. In your case it's by no means necessary and I should aim at a division. I'll keep you in mind. General Nolan often asks me for recommendations. But you can't go now. We're going to pull off the biggest thing yet. But someday — I'll keep you in mind — when this offensive is over. And don't think I enjoy it either being back here with the Corps. I'd rather be with a division, too."

When Craig left the Corps after the Armistice he wrote in my Officer's Note Book:

This is to certify that Captain George Biddle, U.S.A., served in the G2 Section of the First Army Corps from the organization of that unit in January, 1918, through the Marne Offensive, the St. Mihiel Offensive and throughout the Meuse-Argonne Offensive, which constitutes the entire combat service of the First Army Corps.

Captain Biddle proved himself exceedingly dependable and contributed as much as any one man could contribute to the success of his section.

During the four months the First Corps was in line, between July fourth and November eleventh, it captured two hundred seventy guns of all calibers and 10,298 prisoners from thirty-three different divisions. Many of them were among the best enemy shock troops, such as the First, Fourth and Fifth Guard and the Sixth Bavarian Divisions, which were thrown into line during the German Retreat of the Marne. Others, such as the Fourth Erzats, the 255th and the Second *Landwehr*, were old reservists, employed either on quiet fronts, or to be placed in line for deceptive purposes before a major offensive, while the shock troops were being quietly moved up to positions immediately in the rear.

Part of my duty was to superintend the examination of prisoners. When we knew there was to be a big push we had an open pen, reinforced by barbed wire, constructed by the engineers. Sometimes the prisoners came in batches of several thousands. It reminded me of the cattle herding in the Texas corrals after the long drives from the fattening range to the railroad. The men were completely dazed, shellfire drunk. They had taken a terrific artillery pounding for a couple of days on an empty stomach. It was nervous work, too, getting to the rear from the front lines after they were captured. Not all of them got through alive. It was a temptation to some of our less disciplined troops to take pot luck at them, as they filed by in the narrow trenches. The Alabamans had a particularly unsavory reputation. This would be the result of propaganda, as filtered down through Headquarters Staff at Chaumont. I remember one juicy atrocity story, clipped from some French newspaper, translated, underscored with red staff pencil, shot down to us from G.H.Q. with the accompanying comment: "Red meat; feed it down to the front line trenches." Fed on red meat — and brandy — one went over the top; and if one were an undisciplined Alabama hillbilly one poked the Huns in the guts, as they stumbled by to the rear through the narrow trenches.

Our first chore was to delouse, bathe, feed and rest the prisoners. They were too exhausted and terrified for a proper examination. This in the great majority of cases was perfunctory. Shoulder straps and badges were clipped for purposes of troop identification. They were searched for knives and concealed weapons. Orders, letters and documents were taken, hastily examined and dispatched to the Army G2 for thorough analysis. Officers were examined more carefully.

I had two commissioned and two noncommissioned interpreters working under me. Prisoners never deceived us or tried to deceive us, not one out of a thousand. We were working on somnambulists. Our job was to help the prisoner to remember. In the second place we knew all the essentials about that prisoner's history in more accurate detail than he could possibly remember it, everything except the one vital point which we concealed among a host of unimportant questions. We began by asking him his company, brigade or divisional commander. If he had forgotten it, or if he tried to deceive us, we corrected him. We could tell him when he came into line, via what towns he had derailed, via what woods, hills and trenches he had walked to the front line. To him it was usually a shadowy dream, a vague blur, a foggy nightmare. We could sharpen and clarify his memory. We worked on him, and with him, as a psychoanalyist helps his patient. Then there was the one essential point — it doesn't matter what — about which our staff wanted to be informed. Were they building additional gun emplacements? How far back of the front? Was the heavy artillery moving to another sector? Had the officers' leaves been recalled? What was the age of the replacement reservists? All questions in general had bearing on only two issues which could be of interest to a corps staff command: the immediacy of an enemy attack on us and the power of resistance of the enemy to our threatened attack. We always got the right answer up to the limit of the prisoner's memory.

Half a dozen times in all my officer interpreters reported to me that a guard division officer refused to talk. I had the German officer brought in. I sat alone back of a desk, seemingly preoccupied with maps and papers. I stationed two or three orderlies with fixed bayonets about the premises. The German officer would be a fine, strapping fellow and would speak French and English fluently. He stood at attention and saluted. I never returned his salute. I said:

"It is reported to me that you won't talk."

He would say: "Captain, how can I? I am a German officer and a gentleman. Would you?"

I said: "I'm not interested in your reasons. That's up to you. But do you know what happens to prisoners who won't talk?" I looked at him, not threateningly, but disinterestedly and coldly.

He said: "No, Captain." I could see his mouth had gone dry.

I said, looking at him very steadily, and enunciating my words more and more deliberately: "You will be sent . . . to . . . [with a jerk of my thumb over my shoulder] to . . . French Headquarters." I looked at him fixedly in the eye, trying to convey to him that we shared a common knowledge. He went white as a sheet and stammered:

"But Captain . . . a fellow officer . . . my honor . . ."

I said, "I'm not interested. I thought it fair to tell you. . . . Take him away," to the orderlies.

In each case the officer shortly thereafter had a complete breakdown. He burst into tears and talked freely. Of course it was all a setup. We never sent any recalcitrant prisoner to French Headquarters. If we had, they would have treated him just as we did. They would have given him a hot bath and a square meal;

(162)

and the French guard would have shoved a Maryland to him through the barbed wire, just as our doughboys would offer him a Lucky. The whole thing was another example of the high suggestibility of war psychology. If you can exhaust a man physically, by loss of sleep or by a two-day artillery barrage, and repeat to him the same thing a thousand times, he will believe any suggestion. In the club initiations at Harvard, in a state of complete exhaustion, we had been blindfolded, run round in circles for ten minutes, given a piece of lard soaked in asafetida to smell, and told that we were kissing a corpse in the Mount Auburn Cemetery. Our minds, drugged for a week on lack of sleep and coffee, were lucid; as lucid as a maniac's. We knew it was a corpse and were edged up so that we could have kissed twenty corpses and not minded.

Not a very chivalrous trick to play on a brother officer. No, of course not. I wanted quick information about some impending attack or the placement of a heavy gun that hadn't been located by our artillery observation posts. I might have felt squeamish about twisting a prisoner's wrist. I am not a New York City policeman. But a few private theatricals were all in the routine of the regular army.

It was once my privilege to witness a particularly skillful duel between a French Sixth Army examining officer and a German prisoner. The timing of this particular examination had its dramatic quality. During the entire war there were only two or three occasions on the Western Front as portentous. The latter part of April I had spent as a liaison officer with General Marie Gustave Gamelin, who today is the Co-ordinator and Commander in Chief of the French Army, Navy and Air Force. His division had, as I remember, recently come from the Vesle and was resting in Alsace. At any rate he was intimately acquainted with the fortifications and tactical positions on the Vesle. I remember his describing them to me at the mess, as we lingered over a cognac. He pointed out how for many and obvious reasons

(163)

they were quite impregnable. His expression, then, and that of his staff officers on the twenty-eighth of April, when bulletin after bulletin was telephoned in from French G.Q.G., announcing the German advance in that sector, not in terms of yards but in terms of tens of kilometers, was one rather of absolute bewilderment than of horror. It was after this that Foch altered his entire defense tactics, suiting them to the German method of surprise assault and rapid infiltration. On the eve of the attack of July fifteenth, each division had but one battalion in line and only one or two platoons occupying the *lignes de réduits* — the outposts. These *groups de combats* had orders to hinder the enemy and fall back fighting. The greater part of the division was on the second line of resistance with orders to hold at all costs. Other troops were further in reserve on the *ligne de barrage* — the line in front of which was trained the French artillery barrage fire. The heavy artillery was echeloned very deeply behind the second defensive positions. Here also were more reserve divisions. Artillery positions had been prepared farther to the rear, to which the batteries could be withdrawn on a day's notice. This approximately was the position of the French Army during those fevered moments of waiting early in July 1918. From every captured prisoner from the Champagne to Switzerland our Enemy Intelligence learned of the formidable massing of some thirty German shock divisions back of the line. The prisoners themselves were all from fourth-rate Erzats divisions, which in itself was an ominous sign. The General Staff knew that *this must be the Enemy's final gesture.* Their effectives had been liquidated in an appalling way by the thrust of March twenty-first. By July over a million American troops had landed. The losses at sea had been 291!

On the afternoon of June thirtieth two German army aviators were brought down near Chante Merle farm, north of Château-Thierry. They reached our Corps Headquarters about eight o'clock. General Craig had telephoned to the Sixth French

Army and the latter had ordered him to send up the prisoners with the utmost speed. Colonel Williams gave me this assignment, bidding me — to my mortification — wear a helmet and carry my automatic. I left with the prisoners. They were charming fellows. They, too, had enjoyed ski-running about Oberammergau and had climbed the Zugspitze. At Epieds, which we passed in the dark, camions of wounded men stood in queue before a first-aid station. At Château-Thierry two bridges over the Marne had gone since I had been there, but the town had suffered surprisingly little. Vaux was a complete wreck. The trees along the road were slashed at the height of fence posts. It was quite dark now but I could see the hastily sketched-in elements of trenches along the highway. The woods on either side looked like a cornfield after a cloudburst.

French Army Headquarters were at Marigny. The examining G2 officer was a weasel-faced, paunchy Alsatian. Alone, he said to me: "I only want to know one thing, to what army these aviators are attached. If it is the X Army Group from the Flanders front, it locates the attack definitely in this sector."

The German officers were brought in. The Alsatian spoke perfect German. They answered him in faultless French. He offered a brace of cigars. Had they been comfortably fed? He waved them to an armchair. He bantered them on the quality of the wine he must offer them. "You Germans have all our best champagne." "Ah," said the German, "we shall treat you handsomely, if you will only let us take you prisoners." He asked a dozen questions. The German was voluble. Yes, four guard divisions were in the rear. He believed the 87th had derailed from Russia. He understood an attack was imminent. Perhaps in this very sector. And then the Alsatian: "And what, Captain, is the number of your P.O. unit?" The German looked surprised. "I beg your pardon?" "Your P.O. unit; your military address." "Oh! I beg your pardon, why the Hauptmann Keller Pursuit Squadron." "Yes, yes; but the number?" "The number — why

I never knew the unit had a number. You see I was recently wounded. I have been on leave. I was just transferred from the Italian front. You see I am an artillery officer. Just got my flying license." Thus they sparred together for twenty minutes. The German aviator was willing to give any information he had except the P.O. number which would identify the army unit to which his squadron had been assigned. The Alsatian turned to an orderly. The mask was off.

"Take them away. Close, separate confinement. Guards. Bread and water. Too good for them."

When they had gone: "And will you get your information?"

"Yes, yes. Of course. Tomorrow we shall put stool pigeons in the prisoners' pen with them. But it may take a couple of days. I had hoped to telephone that information to G.Q.G. this evening."

I left him. It was dawn when I got back to the Corps Headquarters at La Ferté-sous-Jouarre.

We had our occasional moments of romance or danger. At any rate it seemed so to us back at Staff Headquarters under the goad of army discipline and staff stupidity. One afternoon I drove up with Colonel Williams to the front. It was at Veuilly-la-Poterie, east of Marigny, on July twenty-second. The 167th French Division had just passed through. Along the edge of the fields were the "fox holes" which the German infantry had scratched into the bank with their bayonets. Some had crawled out in their shattered and ravenous condition and had gathered hurried handfuls of ripe wheat ears, which littered their pitiful shelters. The French sappers had not had time to bury the corpses, so unexpected had been the advance. In the July heat the dead blackened almost immediately and swelled until they burst through their uniforms. French, American and German soldiers and artillery horses had all ripened, swelled and blossomed from their various colored uniforms and harnessings like so many flowering and multi-hued sea anemones or sea cucumbers. They died in curiously rigid poses, legs kicking straight toward Heaven, arms threshing in wild diagonals, black head broken back at right angles. The arrested motion seemed always — as in a snapshot — awkward and unconvincing. The sweet, somewhat sickening smell of decomposing flesh blew heavily over the yellow wheat fields.

The shell holes, the silent troops huddled by the roadside, the clouds of dust and debris made the roads almost impassable. Bits of shrapnel from our own anti-aircraft rattled against the roof of our car. The doughboys stared at us with expressionless eyes, sweating under their heavy equipment. We cut off from the road and zigzagged through the shell holes in the wheat fields. A French 210, prettily camouflaged in gray and black and green, was pounding away from a nearby thicket. We stopped to watch it a moment. The noise and shock were sickening. In the fields were the usual litter of war: iron bedsteads, broken crockery, straw mattresses, abandoned trucks, bedding, gilt mirrors, kitchen chairs, wine bottles; all manner of signs, neatly lettered in German, "*Munitions Depot Verwalter*"; a piano stool, many duds and yellow-cross gas shells. Except for the smell, the blackened corpses, the bayonets and camouflaged German helmets, it was what one would expect to find in any vacant lot in the neighborhood of any American city. To the south of us, we could see the high explosives, gas and shrapnel falling on the Epaux-Belleau road and on the edge of the Bois de Montpas, where was concealed our divisional artillery.

Now and then we were bombed. Each time it left me shaking and white, but trying to smile and appear casual in the presence of the enlisted men. Gas I didn't mind. We never had it in big doses. I got to recognize the rather dull *pflop* of the bursting shell, and could follow the direction of the gas as it slowly spread. It clung so close to the ground, I wondered whether it would reach above the knees, if I stood quite still. It drifted down the wind, like an incoming tide on a flat beach. Nor did I mind very much the occasional light shelling. I was never in a heavily shelled sector and never had a big caliber shell explode very close to me. Only light shelling, generally along a road or near a gun emplacement: 75's and 150's, and very occasional 210's. It was almost like a game. At first I was afraid I should seem awkward or a tenderfoot. I watched the more experienced officers from the corner of my eye and slowed down all my movements — the way you do when you feel shy entering a drawing room. You could hear the thing coming right at you with a low whistle, turning into a crescendo shriek. When it was just overhead — you timed it the way you meet a tennis ball, instinctively — you flopped on your face. You saw gravel shoot up a hundred yards away; gravel and bits of shrapnel rattled down about you; you jumped up, slapped the mud off your knees and pretended it was some sort of a game like prisoners' base or snowballing.

The bombing was real terror. The Staff had just moved into La Ferté-sur-Jouarre. I was billeted at 18 rue Condé, a bit up the hill, with a clean sweep down the river. The Gothas came over almost every evening about ten o'clock on their way to Paris. We had plenty of warning. The sky shrieked with sirens. Up the river we could see through our darkened windows the star shells and searchlights from the hills on the northern bank of the Marne; and hear the rattle of the anti-aircraft and machine guns. We knew they were up there. Then we heard through the chatter of anti-aircraft the low purring of the motors. Then would come the first crash. They were after the bridge — on their way to Paris.

It was as if every atom of every molecule in your brain were splintered to pieces. It was as if someone put your head on an anvil and struck it with a sixteen-pound sledgehammer. It was as if you put a stick of dynamite between your teeth and lit the fuse. You counted very slowly and when you reached six you knew there would be another. The Gothas dropped half a dozen or a dozen bombs and then went on to Paris. They always stopped on their way back — regularly at half-past ten — and unloaded whatever was left over.

There was some pretty bad staff work in the Meuse-Argonne. Troops ran ahead of their objectives and suffered unnecessary casualties. There was bad liaison work. The Lost Battalion of the 77th New York Division under General Robert Alexander was a staff disgrace. You don't *lose* six hundred men operating on a two kilometer front and never advancing more than three kilometers a day. Anyway there they were, shot to hell by our own artillery fire as well as by that of the enemy; cut off, surrounded, finally located by our aviation. The airplanes dropped them provisions, candies and newspapers.

We had a dapper little Major Melville Hall with us. He was Colonel William Mitchell's aid in our Corps Air Service. He had been, I think, with the English; and was all trapped up with an Oxford accent that you could cut with a knife, boots, spurs, silver wrist plates and other gadgets. He was an able little officer. I remember his droll comment when news came in one night of the air service activity over the Lost Battalion. He said:

"It's perfectly ripping. American troops are just different from anything the world has seen. Just fancy them out there now; isolated under shell and machine-gun fire for the past week; starved, punch-drunk, decimated; sitting, swinging their legs over shellholes, or on the charred stumps of blasted trees, reading the *Stars and Stripes* and munching chocolate peppermints."

The Corps Summaries were prepared by a friend of mine who had been an artillery officer in the English Army and was my senior. One day a commanding general blew into our office, hot and irascible. He wanted to know who the hell was in charge of the Corps Summary. My friend confessed responsibility. The general bellowed that the Summary was a falsification of the facts and demanded a correction. There was no reason to be afraid of the general. A shouting man is always at one's mercy. Our colonel came running out at the rumpus. When he heard what was wrong he went green. You see, although the general's division was under the command of our Corps, he was a general and our man only a colonel. That's where the shoe pinched.

Our Summary included a paragraph on the "General Impressions of the Day." Under this paragraph on October ninth, the day after the Lost Battalion was reunited to the fold, my friend had written that "the advance of the Corps on our left, combined with our occupation of Hills 180 and 223, has forced the enemy to withdraw from the Argonne." The general felt personally insulted; and on October fourteenth sent in a memorandum to the commanding general of his Corps, modestly averring that: "This statement is not in accordance with the facts and it is a serious injustice to the Division which I command. The Enemy was forced from the Forest of Argonne by the steady, persistent advance of my Division, and I request that in the interest of historic truth the Summary of Intelligence to be [sic] amended so as to state the facts in the case correctly." Anyway our colonel ate mud. He promised "in the interest of historic truth" to print an erratum in his next Summary. He bawled out my friend, described him as a young civilian, and promised to introduce into future Summaries an additional, highly flavored paragraph on the "Activity of Our Own Troops." We were all pretty mad. We told the colonel afterwards that when he was in the right he shouldn't take it sitting from a lower unit. The colonel snarled at us that "You young civilians thinkya alwus know everything. You make these damn blunders and I pay the bills." We ran back to our files and dug out the Divisional report of October ninth. It stated that "Our advance continues, *the enemy offering no opposition.*" [Italics mine.] The general

(170)

hadn't even read his own officer's report or else was ignorant of its contents.

Here are the facts: From October first to October ninth the 77th Division did not advance an inch from Charlevaux and fought bitterly on the Chêne Tondu. From October first to October eighth it had not been able to make contact with its own lost Battalion. On October eighth one brigade of the 82nd was thrown in to relieve the situation by a dangerous flanking movement. It captured Hills 180 and 223. On the same day the 38th French Corps to the west of the Argonne advanced three kilometers and the following day made a further advance of two kilometers. On the morning of the ninth *the French were approximately six kilometers in advance of the 77th to the west and the 82nd Division was the same distance in advance to the east. These operations had rendered the enemy's salient in the Argonne opposite the 77th untenable and he rapidly withdrew.* That day for the first time in ten days the New York Division advanced three kilometers and the next day about six more. So much "in the interest of historic truth."

The "Activity of Our Own Troops" paragraph was a source of constant annoyance. Our Section had nothing to do with our own troop operations; we were concerned only with the enemy.

One day my sense of humor had all leaked out of me. My nerve was gone. I said to myself: "If they demote me for it I'm going to stew up a sauce tonight that even G.H.Q. will retch on." Under "Activity of Our Own Troops" I wrote something as follows:

Our gallant troops, assaulting on the entire front, met with the stubborn and savage resistance of a most desperate enemy. Notwithstanding their dastardly machine-gun fire we pushed ruthlessly forward, capturing eleven prisoners. Our engineers were engaged in building bridges across the Aire at 296.95–285.0 and at 298.5–283.4.

Aerial Activity — Notwithstanding the most perplexing weather conditions our air squadrons and homing pigeons were unusually active.

I was afraid to go into the staff meeting, where each evening the colonel read his report to a distinguished audience — liaison officers, sent in from Artillery, Aviation, G3, etc. That night after reading the paragraph on "Activity of Our Own Troops" the colonel paused a full minute. He belched, frowned, wiped the perspiration off his glasses, adjusted them very deliberately, re-read the paragraph slowly, giving each word its proper emphasis and glared ferociously at his staff.

"I consider that the best Corps Summary I've seen in a long while," he said. After another pause: "As a matter of fact I wrote most of it myself."

On the afternoon of July fifteenth I had known the War was over. Now, early in November, things began to crumble. From captured prisoners we learned that even shock divisions were being broken up, patched, discarded, thrown into line anywhere as a stopgap. Many of the prisoners were in a state of mutiny. They believed in some sort of a social revolution. They were hurt that we would not fraternize with them. I asked one soldier about the discipline in their army. He was a little, gray-skinned, cross-eyed, bespectacled, crop-haired fellow from the first-class 37th Division, which was hurriedly thrown in on November third. That night the officers had ordered a counter-attack. The prisoner smiled crookedly. At regimental headquarters there was mutiny. As for the officers it was: "*Licht aus; Messer raus; und haut ihn!*" [Lights out, knives out and stab them!]

The Armistice was signed. At noon on November eleventh the fighting ceased on the Western Front. I subsequently wrote in the First Corps History, the editing of which was assigned to me by General Dickman:

(172)

A Soldier in the War of Liberation

Although it was not given to American troops to have fought with our Allies through the trials and reversals of the first three years of the war — reversals which perhaps are necessary to weld an army to its finest temper — yet it is a pleasure to think that we were fighting at the end. Of this fact the following radio dispatch may be considered rather as a tribute from our enemy than as a censure:

"Message from Allied G.H.Q. to German G.H.Q., November eleventh, 1918; 4:15 P.M.

"We have received your radio message of 3:15 P.M. Orders have been given for the American attacks reported on the Stenay-Beaumont front to cease at once.

Signed: General Headquarters of the Allies"

Good fighters our doughboys, and at times intelligent, but to the very end lacking in discipline!

Now that the fighting was over I wanted to get back to Nancy, to get back to my painting, to forget it all. So I begged out of the opportunity to follow into Germany with the Army of Occupation. The Corps was sent to Tonnerre in Burgundy. I stayed on with them, and a couple of months later was appointed by General Fassett as Assistant Chief of Staff of the First Corps. I had time to read and think, even to paint a little — which was all bad. I sank into a state of deep spiritual gloom, which lasted off and on for two or three years. I quote at random from my diary:

January first, 1919. Michelangelo wrote: "If God should give me license to choose from all the gifts which he has showered on mortal man, the one which I should most like to have or obtain, I should ask none other — after divine faith — than the high gift of excelling in the art of painting; and perhaps even in that I should wish to be none other than I am. For this I offer many thanks to immortal and sovereign God; because in this world, vast and complex, he has proffered me this little beacon, my ambition in the noble art of painting; so unique in merit that no other gift seems to me more glorious or more worthy of respect."

Apart from his belief in "God immortal and sovereign," art was to Michelangelo a religion, and so it must be to all artists. Today we — I — are without a religious faith. But I profoundly believe that art — to a great artist of today — must be his religion. I mean that painting or any other art is to the artist a nearer physical expression of divine perfection — no matter what be his divinity — than aught else on earth. Love also gives us that sense of perfection, which makes us think that it is divine.

The Italian Renaissance had reverence for their art, and a reverence for beauty. Without such reverence no period can be great in art; and no painter can be a great artist. This is what I mean when I say that to an artist his art must be divine, since it is that physical unity and perfection, which gives us the closest perception of divinity. And this I believe with my whole soul.

I shall have wasted practically two years from my life's work. I started painting when I was nearly twenty-seven. I had been working for a little better than five years. I had painted four or five canvases of which I shall never be ashamed. . . . I had done a few dry points, etchings and drawings, which I believe were good. . . . If I have not gained during these two years in mental vision, in experience, in moral courage, the war has taught me nothing.

I must begin from the beginning. . . . I must look facts in the face and realize that I may always be considered an amateur. . . . For the next five years I must be patient and study. . . . I shall probably never sell more than a few of my things. . . . Frieseke once told me he would be satisfied if half a dozen people in any city understood his work. . . .

When Titian was well along in years and dangerously ill he wrote to a friend: "I have studied, I have worked and experimented night and day to obtain beauty and perfection without ever being able to reach them; and since my earliest years I tortured myself to arrive at some progress, according to my standards, and only at the age of fifty-six do I realize the fate of my profession. Life is human and suffices not to bring one's painting to the perfection which it cries for. At that moment when I shall feel some little progress in my art, Death will come to snatch the brush from my hand."

One must master technique before getting freedom of expression. But my ambition is that, as I continue to paint, I shall be able to carry further and further the freshness of my vision in the process of completion. So that eventually there may be a fusion between the fresh conception and the finished painting. Let me never be satisfied with a happy start — une ébauche — unless I can carry it through. Let me never be satisfied with technical perfection, if it has lost the sense of vision or the sense of beauty.

January tenth. I must curb myself to realize that time is infinite, and that if I can paint well for five years of my life, my name will survive. I must begin from the beginning. That is what will be so difficult and will need so much courage. But it may save my work. . . .

Romain Rolland speaks of "le même odor di belleza montant de tout l'art français moderne." It is that same odor di belleza that I saw yesterday in a reproduction of Lucrezia Borgia by Pintoricchio. No painting. No technique. Nothing, nothing, but that sense of inner beauty — the "through-shine" look — which is divine.

January seventeenth. . . . War is not an artistic stimulant. It can at best be subject matter. War is a great moral shock. It can only disorganize the creative impulse, which demands harmony, no matter whether the individual seeks that harmony in the country or in the heart of the city. Emile Bernard, Leo Putz, Frieseke, Albert Besnard have all told me the same. . . .

Michelangelo said that drawing is the basis of painting. Artists never draw enough. One can learn to paint with a pencil, i.e. to produce the effect of atmosphere, matter and color. The Germans are essentially line-men — the lovers of the symbolic in the line; look at Lenbach or Dürer. Venetian drawings are paintings; they suggest color, matter, flesh, atmosphere. The great artists of the past century — Degas, Millet, Delacroix, Mary Cassatt all drew passionately. Who in New York draws today? It is criminal the way our schools teach to paint directly in color without a preliminary drawing. Learn and daily practice to paint with a pencil. See to it that it remains *in the medium*. Do not *imitate paint* with a pencil.

February eighteenth. . . . Years ago, in 1911–1912, I asked myself: Cannot Rembrandt be painted in terms of impressionism? . . . I believe the gentle gradations from complete shadow to complete light can be best expressed by glazing. . . . It has often bothered me that, although in a drawing I could get just such an effect of *floated modelling in a very high key*, yet when I painted in a high key I lost all feeling of claire-obscure and atmosphere. Is not glazing the solution?

Am I really an artist? That doubt recurs like a nightmare. It takes moral courage to live through these months of mental putrefaction, of nervous anticipation, of readjustment, of doubt, of anxiety. I am restless, ill-humored, depressed, up and down. I doubt myself, my friends, my life.

To have passion and mind — *une passion intelligente.*

February twentieth. At the officers' dance last night Captain Winslow brought a French girl along and introduced her to his friends. She was having a very good time. Major X of the regular army was standing at the door. A lot of first and second lieutenants were standing near us and overheard the following:

Major: "Captain Winslow should understand that if a girl's good enough to invite to the dance, she's not too good to introduce to the other officers."

I said: "Captain Winslow is a friend of mine and has introduced her to every officer at his mess."

Major: "The regular army isn't run on mess lines. If Captain Winslow intends to stay in the army he had better stop this kind of behavior."

I said: "Are you in the regular army, Major?"

The Major said: "Yes."

I said: "I always supposed in the regular army there was the same standard of manners as elsewhere."

A Soldier in the War of Liberation

Major: "My friend Colonel Gallogly asked this girl to dance with him. A lieutenant cut in and he and Winslow took her out to a restaurant, where they sat out the dance. When Gallogly asked her again she said she had a sprained ankle."

I said: "Major, at times it is as important to behave like a man as to stand on your officer's rank. Women have always exercised some privilege of selection. If you see you're not wanted, why advertise the fact?"

February twenty-first: The chauvinistic behaviour of the allies leaves me very unhappy. They are adopting the same attitude of high-handed robbery and unprincipled revenge which we objected to in the Germans. It is robbery to take the German provinces. The officers argue that Germans should be treated like criminals, mad dogs; locked up or killed. You can't kill and you can't lock up 80,000,000 of the most efficient people in Europe. But you can make trouble in the future. If Germany is throttled she *will* make trouble. It is dogs fighting over a bone. Where is the idealism? There was a criminal in Germany, a force, a group, a growth, a policy, a General Staff. And, my God! this criminal was killed and now Europe wants to bring him to life again! And yet there is idealism among the soldiers, who have been fighting and dying for an idea. Idealism exists in the individual; never in the nation. Nations are criminals. "Hieroglyphics written in mud!"

That is why I so hate the regular army. I could forgive them their narrowness, arrogance, stupidity, provincialism; if they had any other ambition than promotion on the "file." I know about a dozen whom I do not despise — Col. Nelson Miles, Col. George M. Russell, General John Biddle, Col. Grant, General Fassett, General Nolan, General Liggett, General Craig.

February twenty-second. I have been reading Delacroix' Journal: "J'ai senti se réveiller en moi la passion des grandes choses. Retrempons nous de temps en temps dans les grandes et belles productions."

How often have I felt that need of self-purification. The similar need "de se replier, de se retourner en soi-même." To rediscover moral balance in solitude. To get away to the country and to find one's own personality, which feeds the growth of an idea. . . .

Modern art has its intellectual limitations. *But we must live within our age. Let us be modern, founded on tradition.* . . .

Be real. It is the hardest and the noblest thing in life. Real to one's passions; honest with one's mind. Passion and mind. We must be real to both. . . .

February twenty-third. Last night I felt again one of those moments of deep moral anguish; about my painting; about my staying over here; about Nancy. . . . No one can realize what the strain is.

March third. What impresses me most in Dijon is the fine Burgundian Gothic sculpture. Claude Sluter's Puit de Moïse is architecturally perfect. During the past year French Gothic has influenced me more than anything else. Its wistful beauty which French art has lost since it turned from Gothic to the classic.

March sixth: Three years ago . . . I suppose . . . What was the happiest day on earth I shall ever have. It was that suggestive, imperfect glimpse of a future happiness — perhaps perfect — which could make such an awakening love more boundless than anything which might come later. It is what makes a dream more nearly perfect happiness than any actual experience. . . .

I went at once to the Chief of Staff, General William Fassett and told him I must go home. He was very decent. . . .

March seventh: I started for Chaumont this morning at ten o'clock. . . . I determined to take the bit in my teeth and went up to General Nolan's office — past the doors of the rooms where I had spent three hateful months a year and a half ago. . . . My head aches . . . wicked ideas come over me, anger, revenge, unhappiness. It is so hard for me to keep sane. At night all sorts of dreams trouble me. . . . God help me to be wise . . .

March nineteenth. Before going I went to General Fassett with the Officers' Record Books of Taylor, Schmidt and Montgomery. They were all in my Section. I asked him to write an endorsement for them. He said it was not the proper moment and that he should wait until they severed their connection with the Corps. He asked me if there was anything in my record book. I said: "No, but it is far less important to me than it is to them. They are businessmen and it will be of value to them later." He answered: "You mean you don't want something from me?" I answered: "No, only I mean that they would appreciate it more than I would."

He wrote in my Officers' Note Book: "Captain Biddle has been on duty with the First Corps for the past thirteen months. During that time he has been on duty in the G2 bureau of the General Staff; and has performed all duties pertaining thereto in a most satisfactory manner. For the greater part of the last two months he has served as acting G2 of the Corps directly under me, and in every way he has done most excellent service. He has been loyal, painstaking and tactful. He has the necessary qualifications for a successful staff officer.

> W. M. FASSETT
> Brigadier General
> Chief of Staff
> First Corps, U. S. Army."

. . . I am a second rate officer because I hate the life; and only do what I do from a sense of loyalty. But I look after my men and officers and am absolutely honest. Poor Anderson, my orderly, had tears in his eyes when he heard I was leaving. . . . I feel as if the demons of hell were eating into the back of my brain. I feel rage, revenge, disappointment. I am so afraid I cannot keep my control. . . .

Brest, March twenty-first. This evening I looked at the catalog of the third *Vente Edgar Degas*. I felt a wave of deep depression. What is the use? . . . I feel so deeply sympathetic with his work. So aware of my own limitations. . . . Why not be a dilettante? Enjoy the work of others. You are written a failure. . . . But one thing the war has given me is some sense of life and reality. Before I wanted to sell; to make a quick reputation. . . . Now I know what I want; what is essential to my happiness. On November eleventh my interest in life switched automatically from the war to my art. . . .

Degas to me was the great genius of his century. Yet he had the limitations of his century. I should like to kneel at his feet. . . .

I feel the need now of being alone. I must work alone. After two years' cessation from work I must not take it up where I left it. I will not go back. I will go forward. I must be alone and untouched by any influence. . . .

Artists should not marry. There is no question about it. They are bad husbands. . . . But without their love I am unhappy. . . . And then one is bad and perverted. . . .

Degas' facility frightens me. I never realized he was such a virtuoso. And he has such restraint. I feel as if a month of my effort must be worth an hour of his. Sometimes I feel I am going mad with envy and rage. . . .

I should like to go to Honolulu for a year or two. . . . to get away . . . I believe I might do work that would live. . . .

I so need someone to help me. . . . I must not grow poisoned and bitter. . . . I will stay young. I will see youth and beauty and love in life. Life is real. If I cannot be happy I shall at least live. God knows in the last four years I have felt and I have lived.

March twenty-third. I finished reading *Jean Christophe*, which I started almost three years ago. Why do they feel so bitterly about Romain Rolland?

"*Plus d'un esprit allemand — oiseaux égarés dans la nuit — venaient à tire d'aile vers le fanal lointain. Mais qui se doute dans la France la force de sympathie qui pousse vers la France tant de cœurs généreux de la nation voisine! Tant de loyales mains tendues, qui ne sont pas responsables des crimes de la politique! . . . Et vous ne nous voyez pas mon-plus, frères d'Allemagne, qui vous disons: 'Voici nos mains. En dépit des mensonges et des haines, on ne nous séparera point. Nous avons besoin de vous, vous avez besoin de nous, pour la grandeur de notre esprit et de nos races. Nous sommes les deux ailes de l'Occident. Qui brise l'une, le vol de l'autre est brisé. Vienne la guerre! Elle ne rempra point l'étreinte de nos mains et l'essor de nos génies fraternels.'* "

These prophetic and Christ-like words he wrote in October, 1912. Today the French would crucify him.

March twenty-seventh. I drink too much. It never goes to my head. I sit and drink from sheer *désœuvrement:* three glasses of sherry, a bottle of burgundy, cognacs, a quart of beer. I see the prostitutes at the Brasserie de la Marine. My mind is full of repulsion and desire. I think of my work and wait for the designation of a boat. . . . All day I had been alone, reading in my room, roaming about the gray, desolate, muddy streets of windy, rainy Brest. . . .

April fifth. The other night I had a curious dream. I was in an American army truck, driven by two German prisoners. The driver was a heavy, stodgy, unattractive fellow. I took from my pocket a little sharp pen-knife, which had been taken from some German prisoners. I jabbed it into both his eyes. I whittled them out from the sockets as I would slice an oyster from its shell. But I was afraid he was not dead, and I jabbed the little blade into his brain, through his skull, again and again. Abram Poole was in the back seat. I sat talking to him. Then to my horror, the driver turned round and asked me for a cigarette. I was in agony. I saw a steep cliff which overhung the road. A German soldier fell from the cliff and his brains spattered on the ground about me. I took the German driver by the hand and led him up the hill, running, stumbling, dragging him behind me. I ran into some trenches and barbed wire entanglements. I asked what it meant and they said: "Don't you know? This is Children's Day." But I was in agony. I burst through the wire and dragged the German to the top of the cliff. There sat another German prisoner. He too was blind. Children were seated about him, listening; and he read to them from a great book, spread out on his knees.

"How can you read," I said, "if you are blind?"

"These are my stories," he said, "I know them by heart; and I am reading them to the children."

"Listen," I said; "here is a man who will read your stories to the children." I took his hand and put it in the hand of the other blind German. Then I became frightened; and in my agony ran and ran; stumbling over rocks and fallen trees.

I awoke. It was three o'clock. My life seems wasted and stale; a failure. Now my torture was sheer fatigue. As morning broke I grew calm. I only felt tired — so tired. "Life, beauty and love," — the words of the little French *fantassin*, the evening before he died. I do so want in my life affection, beauty, youth, love and life, life, life. . . .

April eleventh. Discharged at Camp Dix, N. J. and returned to Philadelphia.

Tahiti

1920-1922

Moemoe fenua i Tautira e,
O te torea iti apatoa e,
I te ara mau ra e,
O te taha iti i Vairua e,
O te ara iti otuitui e,
Tei Parirerire au e,
Ua mo'e outou i te arioi,
Teihea te ara i Tautira nei?

Tautira, land of reverie;
It is the little sandpiper from the South
Winging down the true path.
It is Vairua's narrow strand,
The little path, trembling to the pulse of the sea;
I am at Parirerire,
While you are forgotten by the noble minstrels.
O where is the path that leads to Tautira?

A *paripari*, or ancient district song of Tautira

I WAS singularly fortunate, among some ten or twenty million puzzled beings, to emerge from the War with a clearly defined orientation and a desperate need to make up for lost time. I had less temptation than before to dissipate what I needed of life in the many rare dishes that life proffered. I chose Tahiti for certain plausible reasons. In order that I might work in spiritual tranquillity I wished to get as far as possible from the memories and psychology of war, and obviously from the tumult of the resultant peace, which seemed to me more cold-bloodedly cruel and ferocious than anything

(183)

I had witnessed in the trenches. Because I knew that time lay ever shorter ahead of me and because — having artistically matured during these two years of war — I realized that it was about time to develop whatever in me was authentic, I determined to isolate myself as much as possible from any mental influence. Since my emotional life seemed something of a wreck, I could gamble my ultimate happiness all the more easily in terms of my art. Considerations of painting came first, but the desire for some adventure on the side was a healthy one. This in sum was the rationalization in which I sailed for Tahiti. My dear old white-haired Nana had died during the War and had left me a bequest of two or three thousand dollars, which I knew would comfortably tide me over the next few years. After that perhaps I might fend for myself.

Excluding an intermediate return trip to New York, I spent the next twenty-three months in a native Polynesian village. With the exception of a friend and neighbor, John Holly Knapp, a Harvard clubmate, the nearest European was twenty kilometers distant. Papeete, the village capital of the Society Islands, was a day's journey by carriage and motorbus, or by the small copra-trading steamers. I worked hard, all day and at night, painting, drawing, block-printing, stone-carving and modeling in clay — but since one cannot work fourteen hours out of twenty-four, I had much leisure time to myself. I had fallen in love with the island, the language, the customs and the people, as before I had been moved by California, Texas, Mexico or the Latin Quarter; and all my excess energy was diverted into an attempt to penetrate this charming primitive people.

At the time I had not had occasion to read Franz Boaz. Margaret Mead, Malinowsky and Spengler's masterful introduction to the *Decline of Western Civilization* were not yet published; and consequently I knew nothing of current anthropological thought trends; yet the more I studied and became intimate with the Tahitians, the more I was impressed by the fact that a primitive people is in no sense an inferior one; but merely one whose civilization, language and moral outlook are based on different life concepts from ours. I noted that their mode of living, mental qualifications and manners were a logical expression of these concepts; just as — though less completely and harmoniously — our own apprehension of life more or less rationalizes twentieth-century civilization. I observed in how many respects the psychology of the Tahitians approximated the approach of children; and I began consequently to ask myself — although at the time I was also completely ignorant of the thought-mechanism of psychoanalysis — whether it be true that a child's mental outlook is necessarily less intelligent than, or inferior to, an adult's, rather than simply based on a different need. I felt very strongly at the time that it should be part of the curriculum of every youthful citizen, before reaching maturity, to spend a year in a primitive community, which is not only the expression of the millions of years of our actually inherited, archaic past, but also, by analogy, of our own immediate childhood. It must be remembered that during these years I was emotionally upset, both in my personal affairs and in the thoughts of the horror of postwar diplomacy. At certain intervals I did not speak to a European for weeks at a time, living in almost every material circumstance as a native. I was then — quite naturally — introspective; and I became interested in whatever lessons or comfort I could draw from the study of a different emotional level, which would help me explain or simplify my own problems.

I noticed, for instance, that the Tahitians lived only in the present, never in the past or in the future. This is true of children; but equally so of the Hellenic civilization, of their attitude toward history, mathematics and religion. It followed that Europeans always considered Tahitians incapable of gratitude in their affections, and improvident in their lives; whereas others of us could never sufficiently glory in their unbelievable emotional resiliency, their so beautiful spontaneity, or the ease with which they satisfied their sexual appetites without the degradation of any personal surrender.

Knapp had bought a few acres of land on a wooded prominence between river and lagoon on the outskirts of the village of Tautira, the nethermost on the lesser peninsula of the island. Here he built himself a native hut with wattled bamboo walls and thatched pandanus roof. The following year I did likewise. In the valley the mountains burst into flame, writhing and licking at the hot sky with their long volcanic tongues of rock. The palm trees, like some eerie and parasitic growth, trembled to the gentlest suggestion of trade breeze, or bent their stubborn pliancy to the island hurricanes. Their rustling fronds in the rising, noonday or setting sun, were clusters of jewelry in as many different shades of hair. Nor had the palms the violent contrast of hues — vermilion, pale green, purple and cobalt — of the mangoes, heavy in fruit, the wealthiest and malest tree of all the tropics. The spit of beach before our point of land, where the villagers fished, washed their clothes, worked the nets, or bathed in the shallows of the Vaitipiha, was blue-black at dawn, orange in the heat of the sun and purple in the twilight, as the sun dropped over the blue ranges of far-distant Tahiti nui.

In our cool, temperate zone, where atmosphere seems to play a greater role in delimitating form, we adjust our focus, as does the camera eye, somewhere on the middle distance. Color and contour melt in the horizon line, and are blurred out of focus at our feet. Indeed since the Renaissance discovered the laws of perspective all paintings are blindly constructed on a recognition of this formula. But in Tahiti form and color denied perspective. The violent pattern, at one's feet, of the leaf of a breadfruit tree or of a palm, of the green of a plaintain or the vermilion of a mountain *fei*, of the monstrous shapes and hues of the sea fish, of the primary colors of the tropical flowers, the scarlet hibiscus or yellow *piti*, all this threw the immediate foreground into the focus of the picture; while the intensity of the mountains, the wine colors of the sea, the fury of the billowing cumulus clouds, toward night, brought the world's horizon similarly into the immediacy of the flat design. The eye no longer sought three dimensions in moving from the near to the far. It adjusted itself to the surface of life and found it a tapestry of unparalleled richness and interpenetrating form.

Very slowly my palette began to spread from the silvery, dewdrenched tonalities of Frieseke and the impressionists to a wider range of dominant primaries, and I began to think of color far less as a harmony of tones than as strong individual notes to be fitted into a design. Whereas, hitherto, I had constructed the elements of a picture so as to suggest perspective, I now did all I could in the arrangement of its parts to deny it. To put the matter more simply, I felt that a design should be so close-knit and should so spread to the edges of a canvas that the painting would be equally stable, monumental and complete in pattern, even though placed upside down or on one of its sides. I was pursuing certain trends which had been formulated, in different language, by the cubists a decade previously in Paris. I merely suggest that, in my particular case, a sojourn in the tropics in 1921 resulted in a certain orientation which a sojourn in Paris in 1911 had failed to bring about; and, second, that any impact or influence, if at all honest and healthy, will probably be translated in some generally current idiom or in terms of world movements.

The pattern of the life about me unrolled in a series of vignettes, which seemed as sharp in their symbolism as in the clarity of their line and color. Painting became a natural transcript of experience. As I looked back upon it in Paris, it had there been the arrangement of life to satisfy an esthetic theory into, let us say, the composition of a napkin, a guitar and an apple, rendered in abstract terms of modernism. This pattern of the native life, which so profoundly affected me for several years, I can perhaps best suggest by a few random entries from my diary.

December sixth, 1920. This morning at seven o'clock Mari the Chief's baby died. For a month it had been ailing and the remedies of the native doctor at Paia did not seem of much comfort. Its feeble hands slowly paralyzed, the eyes glazed, turned purple and started from their sockets. Yesterday Mari's relatives collected at his house to offer prayer. It is evening and the wake has commenced. Pua has run to the Chinaman's for bread. His sister Moo is heating coffee in the cooking-shed. Under a mango tree in front of Mari's house, Raiarii, the second chief, hacked and sawed all day at the tiny coffin. Mari sat watching him in a rocking-chair, clad in a dirty, torn undershirt and red loin-cloth. His wife did not appear but sat weeping within. She loved the yellow, crippled child.

December tenth. Each evening the wife of Taaroa sits in a scarlet gown by the edge of the breakers. She smokes cigarettes, made from the tobacco of Papeari, rolled in strips of pandanus leaf. She watches the hills over Ahui. She and her lovely daughter, the wife of Tetuanui, the district mail-carrier, are stricken with consumption.

September thirteenth, 1921. Yesterday, as we sat at lunch, Tetuanui vahine was paddled, dying, across the mouth of the river. Her husband held her, swooning, in his arms. They had been living in Papeete, where he worked on the docks. Now they were bringing her back to her home to die. This morning her soul vanished, as usual in a puff of rain.

October ninth. The days and nights are so beautiful that the whole world quivers in its heat and glory. I am moved, bewildered, by the terrible palm trees, the lordly tufts of the mangoes, by the long black beach, vermilion at noon and purple in the setting sun. But I suppose others will react emotionally to the power of a loco-motive or to a smelting plant at night. I remember once talking to a Russian lady about the grandeur and variety of our American land-

SCULPTURE
IN STONE

Temehau a Teai

SCULPTURE
IN WOOD

TWO CERAMIC PLATES

scape. She said: "We have little physical beauty in Russia, for the plains are monotonous and flat. That is why the Russian must seek spiritual beauty in his soul. Our peasants often go hungry but they never starve of spiritual light."

November thirteenth. About a fortnight ago little Moerai, the foster-son of Arai vahine, joined my household. He is only twelve years old but full of courage. He washes the dishes, waters the flower garden, and does all the cooking. He will start boldly up the valley with the full-grown men after mountain plantain, returning with a load of twenty or thirty pounds after a two-hour climb. He follows me about like a small dog and sleeps on a pandanus mat, stretched at the foot of my bed. His face is round and smooth; his eyes are hidden in ripples of fat. When he sits down to table, his head just emerges above the board. Ueri will tease him in his dry manner. He says: "Moerai will never grow up. When he is an old man, he will be no bigger than he is now. Indeed you may think he is only twelve. Not at all. He is lying to you. He is perhaps twenty or even thirty. He shaves twice a day, or you would notice his thick, black beard. He is hiding a woman, too, the rascal, up in the village." Moerai squirms and grins and makes great sucking noises of satisfaction, as he drinks his tea and dips his long slender fingers into our bowl of raw fish.

January seventeenth, 1922. Two days ago ten-year-old Uraponi, splitting *mape* nuts with a big *fei* knife, almost severed the end of her thumb. While I dressed it, her two older sisters and the village youths sat about in merry jest, telling her that I was about to amputate her hand. Ueri said, with apparent solicitude: "Run for the big scissors, Moerai, the gig-saw and the small hatchet; and fetch a large basin to catch the blood." Uraponi scowled back bravely at them, thrusting out her lower lip and contracting her eyebrows.

January twentieth. My heart is bitter with the ingratitude of the natives. I lie by the water under the black patchwork pattern of a purao tree. Through the branches glitter the thin pale stars against the blue-black sky. Gray, blue-black clouds drift by and below them lies the ledge of Tahiti nui. I am obsessed with the desire for women.

My head throbs and aches. Above the edge of a gray-black cloud, the Pleiades shiver.

January twenty-sixth. As I sat, in a particularly dark and hopeless mood, a boy was carried by with two broken legs and perhaps a broken back. It was little Terei, who fell from the *fei* path a year ago and was with difficulty rescued by Tauire tane. This time he slipped from the top branches of a mango tree. Cruel thoughts torture me. Why should such suffering move us? Beauty is in itself complete. I can see it glowing in orange and silver from the leaves of the giant lily outside my window; and in patches of brown and gold in the twisted, frantic leaves of the breadfruit tree. It is sufficient unto itself. My suffering or his is an isolated blemish, detached from the eternal, without significance.

Rimatara, April twelfth. We left Rimatara in a squall of rain from the north — the *toerau*. For a while I could still see the black specks of horses which had brought the copra from the next village; and the red and white dresses of the women who had collected under a pandanus to shield them from the rain.

Rimatara had impressed me unfavorably as we approached it in the rain. It is low with a few white houses up from the beach. I paddled down the muddy road, past the Chinaman's store, whose owner was bargaining with our half-caste supercargo about the price of copra. I entered into conversation with some girls who had taken refuge under the ribs of an old whale boat, wrecked on the beach, and who were watching the little schooner backing up and down beyond the reef. They told me they were the grandchildren of the *arii vahine* — the queen; and they led me to the giant gravestones, just above the beach, which were visible many miles out to sea. On the last of these slabs was engraved:

> *Tamaeva arii no Rimatara i pohe ai*
> *Novema 28, 1866. Tona ariiraa 1897.*

> Tamaeva, King of Rimatara, has died.
> His reign was from November 1866 to 1897.

Tahiti

Tamaeva, the girls told me, was the father of the aged Himataura, the *arii vahine* — the queen.

I asked one of them if she would accompany me to the house of her *tupuna ruau* — her old grandmother. The girl's name is Tamahareia. They call her Tama for short.

The aged Himataura was reclining on a white *tapa* cloth, her head on a wooden head-rest. The house was almost bare of furniture. Pandanus mats were scattered about. In a corner stood a hand-carved settee, made, so the girls told me, by her royal defunct spouse, who had been taught the carpenter's trade by the sailors from American whalers some sixty or seventy years ago. The ancient woman sat by the door and I hastened to make a drawing of her. Gradually her head sank on her breast. When my drawing was finished, one of the girls shouted playfully in her ear that it was very beautiful and that I should take it to America to show all the people the *arii vahine* of Rimatara.

I had also promised to make a drawing of little Tama. She was perhaps fifteen, with a plump budding figure, oblique Mongolian eyes and a trusting smile. I had some difficulty in finding the proper light and turned her head this way and that.

"Now kiss her," said one of her cousins, who sat weaving a mat.

"Wait till I have found the pose and we will kiss," I said. At length I said: "Now the pose is right." I kissed her.

Tama says with pride that she is *Rimatara tumu mau*, of genuine Rimatara stock, or more literally of the very root of Rimatara. I joked her about her slanting eyes, telling her that she must be *afa tinito mau* — a half genuine Chinese. In the afternoon, holding my hand, she walked me about the island and to the next village, Hororau. Invariably she introduced me to every one we met.

"Ovai tera tamaiti?" [Who is that lad?]

"O Tihoti nei," [It is George.]

"A!" they would answer, their curiosity satisfied; instead of the more usual "E" of Tahiti.

I waded out to the skiff, which carried us beyond the reef to the schooner. The *arii vahine* had presented me with a bunch of bananas, a sack of oranges, drinking nuts and a chicken. I had bought her a dress at the Chinaman's and to Tama I gave a box of scented soap.

April twentieth. The little schooner is loaded. In the hold some hundred tons of copra. More copra piled in the cockpit above the rudder-box. In the after cabin sacks of starch above the level of the upper bunks. The water-tanks brought aft to either side of the cabin. On the main deck stalls are lashed together with *purao* poles. They contain some dozen cattle, forty pigs, two hundred chickens, turkeys and ducks in crates. Forward of the ship's galley are great piles of banana, *fei* and grass for the cattle and pigs. Bunches of bananas and two dozen baskets of poi are tied to the gunwales and bulwarks. Additionally the schooner carries some thirty natives from Tupuai to Rurutu.

We ate on deck in the rain. Before eating there was silence. The men took off their hats and a native Mormon missionary prayed a long time.

"*C'est bien le genre kanaque,*" snarled the half-caste supercargo, who had lived in Papeete and acquired some measurable fluency of French.

I lay below on the sacks of copra, a few inches under the ribbing of the deck. Enormous cockroaches scurried over me. I meditated for a long time on certain aspects of art.

If it is true that the entire esthetic value of a painting, a work of art, lies in what Clive Bell calls significant form — the line, color, composition, etc. — if the esthetic value is entirely independent of representational or literary qualities, why not then omit them, as far as the beauty or esthetic value is concerned? This of course is the thesis of the abstractionists and cubists. Why not omit nature?

The answer to this impasse, about which I had been puzzling for the past two years, suddenly burst on me.

Art is not significant form, as Bell, Roger Fry and so many others assert. Art is *nature translated into significant form*. Painting is the visual aspect of nature; literature, the word-thought aspect of nature, translated into form, design, pattern. The other aspects of nature, or preferably nature as apperceived by different senses, sound, movement or three-dimensional volume, can be re-created into music, dance, sculpture or architecture. This all may seem very elementary. But I had been deeply troubled by the postulates of the modernists. Why not omit nature, if its presentation adds no esthetic value to a work of art? The riddle is answered if we accept nature as the necessary subject matter, or medium or material of art.

April twenty-second. William Kemp, the half-caste Tuamotuan captain, who speaks no English but a little French, crouched barefooted on the deck and told story after story of the *tau tahito* — the ancient legendary days. His eyes glistened, his back straightened and he leaned forward as he crouched. His deep, vibrating voice shook the night. The engines throbbed. About us on the deck the sailors slept on pandanus mats, naked save their loin-cloths. Others chatted and laughed, reclining against the sacks of copra, stacked about the rudder-box.

April twenty-third, 8 A.M. About eighty miles away Tahiti nui is plainly visible, pale and transparent on the edge of the horizon. The lifeless heat beats down on the oily, glassy sea. The highest peaks of the mountains are blanketed; they fade out and later emerge from the cumulus clouds, tumbling and swelling on the edge of the ocean.

It is night and still Tahiti is many miles away. William Kemp, the Tuamotuan, and a *petania* — an adventist — from Rurutu, are arguing as to whether Jesus Christ had ever visited America. Both men are versed in the Scriptures and interlard subtle and sophistic arguments with frequent quotations from the Holy Book.

"How, then, could Christ have come to America; since it was not then discovered? No, nor for many generations."

"But did it not exist before it was discovered? And could He not, therefore, have visited it, if He had so willed?"

"But why, then, was it not mentioned in the *Faufaa Api* — the Bible — by all His disciples and friends?"

(193)

"But it is mentioned in our Mormon Bible and that indeed is the evidence of its truth."

"Because something is written in a book, it is no evidence at all. How do you know that it is not all *parau haavare* — lies?"

"But the only evidence you adduce to show that Christ did not come to America is your Bible. Is not that, too, merely a book?"

By eleven o'clock at night we were running by the lights of Paia; and the cliffs of Punaauia were dimly outlined against the blackness. I went below and slept. At two o'clock we dropped anchor outside the reefs of Papeete.

May twenty-second. I lay under a breadfruit tree outside the house of Paea, the *orometua* — the pastor — listening to the singing; the rhythm, rising, wailing, galloping and dying down. I try to smooth out the wrinkles that gather in my mind. The neverending screaming and chatter of the children all day long about the place drives me mad. I look forward every night to the moment when little Moerai, Uraponi and her sister Terae Hara slip up with the lantern to the house of Arai vahine, where they sleep. At last I am alone, with a tumbler of rum. The rats come out, crawl along the top of the bamboo walls and slip down into the kitchen.

June twenty-third. Ten-year-old Uraponi, who recently was cuffed for gross insubordination and returned to her none too enthusiastic mother, has again joined my household, on the mutual understanding that she is to do no work and come to meals or not as her wayward spirit moves her. Her delicate limbs, slim round belly, protruding under-lip and golden skin are an ornament of sheer beauty, like some primitive bronze Venus of the elder Cranach.

She comes up late from her evening bath, a towel wound about her lean person. To foment discord she exchanges her plate with that of Moerai or Terae Hara, shouting belligerently that she cannot eat off a chipped plate. There is a scene. I cuff all three. Uraponi sulks and, by way of demonstration, refuses to eat, rushes from the house and climbs into the topmost branches of a *purao* tree, from which she glares down at us in obvious hostility. Moerai and Terae Hara call up to her soothingly that she is a *vahine oviri*, *taata amu taata* and *uri taata* — a wild woman, a cannibal and a monkey; and that her baked fish and rice are getting cold and will be eaten by the rats. Darkness gathers and impelled by the fear of the *tupaupau* — evil spirits — Uraponi climbs down her tree, skulks into the house and crawls under the table. Moerai insists she is a monkey and flings her scraps of bread and fish. I open a can of meat to satisfy her ravenous appetite.

July ninth. While I was painting this afternoon Terae Hara and her two playmates Teura and Toahite, daughters of the pastor, clattered into the house like three young colts. They spent the afternoon composing love-letters to imaginary sweethearts. Here is a translation of one written to a certain Tauira, supposedly by Terae Hara, but actually by Toahite.

Tautira, the 23 of August, 1922.

To my darling friend at the house. I beg of you to come to me this night. Come to me here. Do not delay. If you do not come all is over. Do not suppose you will then be able to visit me again.

Look for another sweetheart for yourself, get you ready and bedeck your body, and cast me away, your worthless lover. A twig of roses on my heart will be in memory of you.

My little words are spoken. May you prosper.

From Terae Hara [whose age was perhaps fourteen].

August fifteenth. Two weeks ago I was taken down with the flu and ran a high fever for four or five days. My back and legs ached so that I could not sleep. I vomited continuously, and for a week was tortured with blinding headaches. Nails seemed driven in showers between and through my eyes, and a dull lump fastened in the back of my brain. By concentration I could slowly move it, to the back of my neck and around between my eyes. But I could not dislodge it, and after the fever left me it continued to sap my strength.

At night the lizards seemed to rattle the very roof, skipping about among the plaited fronds of coconut. The rats shook the furniture as they jumped from table to box to chair.

Arai vahine and Tehatara vahine — the mothers of Moerai and Uraponi — brought down their bedding and remained in the house. I had no aspirin, quinine or other medicine. They mixed me native drugs of coconut, bamboo shoots and herbs, which drained the fever from my body. About my head they bound a poultice of starch and lime juice, which relieved the pain. Old Maitihere vahine came from the village and massaged me. My legs and back were stiff and bruised. Afterwards I slept heavily.

September first. Against the full moon some twenty men sat in the shadow of a palm, waiting for the work to begin, singing there in the moonlight. They had trussed their loin-cloths between their legs, about to drag the fish from the receiving-nets.

Teura, the unpremeditated beauty of whose every movement fascinates me, conscious of the very air that caresses her, child and libertine, stretches wantonly in the sand, enfolding her head in her curving arm, darts into the salt water, throws fishes at the boys, and buries her head, for a moment, in her sister's lap.

September twenty-sixth. At about five o'clock the island faded from sight. To the west in a bath of gold the mountains sloped to the sea. That must be Point Venus, Arue and the docks of Papeete; with its sweet, sickening odor of drying copra. And there to the east other mountains slope gently to the sea and are swallowed in the sea's haze. That must be Taiarapu, the eastern peninsula, where the breakers roar against the cliffs of Te Pari; and the tiny huts nestle under the bewildering, the frightening tufts of the slender-stemmed palms.

For over two years I led in outward appearance the approximate life of the natives. I ate their food, talked their language, dressed in their fashion, walked barefooted, climbed the mountains and speared fish with them on the reefs, and was initiated into the social life of the village, yet I hardly penetrated the surface of their mode of living. I realized that the island-born

European, who spoke the language as they did, was, without ever having to stoop to the need of social contacts, in far closer spiritual communion with them than I could ever be. Yet even language did not solve the relation. To understand a native, one must penetrate him from the inside out, not, as I had attempted, from the outside in. In sum, I began to see that our many mis-understandings and their apparent lack of feeling was simply because they, as Tahitians, refused to react in the precise man-ner in which I — as an American — believed that, in their place, I should have reacted. Having painfully learned this truth, I made a determined effort to exact nothing from them in return, to detach myself from them, to hold them — and life — at arm's length; to love them objectively, because they were what they were, and greatly worth loving.

If one's adjustment to the natives was rendered so precarious by one's insistence that they give more — or other — than was in them, then the redeeming quality of the women was that they were capable of giving so little. This of course was a limitation which admirably suited the many that dread a mature relation; and it would explain why so many Americans and Europeans pre-ferred Tahitian women. With a few obvious reservations they made indeed perfect wives. Gracious in their ways, of a pleasant odor, scrupulously clean and fastidious about their bodies; com-petent enough to sweep out the house, to grind coffee, bake fish or scramble eggs; without romantic illusions, realistic in approach, affectionate, always gay, faithful by instinct — though weak in the flesh — adoring children and untroubled by maternity; afraid of any intellectual effort — and consequently far happier in the cooking shed, if professional talk or good conversation flowed with the wine — they seemed created by Providence for the needs of the emotionally timid, devitalized and egotistic sort of male. For they created the minimum of obligation or respon-sibility. They were almost independent, too; for they made up their own dresses and did not have to be much entertained. They were blissfully happy with a guitar or an accordion, a few yards of printed cotton and satin ribbons, a bottle of cheap eau de Cologne and each other's company.

I lived with such a gentle housewife and companion for many months during my stay in Tautira. Temehau a Teai was very beautiful in a full-blown, dusky manner; and fitted into the bold, lush, richly colored pattern of the island life. It is a pity that such an experience, too, cannot be part of our routine educational curriculum. It would undoubtedly help to initiate us into the better understanding of a more mature tie. The dissolution of this particular relation was somewhat precipitate. Coming from the Tuamotu and having lived overmuch in the narrow back alleys of the native quarter in Papeete, Temehau may have assumed with the villagers a certain demeanor of arrogance. At any rate there were those who were glad to do her a turn of mischief. The dénouement was somewhat petty and sordid: eavesdropping, spying, bearing of false testimony, lies and so on. We had a turbulent scene together one heavily electric night. She was about to go on an avowed visit to her sick father in Makatea, an atoll of the Dangerous Archipelago, but she promised me to return in the near future to Tautira. The next morning she dressed herself in a pale blue cotton gown, spotted with white. She had a Chinese shawl of white silk and wore a garland of pink and purple asters, which she had woven from my garden. Her color glowed through her dusky skin and I thought she had never looked more beautiful. I accompanied her to the beach with her two friends and gossips, Arai vahine and Pepe. Before stepping into the low outrigger which bore her to the copra boat beyond the reef, she offered me a pearl, which her father had sent her from the Low Islands. Arai vahine and Pepe stood on the bank and wept. Pepe rested her head on her arm and leaned against a *purao* tree. That was the last I ever saw of Temehau a Teai.

Tahiti

I knew that our relation was not a deep or a permanent one, but for many months I felt lonely and bitter. It began to dawn on me to what a great extent habit lies in the shell of affection and how often wounded vanity is the kernel of a broken heart.

New York and Paris
1923-1926

> They spill out in all sorts of ingenious patterns, the contents of
> the upper levels of their minds; they fetch up the tags and tatters
> of a badly assimilated erudition, so that one can almost say with
> the Florentine humanist, that "diphthongs and consonants are
> the talk of the town"; they no longer seek to shock the grocers,
> they are satisfied if they can dazzle one another.
>
> VAN WYCK BROOKS: *Sketches in Criticism*

DURING these years that I had been in Tahiti, others
had also been intent upon putting the island on the
map. Freddy O'Brien had spent six weeks with
Knapp and myself in Tautira kneading into shape
the final dripping pages of the *Mystic Isles of the South Seas*.
We supplied him with photographs, translations of love letters,
bawdy dance songs and epics of Polynesian cosmography; introduced him to the granddaughters of Ori a Ori, whom Robert
Louis Stevenson had called his friend; and drank with him
copious rum punches, flavored with vanilla beans and lime-
rind oil; while he expounded to us his literary credo, far more
startling, indeed, than his wildest adventure in the Philippines,
the Straits or the Marquesas Islands. *Noa Noa* and Lieutenant
Bligh's *Voyage to the South Seas* had been reprinted that year.
James Norman Hall and Charles Nordhoff, with whom I had
tramped about the island or talked art, literature and aviation
at Mauu's Hotel Tiare or Johnny Gooding's Aina Pare, were
publishing their first successful stories. All this revived post-

bellum interest in the South Seas had to do with the success of
my exhibitions at the Kingore, the Weyhe and the Wildenstein
Galleries in New York; at the Boston Art Club, and subsequently
in Paris and Vienna. For the first time I sold many canvases,
drawings and prints, some of them to well-known collectors
and an occasional museum; and I had, quite honestly, more publicity than I needed. Hitherto I was unknown except to my few
friends. From now on I should continue to be quoted, up and
mostly down, on the ticker tape of the New York art exchange.
I had always been moderately sober in my own estimation and I
remained so, but whatever small notoriety I achieved was a tremendous and wholesome fillip to my avid desire for recognition.

Apart from any personal inclination to keep my feet on the
ground, I believe the criticism of my fellow artists is the healthi-
est guarantee against any prolonged flight into unreality. Marsden Hartley said to me a year or two later in Paris, with one of
his sour flashes of clipped New England understatement, fixing
on me his pale, icy, and judicial glance, and sadistically mouth-
ing his words: "Biddle, I like your work . . . but there are two
things about you, which, in achieving any measurable reputation,
you will have a hard time ever to live down . . . your name and
the fact that you have painted in Tahiti."

I realized that the publicity which my work received was somewhat meretricious, yet I was glad to identify my professional
name with New York. Philadelphia has its own brand of integrity. It believes in itself; although there is nothing much any
longer worth believing in. It respects its own standards, although these standards are inconceivably shallow and antedate
in great measure the birth of our nation. It has the logic and
the courage to love what it likes, and almost always to mistrust
or to dislike anything worth achieving — anything as a rule that
is not Philadelphian. For a century with its tremendous inertia
Philadelphia has relentlessly hated ideas and consequently disliked artists. Artists have in the main reciprocated and have run

away. Benjamin West, Mary Cassatt, Cecilia Beaux, George Luks, Robert Henri, William J. Glackens, John Sloan and myself escaped Philadelphia.

New York, though an infinitely healthier climate for the artist, was not Athens, nor even Paris. It never, of course, wanted the best; it only aspired to the latest. Its influence was seldom quite meretricious, for it made no pretense at anything else. The cornices on Fifth Avenue, which are beginning to disappear, and the sometimes excellent cuisine of the more expensive speakeasies, which, thank God, has stayed, were the symbols of the city's frantic desire to find itself by accepting every standard that was foreign to it. As a friend from Denver once said to me: "We shall make our city not simply the most beautiful in the world but the Florence of America." Yet New York had qualities for which the American artist must always remain grateful. It was absolutely without prejudice; by and large it was generous to the talent of youth as well as to the sins of old age; and it was intensely enthusiastic, curious and eager to see and hear sometimes even the best. It was an enormous lunch counter, to which he who demanded intellectual sensations could step up and slap down his nickel. It was a rich and steaming manure pile, with many a round kernel of nourishment, which every eager fowl could scratch to his heart's content, before waddling off with a full gizzard. In short, one harbored a little love and some respect for Philadelphia; but one loathed it. One could hardly think of New York in terms of affection, but one recognized the burden of gratitude.

These two short winters in New York in 1921 and 1922–1923 gave me a self-respect and confidence in my work which I had previously lacked. I was living at 50½ Barrow Street, in the explosive turmoil of my friend Hunt Diederich's vitality. The house had four rooms, one on each floor. Johnny Roberts, the sculptor, had the ground room; Hunt, Mariska and their two lovely children, Kuku and Sonny, lived in the next one up; I worked and slept in the third; Hunt had his studio on the fourth. A Japanese craftsman lived under the staircase. Sometimes there was the Baroness. All the younger artists at one time or another flowed in and out: William and Marguerite Zorach, Lachaise, Bob Chanler, Rockwell Kent, Louis Bouché, Man Ray, Du Bois, Eli Nadelman, Jo Davidson, Paul Manship.

Apart from laying the background of many close professional ties and half a dozen deep friendships, the next two years marked the orientation of a certain side of my work which needed expansion. I am speaking of sculpture, formal design, and the arts and crafts. An insistence on these aspects of art is characteristic of the entire modern movement, but I was extremely lucky at this impressionable moment to see a great deal of Hunt Diederich, Gaston Lachaise, Bill and Marguerite Zorach. For the next two years I almost stopped painting. I modeled and did some stone and wood carving, never enough; block-printing on silk, designs in marquetry, embroidery, tapestry, batiking, furniture, lithography, a little pottery. It is the way a painter should begin his career, learning the techniques of several of the crafts. Hunt used to say: "I am not a sculptor but an artist; and so I must have the instinct and the skill to execute a problem, a design, in any medium." This is the wholesome and intelligent approach. An artist is most completely individual in that particular medium which is suited to his personality and style; but if he cannot express himself fluently in half a dozen different media, he is somewhat limited in his expression. I may have obtained an adequate style only in painting, drawing and lithography but the years spent in sculpture, formal design and in the arts and crafts added immeasurably to my idiom in painting.

Early that spring I met Grace Moore at a party at Alma Gluck's. We were engaged to each other for a year and a half. We deeply loved each other from the start. I believe that we tried desperately to make a go of things. I know that we had, and still have, the greatest feeling of loyalty and respect for one another and for our mutual careers. Indeed, it was this honesty and mutual respect which occasionally resulted in broken bones and blackened eyes — metaphorically speaking. We tried hard, for we were much in love, to conform to each other's ideal; and I think we improved one another a trifle; but the strain occasionally was too severe and then we slugged one another. Neither of us was quite pliable by nature. I was far too Quaker and Grace was all Tennessee Scotch-Irish. My general appearance, my language, my cursory way of living and many of my friends must have struck her as fascinating Bohemianism, but something to be kept a little in the background. I wondered how I could ever achieve for her the very first rank in my career, the turnout of Adolphe Menjou and the manners of a third secretary of the embassy.

Slowly it dawned on us both that a career, love and marriage, by the very nature of the qualities that make them valuable to us, may well be three separate forces, pulling in opposite directions, and not necessarily trotting smoothly together in the same harness. Love and marriage are after all two different facts, not necessarily antagonistic in intent but rather supplementary. Desiring to love before we marry; and falling in love instinctively and immediately — which seems the logical and is certainly the preferable manner — can there be any other solution for love and marriage than trial and error? Certainly one will entertain no regret for the error and will always feel proud of the integrity of the effort. The greater perhaps the disharmony of the attempted relation, the greater may be the loyalty toward the person who evoked that effort.

Hunt introduced me to Bob Chanler. We used to go late at night to his house on East 19th Street. Here one met much of the youthful eagerness, the post-bellum intellectual and

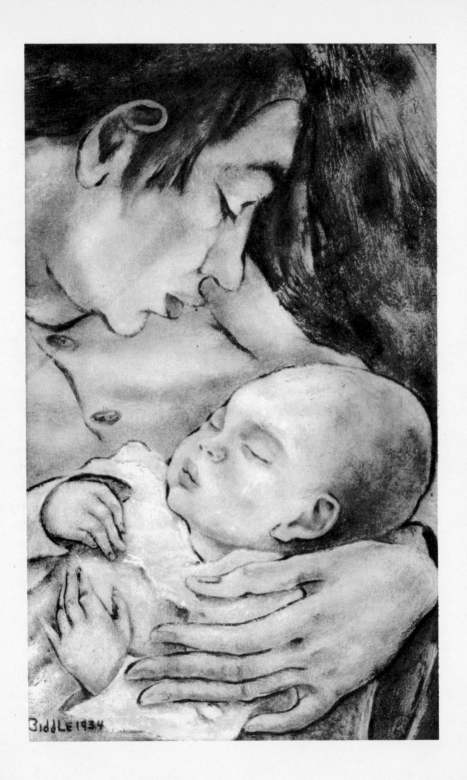

Painting owned by Denver Museum   MOTHER AND CHILD

"HERE'S HOW!"

Photo by Peter A. Juley & Son

sexual emancipation, the esthetic curiosity, the Bohemianism and the promiscuity of the period. It was the decade of *This Side of Paradise*, Gertrude Stein and *The Sun also Rises*. One met *Dial* editors, grave, humorless and high-purposed; dozens of Russian artists, trekking over from Paris, in their first invasion of the Broadway night clubs and Fifth Avenue galleries; prostitutes, pimps, gigolos, sycophants, parasites, alcoholics, musicians and artists. There was good talk, plenty of hooch and a certain gaiety — what the French call "*du mouvement.*" One recalls the occasion when Paul Draper, quite drunk for days on end, had been badgered into singing "Swing Low, Sweet Chariot" in order to sober him up a bit and finally, realizing that his voice had completely gone, burst into floods of tears, while Bob, spinning plates on his head, whistled, belched and whinnied his approval; or the evening when Pascin knocked down the lady who was dancing with him and was bodily evicted by his host; or the family birthday party, when Bob shied a coffee pot at a girl friend because his nerves were on edge and he felt she had not been behaving like a lady.

Only two of the occupants of the house on East 19th Street seem in retrospect entirely sane and sober: the splendid, bold-eyed, deep-bosomed Negress, who brewed Bob's hooch and could repel in masterful fashion any inroad, during her master's absence, on his hospitality — or more frequently, during his soirées, on her own charms; and the silent, heavy Chinese cook, who carried about his person, so Hunt averred, weapons never destined for carving ducks and capons.

Whatever mural talent Chanler had — of a humorous, eclectic, alcoholic sort — flowed over the walls, the stairways, ceilings, bedrooms and lavatories of his house. Its validity was its very definite reflection of the artist, yet he himself, as a human being, was far more magnificent than anything he had created. Sweating, boiling, shouting, cursing, gesticulating, raving, he towered above most people in this madhouse. There was something in

(205)

him of Rasputin and the Brothers Karamazov: the vehemence, tenderness, sensibility, furies, mental eagerness, childlikeness and diabolism. With all this splendid vitality there was something of the showman in Bob, something of the small, white-faced, squealing, pushcart monkey.

Guy Pène Du Bois relates about him the following story. Du Bois was waked up late one night by the ringing of his phone and Bob's insistent pleading. He was evidently frightened: "George Luks is down here, Du Bois. He's ugly. He's been drinking all night and he's tough. We can't get him out. I'm frightened. You can handle him. For God's sake come down quick. I tell you he's ugly, Du Bois. Hurry." Du Bois came down. George certainly looked tough. A small man, at one end of the table, coatless, his sleeves rolled up, his felt hat tilted over one eye, he sat scowling pugnaciously at Bob, whose huge form huddled nervously opposite him. The girls looked rather shattered. Du Bois sized up the situation. He sat down beside Bob and whispered to him: "Throw him out, Bob. He's scared of you. He's bluffing." Bob gulped. "Do you really mean it, Du Bois? He looks pretty tough." Du Bois said: "Bob, he's scared of you. He's yellow." Bob gave a roar like an angry lion. He jumped across the table, seized little George, who was so drunk he could not stand, by the collar and actually got him downstairs and out of the house without the assistance of the Chinaman or the Negress. We all loved Bob. Aside from his liquor and his girls, he was generous with young artists. He bought their work and encouraged them. He was something of a bluff, a bit of a madman and a second-rate painter. But he made the world pleasanter to live in. I wish there were more like him.

I left New York for Paris in the spring of 1923. I stayed there three years. I went there for two reasons. I wanted to do a lot more sculpture and crafts. These could be better executed in Europe at about a third of the price. Second, I felt that New

York success came a little too cheap. I wanted to pit my work against the best French, to exhibit over there, to gain a European recognition. I thought that counted. I was still thinking, romantically and with my American inferiority complex, in terms of John Singer Sargent, Mary Cassatt and Whistler. This was not a mature approach and it took me three years to learn my lesson. I could have pitted my own work against the best paintings in the Metropolitan Museum, which were better than anything being done in Paris. I could have pitted my actual achievements against what I really wanted to achieve. That would have been better still.

Instead I settled down in the Impasse Boissonade 15, in the Quartier Montparnasse, in Paris. I exhibited frequently and was given three one-man shows. My work was handled by one of the smaller Paris dealers. I met most of the French artists and saw something of whatever Americans happened to be living there: Adolphe and Edith Borie, Waldo Peirce, John Storrs, George Antheil, Marsden Hartley, Adolf Dehn, Harold Stearns, Clive Weed, Leo Stein. During those three years I made many pleasant friendships, ate good food, drank good wine, heard much good talk, and learned by experience that I belonged in America. Instead of realizing that whatever mind I had worked in American grooves, I began thoroughly to dislike the French mentality. It seemed to have a jack-rabbit quality about it, leaping and darting pretentiously in every direction, in search only of the unexpected, and anxious only to leave the pack panting heavily up the wrong scent. Paris had a genius for always discovering, in lovely, fresh, French imagery, what the rest of the world had known a hundred years before. The first winter I was there they discovered Samuel Butler, Herman Melville and Josephine Baker, with all their intellectual French ardor. They were serving them up and selling them to me with the same enthusiasm with which they had tried to sell me during successive seasons cubism, futurism, dadaism, expressionism, surrealism and so on. Similarly, instead of seeing in *l'école de Paris* if not the French at least the Paris mind, I began instead to deprecate it heartily. With Matisse's inimitable sense of style, which one also found in any French dress designer, with his light, unlabored surety of touch, so different from the romantic vulgarity of the German modernists, so in the best French lineage of Chardin or of Manet, with all Picasso's exuberant and creative flow of borrowed or stolen design, in all Léger's intellectual intransigence or Braque's fragile aristocracy of pattern and muted color, in all this Paris modernism, was there one spark of passion or love, of interest in life, anything but a cool, polite, elegant, well-ordered preoccupation with esthetic problems? I began to dislike contemporary Paris painting. It dawned on me, at the end of three years, that my natural predilection for something a little different was simply that I was American.

Meanwhile, although it was no longer the mimosa-fragrant spring of one's Latin Quarter youth, the gray mist-laden winters in Montparnasse had an undeniable, urbane and cosmopolitan charm. Wrapped in one's overcoat and woolen muffler, one's feet by an open charcoal brazier, one sat the evening through in front of the Dôme or Rotonde, sipping one's *porto à l'eau*, gossiping in four or five languages; smugly aware that this was the intellectual, the artistic hub of the civilized universe. Sooner or later one met them all, or nearly all of them, these genial, bourgeois, unshaved members of the world's Who's Who in art, who had blazed a path from Paris to Moscow, from Tokio to Dr. Albert Barnes's mausoleum at Merion.

There sat little Pompon, droller in the flesh than his own round, polished, bronze animals, or his own name for that matter. Brancusi would wander by, inveighing with sly peasant wit against "*la sculpture biftex de Michel-Ange et de Rodin,*" chaperoned by the Princess Bonaparte, always ill-dressed and always intellectually hungry. Despiau and Leo Stein sourly sipped their glass of hot milk at their several tables, lone wolves, suffering from chronic indigestion. At another overflowing table, like some huge bourgeois family on a Sunday outing, crowded "les amis de Pascin": Chana Orloff, solid, strong-jawed, matronly; Zadkine, keen-eyed, energetic and grotesque in plus fours, loud-checked cap and blazing waistcoat; Marie Laurencin, short, heavy, nondescript, dull; Hermine David, sadder, grayer, more completely out of drawing than ever dear Pascin painted her; Lipschitz, powerfully built, white, paunchy and alert. Yes, they were all there: red-haired Léger, simple, one-tracked, loudly vibrating, as any other Norman peasant; Derain, heavy-jowled and somewhat over lifesize; Friez, as solid of façade and quite as empty as any successful rubber-tire salesman — each with his own little claque of American admirers. At another table perhaps were the Russians, Larionov with his eager boyish smile; Gontcharova, ascetic and a little stern; Grigoriev with bony chiseled face and long, smooth upper lip, like some tall, fragile Western sheriff; Chagal, sensitive, poetic, with gentle eyes and billowy hair; or little Marie Vassiliev, vital, gesticulating, male-bawdy, Rabelaisian with her third fine, as with her twentieth. They were all there, or most of them, gay, witty, tolerant; on the whole cordial.

Intelligence? Yes. Sensitivity? Enough. Here and there a good bit of originality, of creative talent. Not much passion among the lot. Nothing that glowed or was consumed by any great inner burning. They never bored one; never were too insistent. There was always good talk though it was mostly sauce and spices, rarely a bone to get one's teeth into. One thing they prided themselves upon: They were, each one of them, personalities, originals — not rugged, but individual — as Adolphe Borie said, an edition of one, a single proof struck off, and the plate destroyed.

Three or four conversations — rencontres — of these Paris days stick in my memory.

George Antheil, the composer, was very much the rage. He was almost better known in Germany than in Paris. This made his position among the intelligentsia unique. He was constantly being written up in *Queerschnitt* or Ford Madox Ford's *Transition*. Walter Damrosch heard him play one evening at Bill Bullitt's and was delighted. The maestro said his music had real wit; "*Es hat etwas.*" He would do something for George next winter with the New York Symphony Orchestra. George played round with Sylvia Beach, Ezra Pound, Man Ray, Ferdinand Léger and Gertrude Stein. He took me to the latter's house one evening. Nothing seemed very comfortable and there were some Picassos and a good many Juan Gris hanging around. Gertrude was a dominating personality, massive, powerful and always, I would suppose, by way of indirection. I felt that she might have been a Bethlehem Steel magnate — she had the same thin lips and breadth between the temples; better still a labor politician or a Catholic cardinal. For there was that about her that sized up people and situations — perhaps even better than pictures. She said something about Juan Gris being one of the great unrecognized creative spirits of his epoch. I have forgotten her exact words, but they were, with a certain calculating, inscrutable inflection, in the superlative.

I said nothing. She and George kept up the conversation. She asked us if we would like to see some of her very early Picasso drawings. They were quite unknown to the outside world, she said, looking even more sapient and impenetrable. We said: Yes, indeed; we would love to see the early Picasso drawings. We sat around a table and from an album Miss Stein selected and presented for our delectation one after another of the master's earliest moods. They had real charm and gaiety and life; and evidenced his vigorous, fluid draughtsman's line. Many of them were playful little pornographic sketches; men, or women, or birds, or beasts of prey with monstrous, comic genitals; vivacious little *cochonneries*; all sorts of inventive couplings and witty copulations. We knew that we were in the presence, in this unostentatious and somewhat uncomfortable house, of the early, unpublished masterpieces of a very great creator.

"May I see that one just another moment, Miss Stein? Amazing formality of line. What delicacy and yet what packed design! Interesting the way he echoes his diagonals — don't you think so, George? — in reference to his masses."

Something inside me kept getting tighter and tighter, more and more belligerent. Toward the end of the séance Miss Stein asked me, politely, if somewhat conventionally, what at the moment I was painting. I was ungracious enough to say that I did not think my work would interest her. Miss Stein, who in her own massive and rarified manner had also perhaps been inwardly smoldering, broke out in an Old-Testament-prophetic indictment of my attitude toward art and my own limitations. I would never "understand" or "realize," because of my birthplace, my background, my family, my morals, the Quaker, the Puritan in me. I have forgotten just what. We shouted at each other. I argued with her coldly. I think she called me a lawyer. We parted not entirely on unfriendly terms.

I had of course often seen James Joyce eating his "*rognons à la casa*" at the Petit Trianon, opposite the Gare Montparnasse. The very extreme lenses on his glasses gave him the expression of a huge, pale, emaciated carp. There was something about him a little unbending. When he moved his head to talk or to listen, he ever so slightly moved his whole torso with it, as if he had a chronic case of torticollis, and when he looked at one, he seemed always to be leaning backward and peering down through his cloudy lenses from a great height.

I sat beside him through a whole evening at some little restaurant on the Butte. Like Pascin, he was on a white-wine diet;

and I had been warned that until he started on his second bottle his nerves were apt to be a little taut. Yet he was so aggressively silent and achieved such an opaque front that I was beginning to count my evening as wasted.

Only once during the meal he became excited. He was relating a correspondence between himself and some professor of the classic languages, then living in Switzerland, as to the impropriety in translating Homer's ἐπὶ οἴνοπι πόντῳ as "the wine-dark sea." The proper rendering should have been "of the quality of wine" or perhaps "wine-sparkling." I have forgotten. But as he expounded the etymological and poetic justification for the precise connotation which he gave the phrase, he relaxed; became a little heated; almost glistened through his cloudy glasses in his brief enthusiasm.

After his second bottle of Chablis he opened up a bit. Someone had leaned across the table and had wondered — very point-blank — what Mr. Joyce thought of the last book by Sherwood Anderson, or Carl Sandburg, or James Branch Cabell. He drew himself up as if his interlocutor had wondered what he thought of fornication, and said rather primly:

"I haven't read *belles lettres* for ten years."

I said: "What do you read, Mr. Joyce?"

He said: "Oh, farmers' almanacs, fishing guides, hotel circulars, catalogues of department stores and mail-order houses, dictionaries of modern slang, and of course the advertisements in your American quality magazines."

He was not interested in contemporary literature, or yet in life. Like some ardent geologist, with hammer and receptacle, knocking his way over the earth's crust, collecting pretty pebbles, garnets, semi-precious stones, he, essentially the poet, the mouther of words, was ever searching, in almanacs or sport catalogues, for some new, earthy, glowing bit of imagery. I thought of the Baroness Elsa von Freytag-Loringhoven, who, equally sincere and fastidious, collected old tin cans, broken electric bulbs, milk bottles and automobile tires from the New York garbage pails. Both, in a rarified, intellectual atmosphere, were in search of new forms of beauty in the little, ordinary facts of life about them.

Louis Rittmann, whom I had known in Giverny in the summers of 1915 and 1916, brought the eminent Russian artist Soutine to a party I was giving in my studio at 84 rue d'Assas. It was a mixed crowd. Jane Belo had invited some New York college friends, a debutante or two. They would enjoy meeting the French artists. Chagal was there, Guy Arnoux, Chana Orloff, Hunt Diederich, Marsden Hartley, Ferdinand Léger, Pascin, Marie Vassiliev. Louis came in later with Soutine. He was crumpled, pale, damp, disordered and forbidding. I introduced them and poured drinks. During the evening Soutine came up to me several times and asked me in a tense and irritable manner when the show was to begin, which were "the girls" and whether this was or was not a whorehouse. I supposed at first that it was his dry Latin Quarter humor, but Louis looked a little disturbed at his friend's rather truculent curiosity, and I put him down as very tight but not disorderly. Subsequently it transpired that he had approached most of the ladies present, young and old, with the same harassing inquiries, wondering when they would begin to undress and what the hell sort of a show was this anyway. His French was fortunately a little over their heads. Poor Louis, who is the soul of chivalry, was completely distraught and came to me the next day to offer an apology for his friend's behavior. Someone had suggested to me that the Russian artist felt himself insulted at being invited to a party in which Chagal and Léger were included, the esthetic approach of these artists being inimical to his own credo and artistic standing. Louis admitted that certain of the guests might have ruffled his friend's over-sensitive and high-strung nerves, but there was a simpler, more obvious explanation.

Soutine felt that he had inherited the mantle of genius and

Bohemianism which had cloaked Mogdiliani's shoulders. Of late he had had enormous success and he wanted to live up to his reputation. Mogdiliani had been a tough guy, a rebel, an outcast, a real Jean Foutre; and he would be the same. To hell with what these society people thought of Soutine! He was hardboiled; he was nuts, *détraqué!* This role was condoned by a very smart dealer. After all one must help build up the appropriate personality for a great artist.

"It is a pity," said Louis, "that you met him in one of these moods. He is a regular guy. Perfectly simple — and sensitive."

The Russian sculptor Kogan took me one late spring afternoon to visit Aristide Maillol in his summer home at Marly-le-Roi near Paris. The house and grounds were somewhat nondescript, without any particular character or authenticity. It was the little stucco villa, with gravel paths, vines and pergola, so typically French in its bourgeois mediocrity. The old man was working out of doors on a lifesize figure, cut from some gray limestone. He worked by preference, he said, "en *plein air,*" as this would be the eventual illumination. The violent out-of-door glare obliterated half-tones and called for a bolder treatment and a more vigorous statement of form. Only in finishing he loved to model at night, because the artificial light threw into immediate relief any slight unintended divergence of plane or imperfection of modeling. As he spoke to us, quietly and without ostentation, as an old workman would address two younger craftsmen, he caressed the round limb of his figure with his callused peasant hand. He worked much with the stonecutter's toothed Bouchard hammer. It was adapted to large, generous planes. He offered me the hammer and bade me tap the surface of the stone to get the feel of it.

The inside of the house seemed as shabby and lacking in grace as the exterior. The old man apologized for inhospitality in not asking us to supper. Mme. Maillol was away and he was not much of a cook himself. I asked him where he baked his lovely little figurines, which are as complete an expression of serenity in the fulfillment of form as anything since the fourth century Tanagras of Bœotia. Often, he said, he baked them himself in the castiron coal stove which stood gloomily in one corner of the parlor.

"Sometimes I break my figurines, lowering them with a wire on to the hot coals; but often I obtain beautiful, accidental firings from the ashes and the escaping gas."

A year or two later Jane Belo and I, motoring through the Rouissillon, stopped at Banyuls-sur-Mer, his native village. At the post office we inquired where Monsieur Maillol lived.

"Mais quel Monsieur Maillol, voyons donc? Il y en a tant. Est-ce l'épicier? ou le marchand de tabac? ou bien, monsieur le notaire?"

I said that it was Aristide Maillol, the artist.

"Ah! Ah! Ah! c'est donc celui qui fait les images et qui habite là-haut dans la maison rose." She pointed us the way.

Maillol was unfortunately out. His old peasant wife, when she heard that we were friends from Paris, wiped her hands on her apron and courtesied.

"Bonjour, m'sieur et 'dame. Entrez donc. Entrez."

Their Banyuls home was as simple and almost as uninviting as their northern villa. There was a small studio with two or three unfinished plasters and drawings pinned to the walls or lying about in the dust. There was a tapestry above the door, which he had designed in the early days, when he had known Gauguin. We paused to look at some of the drawings, which obviously the sculptor made use of as he worked.

"Monsieur has such trouble getting models in Banyuls," said Madame Maillol. "Often he works from photographs which he clips from the magazines."

The old lady was proud of her husband and heartbroken that

he was not at home to see his Paris friends. She begged us to stop in another time and courtesied to us from the door.

I believe that Maillol is the greatest living sculptor; and one of the few very great sculptors since the Renaissance. He towers above most of his contemporaries in that he has expressed, directly and without effort in almost everything he has ever done, the spiritual dignity, the earthy strength, the simplicity that are his outlook on life.

I have never met as great a man as Aristide Maillol who was quite as simple; so satisfied, apparently, in being and remaining what he was: a French peasant, an artist, a dignified, unspoiled, gentle human being.

I have tried to convey some idea of French modernism and *l'école de Paris* in flesh as well as in theory. The influence on American art, whether we deprecate it or not, was very real. One recalls the charming bon mot of Charlie Demuth.

"All of us drew our inspiration from the spring of French modernism. John Marin pulled his up in bucketfuls but he spilled much along the way. I had only a teaspoon in which to carry mine; but I never spilled a drop."

Conversations with Mary Cassatt

1911-1926

Claude Monet avait envoyé des toiles particulièrement caractéristiques et c'est l'une d'elles, qui allait faire sugir le nom. Il en exposait cinq, dont l'une avait pour titre: Impression, soleil levant, une vue prise dans un port. . . . Au titre Impression correspondait une touche rapide et légère et des contours fondus, dans une enveloppe générale. Cette œuvre donnait bien la formule de l'art nouveau, aussi par son titre et sa facture fit-elle naître l'expression qui paraissait le mieux caractériser les artistes qui le représentaient, celle d'Impressionistes.

*　　*　　*

Degas n'a de commun avec les Impressionistes que le coloris, qu'il leur doit pour une part. Autrement il n'a pas pratiqué comme eux la peinture en plein air, qui leur reste propre, sa technique est d'un autre ordre. Il a son point de départ dans la tradition classique, il est avant tout un dessinateur. Ses ancêtres sont Poussin et Ingres.

THÉODORE DURET, *Histoire des Peintres Impressionistes*

DURING these years in Paris I saw something of my old friend Miss Mary Cassatt. She had influenced my work more than any other artist whom I had known. I had never studied directly under a painter for whom I had any great respect. At Julien's and at the Pennsylvania Academy I had felt myself to be something of a lone wolf. Nor do I forget the unpaid debt of gratitude which I still owe to Adolphe Borie, Fred Frieseke and Henry McCarter. No one of them was a teacher; yet they helped me in my student days with their advice, their critical intelligence, their intransigent standards and with their faith.

From the very beginning I had been directly and consciously influenced by Degas; and quite naturally, then, by Mary Cassatt, who not only reflected through her own sharp and colorful personality the fine tradition of his masterful drawing and free, bold design, but who also for me became the living word and the authorized commentator on the master's work. It is not surprising that, romantic as I was, full of high resolves, yet artistically unformed and immature, I should have knelt at her feet. She was a Philadelphian, who as a young woman had discarded her Philadelphia milieu, shedding it rather than escaping it; she had the most vivid, brave and magnetic personality I had yet known; and she was the aunt of a niece with whom for a year or two I was in love, but for one who knew Miss Cassatt, it would seem superfluous to offer any reason — except herself — for loving her.

I saw Mary Cassatt for the last time in January, 1926. It was bitterly cold and rained all day. I had received a letter in a trembling and uncertain hand, asking me to lunch with her at her château at Beaufresne, Mesnil Teribus, near Beauvais. An accompanying note from the faithful Mathilde explained that several months before her mistress had fallen from bed; since then she could not walk alone, but was carried almost daily to her automobile, for she was still fond of driving. Often she had serious attacks and at such times her memory failed her. She looked forward to seeing me but I must not be shocked by her altered condition.

Mathilde met me at the gate. She had telegraphed at the last moment not to come, but I had not got her message. Miss Cassatt had had a bad relapse the previous day. She had been ill all night and unable to take any food for the past twenty-four hours. Perhaps she could see me later.

After lunch I went up to her room. She lay quite blind on the green bed which I knew so well from the painting in the Metropolitan Museum and other paintings I had seen at Durand's. She was terribly emaciated. Her thin gray hair straggled from under the lace cap over the blue veins on her high white forehead. Her hands, once such big, knuckled, capable artist's hands, were shrunken and folded on the quilt. When she began to talk they waved and flickered about her head; and the room became charged with the electric vitality of the old lady.

"Well," she fairly shouted, "have you ever seen such weather! My doctor says that in forty years there has not been such a storm." She was terribly put out that the weather had prevented her coming down to lunch. She would have ordered chicken but really hadn't expected me at the last moment. She hoped the Château Margot was really good. It was the last bottle of a case of wine presented to her by her brother J.G., just before his death some fifteen years back. It was all such bad luck. She had driven too far on Friday, and this terrible weather!

Miss Cassatt as usual did the talking. Her mind galloped along, shaking the frail human body, lying propped up, thin and impotent. Every few minutes her memory would fail her, and her face became tortured in the effort to recall or concentrate on a word. She writhed about frantically snapping her fingers. The faithful Mathilde leaned over the bedhead, painfully intent on interpolating the missing links of the conversation. She could almost read her mistress' mind, and would make hurried suggestions to the snapping fingers. Miss Cassatt would pounce upon the right one and gallop along in her talk. Every now and then, for but a moment, she would gently subside, and Mathilde or I would inject a few remarks. What abysses and reinforcements of courage and life and enthusiasm still lay hidden inside the frail body, under the gentle exterior of an old lady's hospitality. Mathilde was to show me the little drawing of the family group done, I think, in Heidelberg, when she was quite a child. There she sat, with a book in her hand, prim, erect, intense; the corners of her eyes slightly raised, looking very straight and hard at one. She wished Mathilde to go and fetch the Egyptian jewelry of lapis lazuli and carnelian. Now there was a terrible snapping of fingers, and various words and suggestions were proffered. At last the jewelry was brought in and spread upon the bed.

Miss Cassatt was becoming exhausted, and I told her that I should see her again. It was too bad the weather had prevented her coming down to lunch. She would motor to Paris as soon as it got a little warmer. I think she hardly remembered me as I tiptoed out of the room, down the long corridor, pausing to look at her dry points and colored aquatints along the wall, then through the darkened salon among the incoherent medley of Empire and Louis Philippe furniture. The drawing by Ingres over there was hidden by the silk window curtain. Most of the Degas, the Courbets, and the Sisleys were in the Paris apartment. On a little table was the set of dark blue English china so brilliantly painted in the Portrait of a Lady in the Metropolitan. Then I went out through the cold glass-covered veranda where hung the Utamaros and one or two Hokusais. With one last peep across the meadow, the chestnut trees, the little formal stream beyond, I drove away in the rain. I should never again talk with this extraordinary woman. She died two or three days later.

I first met her in 1912. She was then an old lady already becoming blind, and recovering from a nervous breakdown brought on in part by the death of her brother J.G., whom she adored. The qualities that made her very great to me were her integrity and her passion. She drew that almost impossible line between her social life and her art, and never sacrificed an iota to either. Socially she remained the prim Philadelphia spinster of her generation. She loved to gossip about Philadelphians; and picked with relish on her family, some of whom she adored — but she would never forgive them for not going to see her exhibitions in New York. She lived most of her life with her mother in her

Paris apartment, or in the country at Beaufresne, and I fancy would have led much the same life had she never painted or left Philadelphia. Her moral code was as inflexible as were her ways of living. She was more angered than shocked at the discovery of irregular relations and an unexpected baby in a peasant family who lived at her gate.

I recall with pleasure certain conversations, monologues. My ring at the door was answered by the barking and scampering of the ill-natured and overfed Griffons who lived with Miss Cassatt. Their churlish yappings would finally subside to an asthmatic wheeze when the tea had been brought in; and they would settle like withered chrysanthemums on the rugs. I steeped myself in the old lady's reminiscent talk. She had known Berthe Morisot intimately; had seen much of Renoir during those last years at Grasse. Chiefly of course she spoke of Degas, for whose work she had a passionate admiration.

"And what do you think of John Sargent, Miss Cassatt?" I had once asked her during my art student days.

Sargent, she said, had shown ability, and at one time Manet had spoken of him, but he preferred notoriety. "You know what Claude Monet said to me about Sargent? '*Miss Cassatt, Sargent est un brave type mais quand il déjeune avec moi je ne parle pas la peinture.*'" I found that a judicious amount of opposition spurred her on. "But you will admit that he has painted some fine portraits?" "What!" she shouted, "have you seen that thing he did of my brother Alec? And did you know the price he charged? And did you notice the way he smudged in the background?" Her voice quivered. "I call it dishonesty. I told Alec he ought not to allow that thing in his house."

She tolerated few among her contemporaries. I once asked her what she thought of Albert Besnard. "You know what Degas said about Besnard," she snickered. "'*Il a volé les plumes de nos ailes.*'"

"What masters would you advise my copying, Miss Cassatt?"

I had once asked her. "How about Rembrandt or Rubens?"

"By no means," she had said, "Rembrandt is 'le dernier mot.' They are finished masters and the purity of their line and design would be hidden under the brilliant technique." Above all she valued line and design. "Do you know what Degas said? 'Il faut se plier devant les primitifs!' "

She herself had copied Correggio in Parma as a young girl, and perhaps Moroni in Bergamo. She made me study his work one summer in museums. She had a veneration for Degas. What he felt was actually her law and standard. Pointing to a little grisaille on her wall she added: "And no painter since Vermeer has mastered atmosphere the way he does." That was that. I have never seen a great and successful artist who so ungrudgingly acknowledged the debt to an earlier and lifelong influence, but it was not generosity with Miss Cassatt so much as her splendid detachment.

Many of her friends must have speculated, as I did, on the relation between the two. She had been a young and brilliant disciple. They were both lonely idealists who lived in their art. One personality fired and directed the other. How often had I wanted to ask the prim old lady pointblank, "Was he ever your lover?" Once she was telling me about Degas's occasionally shabby behavior. I have forgotten the occasion. I think she had sent an American buyer to his studio. Perhaps he was jealous. At any rate he said something about her painting which deeply embarrassed her. It was the markedly indifferent intonation with which she said: "After that for years I stopped seeing him," which revealed to me that relationship. Miss Cassatt's passion for Degas was the generous and detached enthusiasm for his work. About him socially she must have felt as any Philadelphia spinster might feel about the queer Frenchman whom she met in business relations.

With the intellectual world of Paris sitting at her feet Miss Cassatt still wanted more than anything else recognition from Philadelphia and her family. She was given neither. At one time she had wished to present to the Pennsylvania Academy of Fine Arts two portraits by Courbet. "I felt it would mean so much to the students to have these two fine examples of French portraiture. I went to Durand-Ruel and asked him the price, telling him I could not pay for them at the time. 'That's all right, Miss Cassatt,' he answered, 'I will take some of your work in exchange.' And do you know what the Academy had the audacity to write to me?" she shouted. "They thanked me and added that by the way they noticed that the Academy had no examples of my own work and would I send them something, hi! hi! hi! I told them I had been exhibiting for years at the Academy and they had never asked me my prices, although they had funds for buying contemporary American art."

Miss Cassatt was almost unaware of anything that happened in the world of art after 1910. She was after all a very old lady and nearly blind. She never quite forgave Marie Laurencin for omitting noses on her portraits. "Why," she snapped, "I don't quite know what the world's coming to if they call that painting."

In the autumn of 1912 I met her niece Ellen Mary, who was coming out that year in Philadelphia. I must have talked to her about "the cubists and others" whose first exhibition I had seen in Paris the previous winter. At any rate her curiosity evoked from her aunt the following letter, which Ellen Mary gave me. Despite her violence and prejudice, her integrity saw things in truer values than was generally possible for twenty years to come. A certain social intimacy mingles with the biblical scorn, setting her remarks in a background nearer indeed to the mauve decade than to "the present anarchical state of things."

Villa Angeletto, route De Nice
Grasse (A.M.) March 26th, 1913.

DEAREST BROWN:

Yours of the 17th is just here; and as the weather is storming and a pouring rain has been our portion all night and likely to be all day, I have plenty of time before me to answer some of your

questions about cubists and others. No Frenchman of any standing in the art world has ever taken any of these things seriously.
As to Matisse, one has only to see his early work to understand
him. His pictures were extremely feeble in execution and very
commonplace in vision. As he is intelligent he saw that real
excellence, which would bring him consideration, was not for
him on that line. He shut himself up for years and evolved these
things; he knew that in the present anarchical state of things —
not only in the art world but everywhere — he would achieve
notoriety — and he has. At his exhibition in Paris you never hear
French spoken, only German, Scandinavian and other Germanic
languages; and then people think notoriety is fame and even buy
these pictures or daubs. Of course all this has only "*un temps*";
it will die out. Only really good work survives. As to this Gertrude
Stein, she is one of a family of California Jews who came to Paris
poor and unknown; but they are not Jews for nothing. They —
two of the brothers — started a studio, bought Matisse's pictures
cheap and began to pose as amateurs of the only real art. Little
by little people who want to be amused went to these receptions,
where Stein received in sandals and his wife in one garment
fastened by a broach, which if it gave way might disclose the
costume of Eve. Of course the curiosity was aroused and the
anxiety as to whether it *would* give way; and the pose was, if you
don't admire these daubs I am sorry for you; you are not of the
chosen few. Lots of people went, Mrs. Sears amongst them and
Helen; but I never would, being too old a bird to be caught by
chaff. The misunderstanding in art has arisen from the fact that
forty years ago — to be exact thirty-nine years ago — when Degas
and Monet, Renoir and I first exhibited, the public did not
understand, only the "élite" bought and time has proved their
knowledge. Though the Public in those days did not understand, the artists did. Henner told me that he considered Degas
one of the two or three *artists* then living. Now the Public say —
the foreign public — Degas and the others were laughed at; well,

we will be wiser than they. We will show we know; not knowing that the art world of those days did accept these men; only, as they held "*L'assiette de beurre*," they would not divide it with outsiders. No sound artist ever looked except with scorn at these cubists and Matisse.

Her political prejudices were equally violent and they varied from year to year. Toward the end she became incensed with the French, for no reason that I can recall. They were becoming quite worthless and immoral. Earlier in 1915 she used to quote Schiller to me to show how the Germans had changed since the eighteenth century. The last year I saw her she became interested in contemporary American art. I rather think she felt in so doing she was snubbing the French. Perhaps it was a sudden yearning for the country where she had been so little but where she knew she would always live. She had Mathilde accompany her to see a little group of American artists that Pascin and I had organized and that were exhibiting at the Galérie Briant-Robert at 7 rue D'Argenteuil. Léonce Rosenberg had written the preface. I was never more flattered than when she told me that she had been led in front of one of my paintings and could make out that it was a still life. "But the others," she said, "I could not see very distinctly. It must have been a very bad light."

Miss Cassatt, more than any man I ever knew, through the youthful intensity of her feeling, could make her hearers share her enthusiasm for ideas. I loved this prim old Philadelphia lady. How slim and upright she would sit in her white serge jacket and lace cap, her shawl sometimes spread over her knee, as she poured tea in the apartment in the rue Marignan, the wheezy, chocolate-eyed griffons subsiding in a coma of indigestion about her chair. Then as she caught on fire with some idea her eyes blazed and narrowed; her capable bony hands jerked hither and thither. The lace cap would slip to one side and the shawl slide from her knee. As the time to depart approached I would retreat step by step to the door. Once started she literally could not stop, and one was compelled to take one's leave by inches. She would rise, snapping her fingers and talking ever louder, as she heard the visitor's voice recede toward the door. She would follow me out on the landing, and perhaps scream over the banisters some bit of family gossip which she had saved from the last letter from Philadelphia. Such are the moments which I like to recall. There were the other moments when she must have sat alone, prim and straight and nearly blind, alone for months and years, nursing her passions and her enthusiasms. At the end of her great and successful career she once said to Adolphe Borie, to whom she was devoted: "After all, woman's vocation in life is to bear children."

Memories of Jules Pascin

1923-1930

It is just as when one lowers a glass over a candle: the flame devours what oxygen there is, quivers desperately for a moment, and then vanishes, leaving behind a wick that will never be lighted again.

VAN WYCK BROOKS: *Sketches in Criticism*

URING these same years in Paris and subsequently in America I saw much of Jules Pascin and grew to love him. To some degree he influenced my development, but actually far less than I, or others, at the time imagined. In many ways I found Pascin's art deeply sympathetic. Although he received his training in Munich and Vienna he was a *déssinateur* in the finest French tradition, perhaps the finest draughtsman then in Paris. He was an artist to his finger tips, as deeply sensitive as any I have ever known. Then, too, he had the unerring instinct to sense that a drawing or painting is complete when the artist has expressed everything he has to say and has added nothing unessential to the expression of his meaning. The example of this absolute tact or artistry became an actual release to his friends. All of us are sometimes driven by lack of public understanding, by some middle-class morality, by our inhibitions or cowardice to conceive of art as cabinet work, not duly completed until it has been sandpapered and varnished.

In retrospect, however, I find that Pascin's figure grows, not through those gifts of artistry, humor and friendship of which

(227)

he was so prodigal, but as the symbol of a period which influenced all of our generation yet which today has almost disappeared.

Jules Pascin was undeniably a great and successful artist yet his art became warped and life finally defeated him. Of Spanish-Jewish stock his family had settled in Bulgaria and were well-to-do middle-class merchants. Before he was twenty his drawings had achieved fame. Most of his life he lived in Paris, was at the center of every movement, and accepted disdainfully every honor that an unofficial painter could achieve. During the War and at the height of his career he wandered to America, almost starved and became an American citizen. About ten years later at forty-five he slashed his wrists, just after one of the most successful exhibitions that a boom-time Paris dealer could offer him. As far as I know he had no enemies, countless friends and through his wit, debauches, and hospitality had become a myth in Paris, New York and Berlin. Born with worldly goods, achieving success immediately, never outliving fame, what was the canker that poisoned his life, warped his line and finally killed him?

I was once asked by Marc Chadourne to draw for him the death mask of his beloved older brother, the author of *Pot au Noir*. I had not known the latter, but through his family had heard of his early literary promise, the cerebral shock which he received during the War, the trip to the Caribbees to restore his health and the long mental agony which had ended in a *Maison de Santé* and his tragic death.

Sitting for the first time in long and close propinquity to the death of one I felt myself to have known and understood I was brought face to face with two new facts about him: first, the possessed and static serenity of this being, who for a year or more I knew to have been seized of nervous tension and despair; and second, the energy which radiated from this dead nothingness, and seemed to flow over, and into me, and fill every crevice in the room.

So I would like to have seen, emanating from Pascin's death

mask, that channeled and serene vitality that was never his. His life was one long sequence of frustration, concealment and despair.

The author of *Death in the Afternoon* somewhere in his dim childhood must have witnessed the killing of a mouse, and gone screaming to his nurse with the horror and cruelty of it, which image, forgotten, was to warp, condition, forge in him the resistance to death.

So I like to fancy in Pascin's childhood, some tiny wound to his pride or sensibility must have driven him from an acceptance of the world into an escape of mistrust and cynicism.

"When I was very small," he said, "I was the ugly duckling and took refuge in the servants' quarters and the kitchen. I avoided my brothers. *C'était des épiciers.*" So he escaped to the kitchen and, to the delectation of the cook and chambermaids of a well-ordered, prosperous Jewish home, commenced to draw the naughty and whimsical pornographies which would shock the world of *épiciers.*

Pascin was born with a silver spoon in his mouth and he resented it. He had the phobia of success. He identified himself with the scum and jetsam. Only thus, in a family that identifies itself with success, can the martyr exact his quota of self-pity.

He ran away from home to Vienna. He showed his drawings to an art critic, who begged permission to send them to the editor of *Simplicissimus.* In his teens he was already the prodigy of Europe.

"My brother came to bring me home. I was in bed with a prostitute. The concierge knocked to warn me. 'Show him in,' I said, 'his behavior is irreproachable. *C'est un épicier.*'"

Once years later in Paris he said to me: "It was heavy going last night. I dined with my brother. He always wears a *smoking.* But he thinks I have none and so dressed down to the occasion."

These were the only times when Pascin spoke of his family. His early life may have been sheltered with love and security;

but somewhere hidden under childhood memories was the dead mouse. So he spread the legend that he was born in a house of prostitution; and had been christened Jesus; that the French functionary who examined his papers at the frontier protested there was no such Christian name. *"Tiens cela doit être Jules."* His family name was Pincas. He changed it to Pascin. "A further reversal of vowels," smiled his friend, Maurice Sterne, with a twinkle, "would not have been inappropriate."

Hunt Diederich told me to look him up in Paris in 1923. Early one afternoon I went to his studio at 36 Boulevard de Clichy. A decade ago the artists had begun the trek from Montmartre to Montparnasse. Pascin stayed on. I knocked at the door and after a longish wait a small person appeared clamping his shirttails with one fist below his crotch. He had small, deeply set, tragic brown eyes with heavy Byzantine lids, a prominent, well-ripened, debauchee's nose, and thin white legs. He apologized for his studio, which was a nightmare, and agreed to lunch the next day at the Restaurant du Lac in the Parc Montsouris.

There he appeared punctiliously in his closely buttoned blue suit, gloves and derby. I said the procession of nursemaids and baby carriages with the swans and the ducks in the background reminded me of Rousseau's Paris.

We talked of the tropics, Tahiti and the West Indies. I asked him if he would like to go to Bali. He said Sterne told him he had been unable to paint for two years after leaving Bali. It was all so overpowering, everything else looked dry and tasteless by comparison.

We talked of Pascin's American friends. He knew a great number of the young painters, and especially the cartoonists, whom he loved. He was acquainted with a surprising amount of contemporary American poetry and literature. I do not think his mind was analytical. It was very observant and receptive, with a rich play of whimsical fantasy. His voice was vibrant and warm, always a little hoarse, with an undertone of wistfulness. When he was drunk it got very edged like a cicada's, and when he was naughty and whimsical it would trail off in a gentle minor key of playful sadness.

He was on occasions quite filthy himself, especially when drinking, mentally and physically a guttersnipe, but often fastidious about other people's manners and appearance. "When I was young I was very snob and wore spats and gray gloves to the Académie Julien."

Later he came to my studio and examined attentively every drawing and painting. I don't think he ever forgot anything or person he had seen, beneath the heavy-lidded, veiled scrutiny of those sad sharp eyes.

He asked me to one of his *samedi soirs*. He had a patriarchal, tribal sense of hospitality, and wherever he moved with gentle Byzantine languor became the magnet for a swarm of parasites and wastrels, prizefighters, dentists, prostitutes, Hungarian artists, Martiniquan Negresses, Marcoussis, Laborde, l'Espinasse, Henry McBride, almost anyone. One must not be too successful, one must drink his white wine; he, Pascin, must pay for it. That was the nearest definition of this swarm — not exactly of friends or acquaintances — rather satellites. His studio had an etching press covered with half-empty wine glasses. He was working on a dry point and explaining something or other to a Czechoslovakian art student. There was an empty coal stove in one corner, with a cold pork chop on it and a bowl of macaroni; there were canvases all over the place, mostly unfinished; litters of drawings. His place was rarely swept; and so his cat, as she prowled over the drawings, could sign them for him. The bed was unmade. I don't remember furniture; perhaps a kitchen chair or two. Plenty of empty wine bottles. White wine, for he was taking one of his liver cures and on a white-wine diet.

When Pascin came to America in 1914 he experienced as an artist an emotional shock, perhaps the greatest in his lifetime.

Born in security and from a conventional background he had fled to Bohemia and sought his expression in a suave Parisian pornography, that might have had its roots in Watteau or Fragonard. As a mature and successful artist he came to America and for four years almost starved. Dr. Albert Barnes was shown his drawings but bought them later in Paris, not when Pascin desperately needed the money for himself and Hermine David, but the thing in America which thereafter tempered his whole outlook on life was not so much the realistic struggle of economic necessity as a certain comical integrity and clean hard American vulgarity and vitality which recharged his jaded fatigue like a horse lick. Opening his eyes from a dream fantasy of naughty prostitution he gazed with the freshness of a child at life about him: the Cuban Negroes with their burros, the Boston police strike, crap players, the subways, the dust of the garbage dumps and the garbage pickers, Southern colonels, Pullman car porters, the elevators, Western plains and the New Orleans levees. Half-starving he wandered about America and in four years of creative energy blossomed into his supremacy.

Creature of paradox, he expressed his gratitude in three sentimental and bourgeois gestures. For the first time in his life he associated not with parasitical inferiors but with his equals, the young artists, poets, and writers of his decade. He became an American citizen and to cap all went through the legal ceremony of marriage, but here his courage failed, and so he builds up the myth that the reason for marriage was the unwillingness of his grocer to deliver provisions to one living in sin and that of two evils there was less paper work involved in marriage than in the alternative search for a new apartment where he could patronize a less morally temperamental grocer.

George Grosz once said to me: "I was brought up on Fenimore Cooper. When I came to America I was afraid it was not true. Perhaps it has changed. Perhaps Fenimore was lying. But when I had got through the custom docks I knew in my excitement that it was still true that all Americans under their skins have something of the pioneer, Leatherstockings." That is what Pascin found and loved in America.

He had promised to visit me in Croton and one day came out with a trunkful of drawings, a few flannel nightshirts, a silk handkerchief or two and a wooden palette. Sterne told me that he had once before brought Pascin to Croton. He found him late one night, standing forlorn and lonely on a street corner, and insisted on driving him out to the country.

"Maybe it will do me good," said Pascin.

"Well, run in to the drugstore and phone to Hermine David."

"Oh no," said Pascin. "I guess I don't have to."

"Well, buy a toothbrush. I'll fit you out with pyjamas."

"Oh no," said Pascin. "I guess I don't need one."

Uptown Sterne stopped his car at the apartment where Pascin was living. "Just run up and tell Hermine David I'm taking you off for the night."

"Oh no," sighed Pascin. "She'll understand."

She would have to.

At Croton the chief problem was to ease him to bed with not too much red wine by midnight.

Pascin loved Pop Harte and one night the latter turned up for the evening. The talk ranged over various subjects, tonsilitis, the West Indies, New York art patronage.

"Yes," said Pop Harte, "until then I had never heard of tonsils. I was working with a sign painters' outfit in Nebraska. 'What's that they're doing to the fellow on the soapbox?' I asked. 'Taking out his tonsils.' 'Is he sick?' I asked. 'Oh, no, but it's good for the system.' 'What's it cost?' I asked. 'Two dollar, four bits, a crack.' 'Well I guess I'll have to wait over. I've only got four dollars.' 'That's all right. Have one of them out now and the other one on pay day.' So I sat on the soapbox and he took out a tonsil. But the next day the outfit was moved down to Nevada, and I've still got my other tonsil."

Black Sarah came in with the lemon meringue pie, her specialty.

"Yes," continued Pop Harte, "I love the West Indies. Beautiful climate, beautiful scenery; but the cooking was awful. It got me. That and the damn dirty smelling niggers."

Pascin was kicking his shins under the table. Pop Harte jerked himself into consciousness and continued, as Black Sarah removed the dishes: "But they're a wonderful race, the colored people. They've given us our music and our poetry. From them stems the folk art of America." Pascin's face was a mask of polite attention.

Later, outside, Pop Harte discoursed on the Fifth Avenue art situation. "The dealers are all right if it weren't for the damn dirty Jews in the business. They'll double-cross and cheat you."

I glanced at Pascin whose face registered a bored and urbane attention. "But," continued Pop Harte, jerking himself into social awareness, "the Jews are the most talented race in America. It is after all they who have most generously contributed in creative talent to our art, music and literature. I am proud of the large numbers of them that I count among my friends."

Pascin's heavy lid flickered at me for a moment.

Pascin and Pop Harte had lived together in a garret in the Vieux Carré, the old French section of New Orleans. Pop had immortalized their hang-out in the lithograph entitled "Spring Time in New Orleans." On the original proof in bold architectural lettering he had traced the words "Veau Carre." Pascin had questioned his orthography. Then it became "The Early Morning Razor." But had razor one or two z's? "Oh hell," said Pop, "call it 'Spring Time in New Orleans.' "

Max Eastman, Eliena Krylenko, Arthur Garfield Hays, Doris Stevens, Alec Brook, Peggy Bacon, Louis Bouché sometimes came over for the afternoon or evening. With red wine in a jug Pascin invented endless games in drawing. A subject was chosen and everyone must illustrate it beginning at a point and never lifting the pencil from the paper. There was another competition. Each of us wrote the name of an artist on a slip of paper and dropped it in a hat. A book of poetry was opened, once at the lines of Vachel Lindsay:

"Fat, black bucks, in a wine-barrel room."

Selecting a slip from the hat each of us would illustrate the lines in the style of the designated artist. Pascin drew the name of Arthur B. Davies, and I think did both the poet and the artist justice.

One night we were alone and in a sketching mood, and I said I thought Black Sarah might volunteer to pose, if she were approached with sufficient circumspection. While she climbed upstairs to make herself ready, Jane Belo explained that she might be sensitive about her thick lips. "And," I added, "we shouldn't make a caricature; a simple, direct likeness." "And," said Jane Belo, "we can always explain to her that you have made many sketches of Hays and Eastman and European celebrities." Sarah came down an hour later in maroon velvet, white gloves, earrings and pendants, and draped herself in a François I chair. Pascin's sketch of her was tepid, academic and wavering. He later said: "I was too frightened to look either at my drawing or the sitter. My hand trembled so I couldn't hold the pencil."

Pascin returned to Croton after a visit to Dr. Barnes at Merion. They dined on terrapin, canvasback ducks, sherry, white wine and burgundy. The table was cleared and the champagne served. Then Pascin, whose inner being had been mellowed, noticed that servants had trooped into the room and were standing at attention in grateful silence. The learned esthetician and collector was formally addressing them:

"Tonight," he said, "we have with us an artist who, in Berlin, in Tokio, in Paris is equally famous for the sensitivity of his line and the dynamic, three-dimensional pregnancy of his composition. M. Pascin, a great *déssinateur* of all time, will now honor us with a few words."

Pascin rose slowly to his feet and started once or twice to speak. The sweat poured down his brow, and the faces about him melted away. It was the first and only speech of his career.

He was awakened by the droning voice of the doctor: "And, Sam, I know that you are interested in having heard M. Pascin, knowing and admiring as you do his water colors."

"Yas suh, yas suh, Dr. Barnes, ah luv dat skich uv Mister Pascin dat hangs in de hallway between de Picasso and de Matisse!"

Leon Hartl, a friend of Pascin's, was decorating with flowers, doves and bluebirds the walls of a speakeasy at 412 West 44th Street. In payment he received board and red wine. The *patron* was French. Pascin had never received such a commission and its terms appealed to him. The bargain was sealed over a glass of *fine.* He was offered a generous mural space on the second-floor front and in compensation as much red wine as he could consume while working. The thrifty Frenchman had shrewdly stipulated the time limit but not the gargantuan elasticity of Pascin's liver.

The subject of the mural was Lot seduced by his daughters. Lot is Pascin himself, a tired, shabby, shrewd old Jew, sitting behind a small green iron table, like those before the *bistros* on the Boul' Clich'; the table piled with saucers, red liquid in a small glass. Above his head, their hands upstretched, united in seduction? in benediction? hovered two prostitutes — or angels? — stemming, one might hazard, from the spirit of Tintoretto or Theotocopuli.

The theme was familiar to him and the painting was brushed in with a certain frenzy of color and execution, none of the tender mauves and delicate gray pastel washes. Color ran on the plaster wall and over it the raw pigment had been squeezed from the tube. He painted a fitting tribute to the heavy drunken lecheries of the speakeasy. Into it he poured all his masochism, his gentle sneer at a contemptible world, his loneliness and delicacy. I am reluctant to say that it was his greatest painting, a fruition of all that was in him, but there is a certain irony in the history of this mural, which would be appropriate to his masterpiece.

Pascin made a final visit to Croton the night he had finished it. He was in a sorry state of nervous alcoholism. Before leaving a few weeks later for Mexico, I gave a dinner in the rooms which he had decorated. As the evening wore on the tempo of the party reached a crescendo. Two of our guests fell through the roof of the glass veranda which sheltered below the tidy trellis-lined garden. It was too late to get a doctor at once, and the floors and bathroom were covered with blood and bandages. To the excitement were added the shrieks of the *patronne* that her relations with the police would be jeopardized. Shortly thereafter the restaurant changed hands. When I returned from Mexico six months later, the place had been redecorated. The flowers, doves, and bluebirds downstairs and Pascin's mural above had been painted over or else totally erased. That is, I think, the way he would have liked it.

It was the early spring of 1930. Pascin was now in Europe. I had projected a trip to the South and had written him, asking whether he would join me. I received from him the following letter:

> Mon Cher Georges, this *is not* a letter but just an introduction to the letter I owe you certainly and I expect to write very soon.
>
> It is very nice you didn't forget me and gave me sometimes your news. I expect to be since quiet long ago back to the states, but allways thinks hapened. First I was proposed a quiet comfortable arrangement and an exhibition by a dealer. This kept me 5 or 6 month in town and after this I was, as a rest from my hard work and "successes" loafing and drinking round a while. I also had to do cure for my bad liver. I wanted to do this summer a trip to Dalmatia and the other Balkans and be back

end of the summer in the states. But now Lucy was quiet sick, she had allmost, and may still have, to undergoe an operation. She is still in a clinique and will for quiet a while be reconvalescend. So I will have to spend most if not all of this frightful hot summer in Paris. A not too pleasant outlook. I should really prefer very much to be back in Croton, drink your nasty homebrews and carry stones (small ones) for your new house. Maybe I am back to your house warmer, but bild a fence please round your terasse or feed my only on Ginger-Ale straight. What I wanted principally to mention: I may have an exhibition probably in March in New York, but don't want to stay the winter there. Do you have any interesting travel projects? Not Mexico. I want some nice, quiet country with pleasant gaie, not gloomy, people where I could do lots of work or have a nice time if I should have the means to feel lazy or preferably do both at a time. Anyway I should be very glad if you wrote me from time to time.

> Alor, à bientôt, j'espère!
> Amitiés
> Pascin
> 36, Boulevard de Clichy

So I spent two months alone in Charleston where Peter Blume was making his preliminary sketches for "South of Scranton." Motoring back I stopped at Lancaster, Pennsylvania. There Charles Demuth told me the particulars of Pascin's death. He had tried to hang himself from the knob of his studio door, and, unsuccessful, had slashed his wrists with a razor and very very slowly bled to death. I was told later that with a brush, dabbed in blood, he scrawled a farewell message on the door to Lucy. His end was the last despairing, masochistic gesture of one who subconsciously believed that life had ill-treated him.

Thus died my dear friend Pascin, the last of the great Bohemians. His work no less than his life embodied all that was decadent and fin de siècle in the école de Paris, yet he had chosen to love and to cast his lot in America. More or less he influenced all the young American artists with whom he came in contact. Today, not yet a decade since his death, he is all but unknown to the student generation. It is not that his stature has shrunk but that since 1930 young America has turned its back on the art for art's sake of Paris. As a symbol perhaps rather than as an artist, in his life as in his work, he summed up that period. It is the attitude of the rebel, the outsider, the individualist; the attitude of the artist, who, shocked by the brutality of life, finds his only escape in disowning its values.

"Pascin," said George Grosz, "was a great artist. What a pity he was so afraid of all moral standards."

Houses Not Built on Sand

1926-1929

I sometimes dream of a larger and more populous house, standing in a golden age, of enduring materials, and without gingerbread work, which shall consist of only one room, a vast, rude, substantial, primitive hall, without ceiling or plastering, with bare rafters and purlins supporting a sort of lower heaven over one's head — useful to keep off rain and snow; . . . a cavernous house, wherein you must reach up a torch upon a pole to see the roof; where some may live in the fireplace, some in the recess of a window, and some on settles, some at one end of the hall and some at another, and some aloft on rafters with the spiders, if they chose; a house which you have got into when you have opened the outside door, and the ceremony is over; . . . where the washing is not put out, nor the fire, nor the mistress, and perhaps you are sometimes requested to move from off the trapdoor, when the cook would descend into the cellar, and so learn whether the ground is solid or hollow beneath you without stamping. . . .

HENRY DAVID THOREAU: *Walden or Life in the Woods*

I HAD MARRIED Jane Belo in Paris in 1925. We spent that summer in the Adirondacks and the following year settled at the Finney Farm in Croton-on-Hudson. During the War the Duncan School had danced on the green patch of lawn under the ampelopsis-covered ruins of its old cement barn, the first structure of its kind in America. Later Maurice Sterne and Mabel Dodge Luhan had wintered there. I had chosen Croton somewhat at a venture but largely at the suggestion of Louise Bryant Bullitt, who owned a small colonial farmhouse on Mount Airy Road. With the exception of the three months at the Fort Niagara Training Camp on the shores of

Lake Erie, I had not spent a summer in America for fifteen years, since 1911; and this absence may explain the enthusiasm and affection that I felt for the lovely Westchester countryside.

This region is unique in America. Ours is a land of many lakes and rivers. The Hudson is among the world's lesser waterways; but I know of no estuary — or lake, for it is that too at its lower extremity — more gallant, male and lordly. This entire section, skin-deep under the earth-mold deposits of the primeval forests, is a wide granite buttress. The channel of the river was cut, transversely, through these low ridges of rock by the slow grinding of the glacial ages. In the neighborhood of Croton the hills form a steep right-angle escarpment, rising some five or six hundred feet in altitude and for several miles jutting out into the broad basin of the Tappan Zee. From the shoulder of this promontory one can see to the north the threadlike beauty of the Bear Mountain Bridge, stretching in the mist across its devil's chasm; to the south, on a clear day, the transparent towers of the Chrysler and the Empire State buildings rise out of the Palisades some forty miles distant; and to the east, here and there in a dip between the Peekskill hills — the last low echo of the Berkshires — glistens some patch or arm of the blue Croton Lakes, whose system penetrates thirty miles or so into the woodlands of Connecticut.

I had been reared in Pennsylvania and New England. Both regions were part of me and could evoke sharp pangs and desires, hidden under the crust of childhood's memory. The Hudson is more than a symbol; it is a barrier, a natural definition, between New England and all that lies south of it. The flora, the conformation of the land, the color of the earth and streams, the architecture and the accent of the people in Westchester, Putnam and Dutchess Counties partake of both, sometimes of one, sometimes of the other, but they are predominantly of New England.

With New England one associates birch copses, stone "fences"

(241)

and the hard, round trap-rock boulders, the "nigger-heads," scattered through the fields and swamp lands of the North. These landmarks are foreign enough to Eastern Pennsylvania; and the balsam and spruce soon disappear as one moves southward. The *ulmus americana*, whose Gothic purity is so characteristic of the New England green and our own hilly Croton roads, forms no part of the background south of the Hudson; although it shows up again in all its strength and elegance on the lawns of the White House. The same is true of the rugged profile of the *acer saccharum* — the sugar maple — which shades every Vermont farmhouse and is still so plentiful on Mount Airy Road; but which I cannot recall in Pennsylvania or the South. Many of the lovely Southern trees, the sweet gum and the Judas, so profuse and full-grown in the Virginia woods and in Pennsylvania, seem here no more than some exotic bush, landscaping the Westchester Parkways. I once reared in Croton the beautiful non-deciduous *magnolia grandiflora*; but it never blossomed and finally perished in one of our harsh winters that drove the frost three and four feet underground. Clear streams, boulders, clapboard farmhouses and stone fences belong to New England and the east bank of the Hudson. Slow, muddy "runs" or "branches," deep fallow earth, red dirt roads and red-plowed fields, stone farm buildings and split-rail snake fences are parcel of Pennsylvania and much that is south of it. Long Island is the last Southern terminal moraine. There are, then, geologic as well as social-historical reasons that mark the Hudson as a natural boundary.

Jane and I were extremely happy together for the next few years, in France, in Cuba, Puerto Rico, Haiti, or in Croton. When, finally, she asked for a divorce, I had learned that marriage is something more than a relation involving responsibilities and obligations. It is also something much simpler — a fact. One must recognize a fact; and at certain moments about marriage —

although one is at liberty to express the deepest regrets — I believe that the clearest obligation is a recognition that the relation is ended.

Deep in all of us at times is the desire to travel, to expand; to see beyond the next ridge; over that blue horizon. There are other moments when we experience as strong a need to sink our roots deep into the soil; to come to some sound anchorage, which will hold against wind and drift and from which we can chart new bearings.

After Jane Belo and I separated in 1928, my obsession for the moment was to establish my identity, the permanence of my domicile, with this region of America; with all its winter ice and snow, its tropical summer heat and its lovely soft spring colors, russet and salmon pink and tender green; with its granite ridges, its swamps, its sparkling lakes and its bold, gallant Hudson River.

This permanence I could best achieve in building a home, a house, so heavy, so solid — in the time, the intent, the emotion involved, as much as in the broad footings, the stone foundations and the concrete walls of the structure — that I could never desert it; that I should always spiritually live here.

To this task I set myself wholeheartedly in the early spring of 1929, and gave myself six months to its completion. I had spent a good deal of thought and study on architecture, even in its simplest — but its most rock-bottom — element, the private dwelling. If architecture — more almost than in any other art — is plastic form which symbolizes, in organized plan as well as in minutest detail, a utilitarian purpose, then the private dwelling must be the outward physical expression of the inner man. If it shows his purpose in life, his standing in society, his taste and moral outlook, then in its unpretentious way the humblest dwelling can be art, for it will fulfill the definition of architecture.

I had, from rubbing up and down America rather than from any theoretic knowledge, three or four architectural predilections. Perhaps I had in mind the solid masonry of the Pennsylvania-Dutch barns, perhaps the pueblos of the southwest or the peasant houses of Europe. First, I wanted a house so strong and well-jointed that it would survive by many centuries anything I painted. I was frankly in open revolt against the flimsy, jerry-built, cardboard-walled, tar-paper-roofed, imitation log-cabin, stucco, marbleized, brick, or birch-bark sausage-stand, pre-fabricated sort of villa; with Sears-Roebuck two-car garage, and all other instalment-plan facilities, whether pyrofax, oil burner, electric icebox, gas stove, Bendix washer or other device. Such luxuries might come later; but, first, twelve acres of woodland and stone footings, even if I had to wait ten years for my concrete foundations, rather than to do it all slipshod and impermanent, overnight, in some superlatively advertised, thin, *ersatz*, un-durable material. I wanted my walls to be of masonry and con-crete, so thick and of such a mixture that it would take a man all day with a twelve-pound sledgehammer to knock a dent in them. I wanted my floors of such hard, wide, hand-ripped, white oak timber — not merely in the living rooms, but in the kitchen and in the bathrooms under the battleship linoleum — that one could not drive a two-inch wire nail into them. I built some of my partitions in fifteen-inch, solid, poured concrete. It was an erratic gesture rather than a structural need. But as a symbol I prefer the idea of masonry partition walls to that of imitation antique "L" hinges, imitation slate tiles and imitation granite building blocks. A home should at any rate purport to be strong and honest and enduring.

As an interior finish there is nothing as beautiful as the white-washed surface of stone masonry, or of the poured cement, which has caught the imprint of the ship-lap of the supporting forms. My architect friends told me that a concrete wall, being hydro-scopic by nature, could never repel moisture, soaking through

A HOUSE NOT BUILT ON SAND

AUTHOR IN
DINING ROOM

Photo by Robert Imana

FLUTE
PLAYING

WINTER ON THE HUDSON

BRONZE: FIGHTING COCKS

from without; and that consequently I should always have damp and sweating walls. I comforted myself with the thought that half the houses in Europe, with a much wetter climate than ours, are constructed in masonry; and in Italy of native Pozzuolana cement. They have outlived the theories of the best contemporary American architects. Someone once told me that the decadence of modern architecture dated from the time when the architects conceived of their buildings in terms of office blueprints rather than in terms of local materials, local needs and local knowledge. I remembered the occasion when a certain encyclopedic-minded and practical-successful New York architect had been asked the necessary depth of footing for the wall of a country garage. He had shrugged his shoulders: "Why not ask some local carpenter? How do I know the depth of frost line of your Croton winters?" I remembered, too, the reams of literature I had gotten from the Department of Agriculture in answer to my query as to how to mix crude color and lime so that it would set, insoluble in water, on a masonry or concrete surface. It was Louis Vespermann, the local carpenter, who told me to add a cupful of salt to a bucket of whitewash. That was practical chemistry that was unknown to the research bureaus at Washington!

How then could I insulate my wall itself, preserving its lovely inner surface, without resorting to the expense of lathes and the horrid smooth-white nakedness of plaster? First of all I built my walls fifteen inches thick. That would help solve my problem. I also constructed funnels of ship-lap and dropped them into the forms as the men poured the cement, thus filling my walls at intervals of two feet or so with insulating air chambers. Later that summer I visited Mr. Harry Mercer, that incredible archeologist, Latinist, ceramist, scholar and architect, in his house, factory and museum at Doylestown. Early in the century he, too, had been intrigued with the same medium and with the same problem. He had solved it in a somewhat similar manner by dropping rolls of chicken-wire, wrapped about by cloth or paper, into his cement forms.

I faced two other problems in building. American householders had a passion, ill-ordered, sentimental, irrational and unbeautiful, for excessive fenestration. They wished, perhaps, to let in God's light and sunshine. They seemed almost afraid, inside the house, to shut nature out of doors; but sunshine does not enter through a north window; nor through an east window, for that matter, to the average American. They could not realize that if one stands between two lights one stands almost in darkness, blinded if the lights are sufficiently strong. All the best lighting — like God's own sun, and moon and candlelight — is single and direct; never indirect or at cross purposes. From outside, many windows destroy the simplicity, the design, the form of a wall; unless, as in a factory, the wall itself is a series of glass units. And from within an excess of openings, whether of doors, windows, closets, fireplaces, radiator spaces, air ducts or other vents, weaken the feeling of wall space. From an esthetic point of view the less openings the better, but if the house is that of a sculptor or painter, unencumbered wall space is necessary to fulfill its purpose; and this need is practical as well as beautiful.

One's house is a symbol of the *withdrawing* of the individual from the outer world into the privacy of his own thoughts and emotions. In France the house meets the street, which is society, with an impenetrability of unbroken wall. The house from within faces its own interior, itself; its garden, benches, pergola and fruit trees. But characteristic of our civilization, where often we have nothing within to which to retire and must therefore, like monkeys in a cage, constantly live in the external goings and comings and chatterings of the open market, is the façade of crowded windows, the front porch and the observer's inevitable rocker.

I then determined, in order to obtain the maximum of sun and light, as well as of interior space, to have my windows, with the exception of my studio north lighting, only on the south side. This would give me three walls in every room free from windows; and wherever possible I saw to it that it was free from doors. Hélène complains that a closet is as necessary to the smooth functioning of a house as an empty wall space. We have indeed had some heated discussions over this, to me still debatable, theory. I have pointed out in rebuttal that the Lee Mansion at Arlington, Jefferson's home at Monticello and Washington's at Mt. Vernon were all constructed, by three of the wealthiest, most intelligent and practical men of their day, without any closets. She counters in surrebuttal that they are also built without plumbing, running water, central heat or electric wiring. My rejoinder that they could not have had these luxuries, but that, in the case of closets, they apparently preferred not to have them, seems to her only partly satisfying. At times she falls back on the argument that she is neither Washington, Jefferson nor Lighthorse Harry Lee. I try to make it clear that when I built the house I had not realized that I would subsequently marry someone with this highly emotional feeling about the necessity in life of ample closet space.

When I purchased my land I had the choice between a three-acre lot, with a view to the north of Bear Mountain and to the south, at night, of the lights of Spuyten Duyvil, or of thirteen acres of wooded swamp land. Hesitating, I asked George Howe, the architect. He said:

"For God's sake take the swamp. It is true that from the open hilltop you have an incomparable and unimpaired view of from twenty to forty miles in every direction, but that in America is not always an unmixed blessing. We are a young and consequently a growing country; nor do we always expand in elements of sheer beauty. You cannot tell what will be added to your view, perhaps some crenelated Scotch baronial manse or Gothic French château at your very gate. In the years to come you will be grateful if the whole countryside for twenty to forty miles cannot view you. Nor should one ever build on that particular spot which gives us what the smelling German tourists call *eine wunderschoenste prachtvolle aussicht*. Little by little, as with every new love, you will grow immune to the dramatic novelty of the landscape. After a while you will not look at it at all. Why not, then, have something in reserve; which is not always at your feet; to which you can make — even a five-minute — pilgrimage with some Sunday guest, for whom you are reserving the opiate of your Croton hills and lakes and rivers. Quite from the *Liber Studiorum*, too. That is the palliative of your Croton landscape. It is eighteenth-century rather than American. It drugs with its loveliness instead of shocking one by a sordid, chaotic American challenge."

George's taste is as infallible as his ratiocination is tortuous. I have never regretted his preference for woodlands over hilltops; and the swamp has brought me several unsolicited compensations. I pipe my water from an old Indian spring, from the sandy bottom of which I once fished up a flint arrowhead. It is a pleasant thought that centuries ago some Mohican hunter lay hidden in the spice bushes; and that he aimed at — and missed — some huge ancestor, crouched at the edge of my freshet, of those full-throated bullfrogs that today still sing and breed there. I have dammed my streams, dug out the swamp to terrace its banks, and given over the resultant ponds to the care of a brood of Marguerite Zorach's wild Mallard ducks, which thrive on the mosquito larvae, the newts and tadpoles; and compose a far more varied, prouder and gayer picture than that of any ships which sail the Hudson. I have counted twenty-four different trees within fifty yards of my house; and as I cleared the underbrush have opened up to easy view two white oaks with diameters of five feet at the base and a spread of thirty yards of branches. It is a pleasant thought that probably before Hendrik Hudson sailed the river and dropped anchor off Anthony's Nose, possibly before Columbus sighted the Cuban headlands, these two old fellows stood there, spreading their branches not, as now, among second growth but in some open meadow.

What one sees to satisfy one from one's window is never the grandiloquent episode but the intelligent selection and arrangement of the commonplace. Gray squirrels chasing each other like cool shadows over a patch of green lawn, the reflection of three white birches in my black pond, the opaque white cloud of dogwood blossoms darkening my window in the spring, or the Chinese arabesque of the same dogwood stems and their clusters of red berries in the winter against a drift of snow — all this was better to look at through one's window, because it was more intimate and human, than the crest of the Matterhorn.

I had built my house on a shoestring, selling a Modigliani painting and a Rodin water color, which I had gotten in barter from George Hellman, the most generous of art dealers, years before for some of my own work. I had also disposed of a Rembrandt etching and two colored aquatints by my beloved Mary Cassatt. I had borrowed from generous but none too trusting friends. Now that the house was finished I was able to convert the loans into a mortgage and pay back my individual creditors. I had broken ground on a lovely warm April morning. The woods were white with dogwood and wild cherries, and the banks of my spring were carpeted with the yellow dogtooth violet. The house was finished by the first of October. Asters, wild sunflowers and goldenrod tiptoed here and there through the russet of the falling leaves. I had been my own architect and contractor and had done manual work during these six happy months with the masons, the carpenters and the pick-and-shovel gangs. Helping to fell timber, putting a hand to the masonry, knocking together forms for the built-in radiators or other insets in the cement walls, adzing and oiling the roof beams, washing the interior walls with color, landscaping the terraces, running errands in my car — there was always something to be done till ten o'clock at night to keep one busy. I was run ragged, but now, for the first time in my life, at the age of forty-five, I had my own home, my house, my anchorage.

One day toward the end of that same month of October I was scratching with diamond and sandpaper at a new stone at George Miller's, the lithographer's, at six East 14th Street. Jimmy Rosenberg came in and started working on a transfer. It represented, I supposed, an earthquake. There were tumbling skyscrapers and stampeding crowds in the narrow streets. Jimmy asked me if I should like a proof as a souvenir.

I said: "O.K. by me; but souvenir of what?"

Jimmy said: "Have you read the financial news, today?"

I said: "As a matter of fact I lunched in with George Miller and haven't seen a paper. But apart from that I don't read financial news. I never owned a stock or a bond but once. During the War we were lined up overseas and told — at the point of a gun — to buy Liberty Bonds. I bought one; and out of protest I gave it away to my oldest nephew for a Christmas present. So I don't read financial news."

Jimmy said: "O.K. by me; but today it's on the front pages and it probably will be for another year or so."

Coming up Fifth Avenue in a taxi Jimmy asked: "Are you in love for the moment?"

I said: "Probably; but she's a married lady. I think she's in love with some one else and she's sailing next week for Latvia."

Jimmy said: "Very well, then. I should like you to meet a young friend of mine, Hélène Sardeau, a very fine and talented Belgian-American sculptor."

This all happened on the twenty-ninth of October; and although I didn't meet Hélène until the following Monday, I have kept Jimmy's lithograph as a souvenir.

I think of every story of a life as a striving for, and if the life is not frustrated or tragic, as the eventual attaining of, maturity.

Houses Not Built on Sand

If this particular story dealt with the search for inward happiness, this chapter would be the final one. Hélène has been capable of creating and holding a mature relation. She is herself a mature person, and maturity is a rare quality. It is never being slightly different. It is only being completely one's self.

I was to have another experience, which chronologically belongs a year or so later, after my return from Italy, but which I shall tell here.

I knew of course that being with child was physiologically and emotionally not only one of life's miracles but perhaps its greatest experience, and I had always averred with absolute honesty that the only reason why I regretted having been born a male was that I should never have that experience. I knew that different women can be affected by this, as by any other event, in divers ways. It is not strange that in Hélène's case I should watch her more closely. It seemed to me the absolute example of creation. All her energy, her concentration, seemed subconsciously and without any effort canalized to a certain achievement. One could not detect any friction of intent, any cross-purpose, any wastage of force. Her whole life was concentrated in one single, ever-increasing, smooth flow of energy. Her life had become wholly a will. One hardly sensed activity. If a river is broad enough and deep enough one does not observe the current. She was not so much unconscious of the life that went on about her as that all of life to her was part of that inner creative flow. She embraced the universe, yet the universe had only this tiny concentrated purpose — her child.

Art and Its
Social Significance
1933-1939

One such wave (and not the least) I raised and rolled before the breath of an idea, till it reached its crest, and toppled
over and fell at Damascus. The wash of that wave, thrown
back by the resistance of vested things, will provide the
matter of the following wave, when in fulness of time the
sea shall be raised once more.

T. E. LAWRENCE: *The Seven Pillars of Wisdom* [1]

FOR ONE who had spent the preceding fifteen months
in an Italian village on the edge of the Abruzzi, sixteen
kilometers from the nearest telephone and forty from
the nearest bath, the landing in Brooklyn from a small
Italian freighter through solid sheets of November rain was like
stepping from the cloying sweetness of a decaying garden into
the salt tang of life. I had not entirely enjoyed my exile, but I
made the most of it. I had stayed on in Italy because I had
nothing on which to come home. History was being made about
me. In Sweden Kreuger had exploded, dragging little nations
down in his collapse. In Germany perhaps the greatest genius
of his day, because more completely than any other mortal he
embodied the hatred and malignity which was spreading its
miasmatic poison over the earth's surface, was rapidly cashing

[1] Doubleday, Doran and Co., Inc.

(252)

in on a ten years' build-up of rancor, frustration, persecution and sadism. On Fifth Avenue corners men were still polishing apples. The crazy pattern of Hooverville was a mad landscaping on Riverside Drive, but the spectacle of machine guns and tear-gas bombs to protect the Capitol from flat-bellied, unshaved, jobless veterans could at best evoke a somewhat hollow laugh.

From Lacco Ameno on the fringe of Ischia one watched the downward spiral of U.S. Steel and speculated on the Democratic Convention in Chicago — Governor Roosevelt is undeniably playing a shrewd hand; almost too shrewd at moments? In his investigation of Mayor Walker he seems unduly circumspect. Will he ever take off his gloves and fight? Is he the sort to pull his punch? Why now all this pother over "the forgotten man"? A good phrase that. It might stick. Yes it's an even bet Roosevelt will get the nomination. And of course he'd be elected. Poor old Al! And Hoover? Fat-head! . . . Bill Bullitt writes from the Berkshires. He's been seeing something of Franklin this summer and thinks he's a swell guy. Bullitt has thrown his hat in the ring. I'm glad he's back again in politics. Politics or diplomacy. All the same game. But he'll hardly want to publish just now, I suppose, that life of Wilson. Rather too Freudian an angle for a party diplomat!

From Ischia, too, mural painting seems very much in the American offing. . . . That fresco panel I did in Rome for the Modern Museum show in a mad fortnight of excitement. . . . There had been a telegram from Lincoln Kirstein. Who was he? Of course, I had met him through Bullitt at Ashfield, the summer before I came to Italy. Many cocktails and we had talked art and Mexico and Rivera, and the Fogg Art Museum, and *Hound and Horn* . . . Harvard has certainly changed since my time. Thank God! Yes, I remember now. I told him how Moïses Saenz had offered me a mural job in Mexico that same spring. The way my heart almost broke when it fell through. How I would give ten years of my life or my left arm to have the chance to do one. . . . Apparently my panel was better spoken of than most of them. The critics certainly rapped the show. There was no doubt, so my friends wrote, that there would be some sort of a tryout for Rockefeller Center. There might be big things, if only one were given the chance. But it's all a racket, like corporation law or dentistry. You've got to get in and play the game. Give Benton his credit. He never gave up hope and he had to wait a long time. . . . Orozco doing something now for Pomona College out in California, and Rivera in Detroit. . . . That was a good letter of Henry Poor's in the *New York Times*. Instead of trying to pick the best thing in the world at fifty thousand bucks why not select fifty artists at a thousand dollars apiece. That way you'll be sure to have something good for your money. Scrap the rest. . . . Oh, it's in the air. It's in the air. . . . God, how I wanted to get back!

Italy was good for a vacation. Even for a year. All art in Europe had sprung from the lap of the Mediterranean: Greek, Roman, Etruscan, Cretan, Egyptian. Here you had it at the source; and what a place for work. No telephones, no business interruptions. Not even friends. Every day a ten-hour day, with occasionally a twenty-kilometer hike over the crumbling foothills of the Abruzzi. Red wine at night with eighteen-century flute music and Hélène at the creaky piano.

Padre Martini, Karl Ditters von Dittersdorf, Corelli, Tartini, Lully, Purcell; Pierre Bucquet's Suite for two Flutes (*Le Plaintif, La Légère, La Folette, La Hardie, La Douce Sarabande*); Pergolese's "Tre giorni son, che Nina"; Rameaux' *Air Gaie, Air Tendre:*

> "*L'amour dort dans le feuillage,*
> *Chut! ne le réveillez pas!*"

Beethoven's Largo in E flat for flute and clavier; Mozart's Andante in C major for flute; Jean-Marie Leclair and Bach's *Sicilienne*.

Remote and tender. To close one's eyes for a moment and pulse to the measured rhythm, the reasoned style, the sweetness of an art which can be no more, an art dedicated to all time. Then to open one's eyes resolutely to the little goose-stepping, black-shirted, lantern-jawed ape; the loud-mouthing barker of a glory that was never his.

I never worked better than those fifteen months. Fifty oil paintings, two hundred drawings, fifty pieces of ceramics; at Ischia a dozen huge hand-decorated and fired bowls; boxes in marquetry at Sorrento; lithographs in Rome. Painting, walking or swimming; gallons and hogsheads of red wine; learning Italian; studying every Italian fresco in central Italy. Over and above all my beloved Piero. Better than Raffaello Sanzio, better than Luca Signorelli, better than Allesandro Filipepe Botticelli, or Domenico Ghirlandajo, and his pupil Michelangelo Buonarrotti, I love him. The scarred and faded walls at Arezzo have the grace and elegance of a print by Utamaro or Koriusai, the harmony and interwoven orchestration of Bach's music, the winsomeness of a tapestry of *mille fleurs*. His *Resurrection* at Sansepolcro is a simple statement of nobility, comparable to Giorgione's *Castelfranco Madonna*, or Michelangelo's *Pieta*, or that most beautiful *Disentombment of Christ* in the Louvre of unknown Flemish origin.

One loved the Italians too: their intelligence, their flashing individualism, their humanity, their humanism and sunny warmth. Mussolini had not yet dragged Italy's name through the mud and blood of Ethiopia; nor had his gallant son Vittorio, in words that transcended his acts, transmuted into fascist art the noble fascist sport of disemboweling women and babies from the air. The peasants remained cheerful if they sang somewhat less than in the years gone by. Next winter, I was told, there would be some insufficiency of corn. That was a serious matter. The increased tax on butchering hogs would hardly affect them. For years they had scarcely eaten meat; and, as with coffee and tobacco, they had almost lost the taste. Just as well indeed. The price of a couple of packages of "Luckies" would keep a family of peasants alive for a week. Clothes, too, were not, strictly speaking, a budgetary item. Just fancy a peasant buying clothes! One doesn't buy clothes; one mends them. Shoes one seldom buys. A slice of an old automobile tire, fastened with raw-hide thongs over the instep and about the ankle, will serve just as well. So on the whole the peasants were a happy lot with few desires and fewer cares. Since child mortality was high there was small need for a doctor. But they must have corn. Next winter there would not be quite enough. One could tighten one's belt. "*Viva il Duce! Viva il Fascismo!*"

Our little Italian freighter bucked its passage through the cold gray seas of the Atlantic from Naples to Brooklyn in twenty-one days. There was time for a readjustment of one's values, a reminiscent glance over the past twenty years at the main currents of art. The tide which had run so smoothly and strong with the last of the impressionists, Cassatt, Degas, Renoir, Rodin, had raced and tossed and sparkled in the high noon of modernism: Matisse, Picasso, Braque, Pascin, Derain, Brancusi, Despiau, Maillol, Bourdelle, Chagal, Segonzac. Zadkine, Gleizes, Orloff. I had known them all or nearly all of them. Brought to a stop by the four years' barriers of international hates, wars, blood-lettings, physical killings, spiritual strangulations; yet this great European estuary, fed from the countless streams of earlier traditions, styles, cultures; and more recently still mingling and enriched by almost every national European source — Russian, Jewish, Germanic, African, Mayan and Mongolian — had still struggled on, until one might expect a universal language, a universal flow. For some time now the current had been slowing up. The tide was at the slack, as if bogged by the inertia of this vast world-economic depression.

American art had reflected to a great degree the warmth and

brightness of the European movement. It had, nevertheless, provincial and parochial accents and inflections, which made it different from European art; no matter how hard it tried to conform to type, to follow the European standard. Although its general direction paralleled that of Europe, yet the American movement had been deflected by local dams, inhibitions, conformations; and fed by regional enthusiasms, prejudices and deep traditional folk springs.

Since 1913 water — and art — had flowed under the bridge. In that year Czar Nicholas and Kaiser William II, John Singer Sargent, Henry and William James were still at their zenith. *Main Street* was published some seven years later. Edna St. Vincent Millay had not entered Vassar. In Paris one saw more of horse cabs than of taxis. Europe was comparatively at peace.

In America prior to 1913 the annual exhibitions at the Pennsylvania Academy of Fine Arts (and of its younger rival, the New York National Academy of Design) were the artistic events of the season. There were other annuals in other cities. Among the exhibitors who have not passed into oblivion, were Mary Cassatt, J. Alden Weir, John Singer Sargent, Albert Ryder, Childe Hassam, Thomas Eakins, Carl Frederick Frieseke, Adolphe Borie and the so-called insurgents: Robert Henri, George Luks, John Sloan, William Glackens (all of them graduates of the Pennsylvania Academy of Fine Arts), Arthur B. Davies, and George Bellows. Modern contemporary French art was seen nowhere outside of Stieglitz' small gallery at "291" Fifth Avenue. Mrs. Havemeyer's private collection contained some fine Cézannes. He had died an old man nine years previously.

The insurgents rebelled against the technical formula of French impressionism; and more specifically against Philip and Lillian Westcott Hale's tepid sub-adolescent nudes, Tarbell's dreary and uninspired academies and Sargent's bituminous portraits in the genteel tradition. Sired perhaps by Thomas Eakins and Frank Duveneck, there was more of Munich than of Paris

(257)

in their blood. They insisted robustly on the actuality of contemporary America, with its slums, street scenes, wharves, saloons
and factories. Of what we speak of as Modern Art there was none.

Then like a crash came the Armory Exhibition of 1913. For
months the whole city surged in to see the hullabaloo and there
were full-page reproductions in Kalamazoo, Waco, Venice,
Athens, Troy, Paris, Rome and Ithaca. *Un roi vite* and *Le nu
descendant l'escalier* became almost incorporated as part of our
American idiom. Post-impressionism, neo-impressionism, cubism,
futurism, vorticism, Lehnbruck, Brancusi, Matisse, Picasso, cul-
minating in logical sequence from Goya, Daumier, Courbet,
Degas, Gauguin and Cézanne, all this was seen for the first time
by the great American public. They saw it, discussed it, thoroughly disliked it and never entirely forgot it. As Arthur Carles
said:

"It was Matisse who put 'nigger-pink' on the map."

But it was different with us artists. I can never forget my own
emotions as I wandered utterly exhausted yet drunk with excitement from one gallery to another, from new sensation to shock,
from fresh knowledge to an ever-growing inner experience. One
had the same generous feeling as twenty years later when Edward
Bruce outlined to us the creation, through Harry Hopkins'
largesse, of the first Federal Art Project; the same presentiment
which electrified in 1936 the organizers and members of the
first American Artists' Congress, that history was in the making
and that we were making it.

The exhibition was the choice and expression of the younger
and more intellectually-minded, and it had the effect of fusing
them into a self-conscious group, alive to the international movement which flamed in Paris before the war, to the currents strik-
ing like electric waves from African, Polynesian, Aztec, Hopi
Indian and Russian folk art, and from the Russian ballet. Many
of us had studied modernism as individuals in France. A few —
Weber, Walkowitz, Diederich, Nadelman, Sterne — had to a

mild degree participated in the Paris movement; but after 1913 we were conscious of forming a group of modern American artists. We were somewhat dogmatic; we were filled with ideals and ideas; we knew that we should achieve recognition; we had pride; we were young.

Our group was not exhibited by museums, annuals or galleries. It was natural then in our glowing intransigence that our art was expansive, experimental, self-searching, probing of esthetic standards. Paris, African sculpture, abstractions characterized our work. Sentimentality, realism, the anecdotal, the academic outlook and John Singer Sargent were anathema. Davies, by some acclaimed the father of the group, draped his Celtic moonlight romanticism with a filmy netting of cubism. The American modernisits of 1913 and the following years were swinging away from the American "human interest" note of the Luks, Henri, Glackens, Sloan and Bellows. And we did not willingly exhibit with these other rebels of an earlier decade.

We were all comparatively or absolutely poor. As to reputation we had none. We could hardly boast that our work was sufficiently known to have been condemned and found wanting. So we clung much together, sucked ideas one from another; drew comfort and companionship one from another; exchanged linoleum cuts or drawings; occasionally bought each other's work. We knew that recognition would be ours and we were young.

And of this group in the earlier and intervening years were the sculptors Hunt Diederich, and Eli Nadelman; and such painters as William and Marguerite Zorach, John Marin, Charles Demuth, Joseph Stella, Alfred Maurer, Andrew Dasburg, Jules Pascin, Max Weber, Abraham Walkowitz, Marsden Hartley, Arthur Carles and Man Ray. And other artists fused with the movement in the coming years.

In 1921 occurred an event, hardly to stir a ripple in the world of art, yet which marked a definite stage in the slow expansion of an idea, the "wash of the wave" upon the "resistance of vested things." William Yarrow, one of us then, Arthur Carles and Henry McCarter, all of them Philadelphians and the latter two members of the faculty of the Pennsylvania Academy, persuaded that august and timorous body — waddling slowly forward, one eye to either side and seeing nothing, with the gravity and self-esteem of any well-fed and successful gander — to hold an exhibition of modern art. Arthur Carles, hollow and prophetic-eyed, his long, unkempt and dusty beard the challenging symbol of the Bohemian tradition and the Parisian modes, had tirelessly sown the seeds of modernism in Philadelphia; Henry McCarter, of an older vintage — he had seen Van Gogh in life, had watched Corot paint, spoken with Toulouse-Lautrec and studied in the atelier of Puvis — had been the link, as he is today, for every outstanding art student, between the high tradition of the past and what there is young in the world about us. How the authorities of the Academy were induced to accept modernism is of no consequence. Modern art was safe for the public. Fifth Avenue Galleries were slowly opening their doors. The number of modern artists was growing and included a somewhat younger crop such as Morris Kantor, Gaston Lachaise, Georgia O'Keeffe, Charles Sheeler, Louis Bouché, Stuart Davis, Thomas Benton, Alec and Peggy Brook, Yasuo Kunyoshi, Preston Dickinson, Niles Spencer and others. There was still an intellectual rift between the modernists and the insurgents of an earlier decade. I am not positive but I think that neither Luks, Henri, Sloan, Glackens or Bellows were invited to the Philadelphia exhibition. "Isms" die hard and the modernists remained intransigent until they would in the fullest sense be accepted by the public. Then they might fuse in the general contemporary art current.

Today this fusion had taken place and another exhibition, in no way charged with dynamite or knocking sparks from rocks, might be taken as a symbol of this near maturity, this coming of age of American painting. In the spring of 1930 the New York

Art and Its Social Significance

Museum of Modern Art, as cautious as it was snobbish in its insistence on modernism — modernisticism, if I may coin a much-needed word — gave its first exhibition of living American artists. Although the general current of the work was distinctly modern, yet the show mingled the somewhat academic placidity of Kenneth Hays Miller, the echo of Allen Tucker's impressionism, the sentimentally realistic sobriety of Eugene Speicher and George Luks with the frank abstractions of Charles Demuth, Stuart Davis and Georgia O'Keeffe. Now the significance of this exhibition was not that the museum sensed that the prevailing current was to lean just a trifle to the right, to be a little old-fashioned, to present a united front of styles; it was rather that American art had matured to the point of shedding for the moment the "isms" and egotisms of its adolescence.

This year also marked the first year of the depression; and the depression was to exercise a more invigorating effect on American art than any past event in the country's history.

At Croton cocktail parties, our minds heated by the final yield of bootleg gin, we discussed economics, socialism, communism, the profit system and technocracy — never at the same parties — with Floyd Dell, Max Eastman, Bill Hodson, Stanley Izaacs, Bill Gropper, Bob Minor, Stuart Chase, Henry T. Hunt and Jerome Frank. Veblen and Howard Scott were the heroes of the day. *Engineers and the Price System* had been reprinted and was selling like hot cakes. One read Tugwell's *Industrial Discipline*, Chase's *A New Deal*, and Roosevelt's *On Our Way*. I was avid and harassed as I had not been, perhaps, since I first began to doubt the existence of Our Lord in the exact terms of my own smug creation.

The months I had spent in Italy had been essentially a period of shifting values. One's broker and banker friends had lost fortunes and gained perhaps a little dignity of manner. They could frequent the subway or carry their own valise, almost gallantly, without a show of deprecation, without even an apology. Perhaps money was not the exact synonym of success. They had done a lot of thinking during the past years. Some had committed suicide. The survivors had profited, one felt, by their losses. The lines of the façade were a little truer to whatever of architecture and meaning there was in the vast emptiness within.

We painters never carried much façade. We had not the wherewithal with which to deck it. There was consequently less frontage to crumble. We took the depression, spiritually, well within our stride. One or two of us committed suicide, too, those drab years: Robert Spencer, Alfred Maurer, Jules Pascin. It was our art and not our bank accounts that was depressing us. Most of us had nothing to lose and we rarely had a "job." We consequently did not understand these lamentations about living without a salary or on a diminished income. Since American culture had denied us wealth as a symbol of success, we did not feel that our stature during these past years had in any degree shrunk or diminished. On the contrary we noted a very marked recrudescence in the interest in American art. There had never been so great an attendance at exhibitions. People had the enforced leisure to see paintings for the first time in their lives.

We, too, were recasting our values. We had problems of living, or of dying, that had to be weighed and sifted. Quite obviously society could do little for us. People could not afford to buy luxuries during a depression. Nor was it ethical or in the best of taste to do so. If collectors bought they sometimes bought anonymously, not to conceal an act of generosity but rather a self-indulgence! Furriers, diamond merchants, artists suffered most.

It was beginning to dawn on us for the first time that we functioned, if at all, outside our capitalist system; in this sense, that our merchandise by itself created no demand and therefore had no open market value which could be controlled by dumping or removing our wares from the market. Weyhe said years ago: "No art in America sells itself. I spend nine dollars promoting and advertising a lithograph to sell at ten."

Oh! we painters did some sober thinking during those years. We had never been completely witless or even dullards. But somehow we had missed the simple truth that by facing life we should achieve maturity. And during these years we grew a little closer together.

I was painting a large mural canvas that spring for the Century of Progress at Chicago. Since it could not be executed on the spot in the truly mural medium of fresco, and had to be completed in three months and would then seem relatively but a two-cent stamp on the vast and boundless interior of the Agricultural Building, I could not think of it as having any great importance, but to obtain a worthy mural commission I must first establish myself as a mural painter.

I saw much of Diego Rivera working at Rockefeller Center and was soon ardently to espouse, quixotic though the defense turned out to be, his cause. I had lived for a month with Rivera in Mexico, watched him paint, and listened to his gargantuan exploits and his Münchausenish tales. I had talked long hours, while I painted his portrait, with the dry-hot, feverish and jealous-bitter intensity of José Clemente Orozco. I had known most of the lesser Mexican satellites of that prodigious pair — Siqueiros, Atl, Montenegro, Pacheco — and had lived in Taxco with the brilliant young architect Juan O'Gorman, and Carlos Contreras, the driving force behind the National Planning Project for the Republic of Mexico. I had sucked to the pulp all the wisdom and scholarship of Anita Brenner's *Idols Behind Altars*, so that I felt a certain sympathy and understanding of the ideology, the causal circumstances, the germination and the quick tropical flowering of the Mexican School. To recognize the same creative seeds, and analogous chemical and physical conditions in our

American soil and climate, might form the subject of a preliminary inquiry. How translate the Mexican method into terms of the American thought pattern and cultural meaning? Could we also have a worthy mural art, and HOW?

History up to now would indicate that vital schools of art followed a rising curve of economic prosperity. Wherever mural art had reached its fullest expression, there had also been a universal religion — that is a common social faith or purpose — which the artist had shared with all classes of society; and lastly the availability to the best artists of public walls, on which they could emotionally symbolize those social, collective beliefs. These requisites — the noble theme, carrying some universal appeal; and the social institutions which could provide the wall spaces and commission the artists — seemed indeed of the very essence of mural painting.

We had not perhaps struck the bottom of the most cataclysmic depression of history. Were there, then, not patent signs that a long period of frustration had set in? Or were there compensating elements that might warrant a more optimistic conclusion?

In the Mexican mural renaissance this classic art pattern had undergone certain modifications. The young Mexican students and artists, flocking back in 1921 from their apprenticeships in Italy, France or Spain, were drenched with the social idealism of the revolution; and the Indian and Aztec culture became the background on which they embroidered their social theme.

A number of the younger, liberal artists banded themselves into the Syndicate of Technical Workers, Painters and Sculptors. The first contracts, based on wall footage, an eight-hour day and an average daily pay of four dollars, were given out toward the end of 1922. Although the Syndicate enjoyed complete freedom from censorship and had the loyal and courageous backing of the Minister of Education, it was savagely attacked by the conservative members of the moribund Academia. The press took up the hue and cry. The frescoes were scratched and mutilated.

Art and Its Social Significance

A few months later a change of presidency brought about a change in the Ministry of Education. Of the entire Syndicate only Rivera was recommissioned. This great burst of national mural art, which had flowered in less than a year, was apparently ended. Yet ten years later thousands of American students traveled every year to the capital to study these paintings. Their influence had spread to Europe and today twenty government buildings in Mexico were being frescoed by younger artists, unknown the previous decade, in the same brave tradition of *social purpose and technical freedom of expression.*

The best liberal Mexican artists had been offered walls to work upon, in complete freedom and with no condition whatsoever. Mexicans undoubtedly had a social faith which burned as warmly as many a religion for which men have been willing to die. But this movement *had not occurred on a rising tide of economic prosperity.* One must accordingly rephrase one's hypothetical law of probability, to make it applicable to this new phenomenon.

Excessive wealth was not essential to pay for mural art. Very little expense was involved. The artist must be offered an uncensored wall space and then provided, while he worked, with bed and board. All else became a surplusage. Mexico had taught us that. *Hitherto art had been considered the superfluity.* In the cycles of the rising money market those artists who could seduce patrons — that is those painters whose pictures were in demand — could exact whatever price they chose. The rest could starve. In periods of the falling market all would have starved, had all continued to paint. But in Mexico *there had been no art price hinging on popularity, on the criterion of taste. The government had offered to employ at a living wage the members of a painters' guild to perform a useful purpose.* The nature of this purpose was to educate the people, to spread the symbols of Mexican socialism — propaganda, if you will. All art is propaganda in the sense that it is a direct appeal to the emotions. It can be nothing

(265)

else. The average human being is ninety-eight parts emotion and two parts mind. The whole force of art is this direct, complete, emotional appeal.

The only valid question then is this: About what aspect of life shall art become emotional? What idea shall breathe warmth and light and vitality into art and give it meaning?

During the War every nation in Europe had mobilized its artists. The purpose might have been an unworthy one. At best half of the art was a lie. That was not the point. The point was this: that during the War for the first time in history *the nations mobilized their artists and hired them at an established wage for an educational purpose, realizing the tremendous, emotional power of art to convert the masses to an idea.* The artists had apparently proved their worth, for today the great tyrants of Europe — all breathing, inflated and puffed up with a war psychosis — had kept their artists mobilized. They, too, were pouring out propaganda of another sort.

Was the distinction I made between social Mexican art and fascist European art a somewhat legalistic one? Indeed no; for it cut to the tap root of the whole matter. The war-minded totalitarian states mobilized their artists — as they did their soldiers — to obey orders and march in serried rank. Otherwise? God forbid! And their art served its purpose and converted the masses to sadism and fear, but the art itself was as sterile of ideas, as lifeless and stillborn, as the monsters that had ordered it were vacuous and blatant. No Mexican artist had been mobilized and marched, goose-stepping in rank, at the point of a bayonet. *He had been given the uncensored privilege of expressing a social faith.*

What were the chances in our America of rivaling the Mexican experiment? We had a wealth of young, anonymous talent. Of that I was certain. It was our generation, the men over forty and on the museum lists, who would have the least to give. The men over forty were beginning to harden and petrify. How many of them would remain young enough to follow a new idea? A few. Of that I was certain. Two or three were all that were needed.

To obtain uncensored wall spaces for the younger men we must work at a plumber's wage, as in Mexico. It was probably the only way to break through the ring of those smooth and efficient architectural henchmen — handmaidens they were sometimes called — who, with well-stocked art libraries and highly-paid assistants, could knock out murals in any style or tradition at thirty-five to seventy dollars a square foot. Mexico, remember, paid one to two dollars; here in America it might be done at five.

But America was without the religion which had burned in New England in the seventeenth century; without the political faith which had carried us through the Revolution and Civil War. Even among our artists there was no unanimity of social conviction. The depression, however, had done much for us. It had made us face life and realize our own social and political power. And the petty European monsters had instilled in us certain wholesome, unifying and rejuvenating hates. Hitler had taught us how much can be built — politically — on hatred. Our artists loathed the destructive philosophy of fascists and Nazis as whole-heartedly as the latter feared uncensored art and freedom and democracy. But a negative faith was insufficient. There must be some forward swelling energy of love. Every artist in America, every intelligent and out-looking student of his times, knew that life here was drab and often pitiful or tragic. They knew that it could have justice and beauty. There was enough for all. No element was lacking. Through trial and error we must somehow reshuffle the constituent parts that formed the dreary design of our national life. For among those elements somewhere lay the picture of democratic justice and spiritual beauty.

This, then, it seemed to me, was a universal faith, dimly as yet seen by all the people, but to which the artist could give expression in a language understood by all: LIFE IS DRAB AND UGLY. LIFE CAN BE BEAUTIFUL. When once realized this truth must become a goal, a magnet, a lodestar of directive purpose, as vivid and compelling as any medieval faith in the life hereafter.

On May ninth, 1933, I wrote to the President:

DEAR FRANKLIN:

I never doubted your ability and courage; and perhaps that is the reason why I have so delayed in congratulating you on your achievements. The sincerest thing I can say to you is that you have grown and will continue to grow with the demands that America and the world puts on you. I am really proud to have known you at school and college.

There is a matter which I have long considered and which some day might interest your administration. The Mexican artists have produced the greatest national school of mural painting since the Italian Renaissance. Diego Rivera tells me that it was only possible because Obregon allowed Mexican artists to work at plumbers' wages in order to express on the walls of the government buildings the social ideals of the Mexican revolution.

The younger artists of America are conscious as they have never been of the social revolution that our country and civilization are going through; and they would be eager to express these ideals in a permanent art form if they were given the government's co-operation. They would be contributing to and expressing in living monuments the social ideals that you are struggling to achieve. And I am convinced that our mural art with a little impetus can soon result, for the first time in our history, in a vital national expression.

You are too busy at present with more serious problems to give this matter any thought. Perhaps during the summer you will let me drive over from Croton-on-Hudson and pay my respects.

On May nineteenth he answered me from Washington:

DEAR GEORGE:

It is very delightful to hear from you and I am interested in your suggestion in regard to the expression of modern art through mural paintings. I wish you would have a talk some day with Assistant Secretary of the Treasury Robert, who is in charge of the Public Buildings' work.

As I read his letter, walking down our wood road from the post box to the house through the heavy-laden glory of the dogwood blossoms, my heart beat with excitement. Here was an entering wedge to the promotion of an idea.

One felicitous expression of the President's — *modern* art — which I had not used and which he had incorporated in his letter, was to guide our frail purpose over many ominous hazards and through hostile forces which stood directly in our path.

I had discussed the matter at length with Gerdt Wagner, President of the Ravenna Mosaics and a Croton neighbor. I now approached a number of painters tentatively. We must form a self-selected group to start with. They must have some cohesion, some faith — esthetic and social — one with another. Henry Varnum Poor was, as ever, helpful. I trusted his taste and integrity. Whom would he suggest? Maurice Sterne and Boardman Robinson and Tom Benton, of course. Thus our nucleus grew. Reginald Marsh spoke of Edward Laning and John Steuart Curry. "Josh" Billings was one of us.

I wrote out a program and submitted it for criticism. It must be the expression of this self-selected group. That was the idea. It never quite panned out. Yet it had some influence on what followed. If, as Henry Poor suggested, a body of artists who were not necessarily the greatest, but who felt real community with

(269)

each other, could work together for a year, encouraging and criticizing one another, gathering ideas from this community of thought, and carrying out a single, social, ordered, decorative theme — not each one blindly thinking of his own space — they might perhaps do something a little different from anything before. As far as I knew no government had ever commissioned a self-appointed group to design and decorate a building. The idea finally bogged down in the morass of the Procurement Division red tape. However, something of it survived. Someday it may be tried again.

Here is a partial statement of the program:

A REVIVAL OF MURAL PAINTING

American art is today ripe for a national school of mural painting, with which to express in a permanent art form the social and democratic ideals for which the present administration is fighting. The younger, liberal artists are socially conscious of the economic adjustment through which America is passing. If given a free hand they would be willing to work at mechanics' wages on government projects.

Three things are needed to give the necessary impetus to such a movement:

1. A few social-minded, creative artists of the first rank, representing the modern movement, and experienced in mural painting.

2. The assignment to them by the government of public wall space on which to express the social ideals of the government and people.

3. The understanding that in the personal expression and technical execution, the artist be given as complete freedom as possible. Interference would only tend to emasculate his work. The government may exercise the right to assign mural subjects and veto any expression of opinion which it considers embarrassing.

With such a general understanding certain artists have expressed their enthusiasm to co-operate with the government.

They would agree to work at mechanics' wages for the government in Washington or in other assigned cities.

Art and Its Social Significance

We understand that the Treasury Department, which has charge of Public Buildings Works, has the authority through its proper administrative channels directly to commission artists to do mural work on government buildings.

TO SUM UP

I. It is believed that a vital national school of mural art can be started through the endorsement and co-operation of the national government;

II. That the free expression of the artist can be galvanized to set forth the social and economic ideas for which the present administration is fighting;

III. That in a period of economic depression the government should give the same relative assistance to our artists as to other branches of labor;

IV. That such assistance from the government will encourage other agencies and that the movement is economically sound and in keeping with the government's policy to stimulate recovery.

I sent copies of the memorandum to Secretaries Ickes and Perkins, to Frank, Tugwell, Mrs. Roosevelt, Hunt and others. I had meanwhile written to Assistant Secretary Robert, who would be delighted to see me and "any of my associates at a day's notice."

On June nineteenth Wagner and I motored to Washington. We dined at 2024 Tracy Place. It was bachelors' quarters, Jerome Frank, Tugwell, Henry T. Hunt, Lee Pressman. Jerome sat me next to Tugwell. I began immediately playing on my theme. He listened quietly, a little professorial, cool, precise. But he had his enthusiasms, too.

"I wish to God," he said, "you could decorate our Department of Agriculture. Yes, Chip Robert is the man to see. If things go wrong get pressure from above. Never go below. You'll get bogged in."

I asked him about the President. How did he spend his day? In bed as a rule until eleven, and no handshaking. The pressure on him was tremendous. It was very difficult to see him.

A star feature writer from the *New York Times* was there for an interview. Feathers flew. Bluntly he "saw no design among you intellectuals; nor frankly do we think much of the cabinet." Tugwell suggested it was "more the case of building up a structure to deal with a practical problem than any fixed plan. A football team has training and a purpose, but may not know the next play. Roosevelt is more a progressive than a radical." Jerome Frank cut in: "In shaping the design one draws an eyebrow and then a hip. The pattern isn't at once clear." Another said: "Much of the President's addresses to Congress were design; much to conceal design. Our schedule was never more than a week late. Much legislation could never have been passed if Congress had realized the implications. At the end of four years the mesh will be woven into the economic life of industry." There was much talk of a certain General Johnson. Tugwell said: "You will hear more of him in the next few months." He said to me: "Why not get the walls of the Executive Mansion for your group of painters?"

On June twenty-first Wagner and myself saw Assistant Secretary Robert and his Supervising Architect. I outlined for them my plan. The Procurement Division, he told me, had the authority to commission artists. The money had been allocated for the Justice Building, but the policy during the depression had been to soft-pedal on murals. Art was a luxury. They must wait for word from above. However he assured me of his interest in the general idea. He would give it his consideration. Thereafter we corresponded frequently and six weeks later he telephoned me from Washington that our group "in principle" would be given the Justice Building to decorate.

On August sixth came a second letter from the President in Hyde Park:

Art and Its Social Significance

DEAR GEORGE:

The enclosed from the Fine Arts Commission speaks for itself. It does not sound very encouraging for the mural paintings.

Someone had shown the President my memorandum. I had not sent one to him. He was enough interested, notwithstanding the pressure on his time, to refer the whole correspondence to the Fine Arts Commission. "The enclosed" constituted what they termed their "careful consideration" of this correspondence.

They had arrived upon reflection at "several assumptions and conclusions" that would "probably prove fatal to the project." Our group were "painters of easel pictures of an incidental nature"; our intention ignored the architect. "The efforts at mural painting by some of the group and others of their persuasion" had "been attended by much controversy and embarrassment," "condemned by the profession for chaotic composition, inharmonious in style and scale with the building and in subject matter, professing a general faith which the general public does not share. I think the government would be glad to avoid such experiences." Our group also ignored "the established tradition built up by its pioneers and fostered by the American Academy at Rome — which has brought forth a younger, more liberally minded and murally trained modern talent."

That was that. There was more to it. These were the high spots. What the President might have done was to file the report and so clear his desk of one more routine correspondence. But he had written a letter, which I believed I might thus translate:

DEAR GEORGE:

You talked of Rivera and "social ideals" and "the Mexican revolution." You stuck out your neck. I can't have a lot of young enthusiasts painting Lenin's head on the Justice Building. They all think you're communists. Remember my position. Please. I wash my hands. But here's the dirt. Now it's up to you.

(273)

The outlook was far from bright. However, I had by now enlisted the co-operation of such friends and wellwishers as Secretary Perkins, Rex Tugwell, Jerome Frank, Louis McHenry Howe, Secretary Ickes and Henry T. Hunt, General Counsel of the Federal Emergency Administration of Public Work. All of these through correspondence and personal talks must have influenced Robert in my favor. When I again saw him on November fifth he had news for me indeed.

"I have had a long talk with Jerome Frank, Tugwell and Ned Bruce. We are appointing a committee of twenty artists, architects and critics representing both modern and academic art. With their backing I will have the authority to go ahead with your project. From them I shall appoint a smaller committee who will have the supervision of the mural work and crafts for public buildings."

That was news of the most complete and satisfying nature. On November eighth Ned Bruce and I had a twenty-minute talk with the Secretary of the Interior. The honest, tired and somewhat suspicious man had never perhaps known such a lobbyist. I begged that for the success of our program the artist's remuneration be sliced to the bone. This revived his interest. He blinked at us through his spectacles, not, I felt, unsympathetically.

"Word has gone down," I said, "not a cent for art. Spend only on essentials. But cannot an artist expect as much in these lean years as a bricklayer? May I quote you as saying, Mr. Ickes, that it is the policy of the administration to do what it can to foster art during the depression?"

He said: "Yes, it has my approval."

I mentioned the idea I had discussed with Hunt of having a percentage of building funds earmarked for mural decorations. Might I ask Hunt to send him a memorandum to that effect for his signature?

"Yes, I should do so."

Bruce spoke of Hopkins' promise to him to spend part of his $400,000,000 pump-priming fund, for needy artists. Ickes referred us to Frederick Delano, the President's uncle, Chairman of the National Planning Board, and to his secretary, Charles Eliot, 2nd.

The next morning we drafted for Hunt the memorandum about earmarking construction funds and the use of the relief money, which he incorporated in a strong letter to Harry Hopkins. The mechanism was now complete. The parts had still to be assembled and the machinery geared. For this task Bruce had been appointed by Robert, officially, as the Secretary of the Advisory Committee to the Treasury on Fine Art.

Edward Bruce had every qualification for the undertaking, the organization of the Section of Painting and Sculpture, the first generous federal subsidy of mural art and the first spending of federal relief funds for artists. He had been a corporation lawyer and a business executive before he took up painting. Back of his painting was a philosophy. He had studied Chinese art in the Orient and the Cinquecento in Italy. He was a promoter, an idealist and an astute politician. He was vastly popular with everyone in Washington and kept open house. He was a very fury for work. He had met Robert on an economic conference, not in the role of a visionary artist but in that of an expert in the latter's own field. He would seem indeed an impossible gift from Heaven to artists and the cause of art. No other at that particular moment could have manipulated the pawns so effectively. He could appropriate another's idea but never lost sight of his own. He was both a skeptic and a sentimentalist; a skeptic about human beings in general, a sentimentalist about art and his friends. His taste was catholic. He stood neither at the extreme left nor at the right. His paintings were in museums; all his life he had talked to politicians, lobbyists, and the upper brackets of industry. He deserves whatever credit there is for the creation and organization of the Section of Painting and Sculpture — now the Section of Fine Arts of the Treasury — and for its achievements and present policy.

Certain modifications of the idea took place during the next few rapid months before it finally crystalized as a function of the Procurement Division and became part of history, in the not always glowing bulletins of that scrupulous and uninspired departmental body.

The idea of appointing a self-selective group had been abandoned. If a precedent were established it must be within the frame of democratic theory. The artists should be selected by a panel of outstanding museum directors. This system has the theoretic merit of removing the choice of the artists from politics. This is not always the case. Political manipulation merely operates on a different level. It has the practical merit of protecting the selection against political interference and criticism. It serves then for the exact opposite end to its supposed one, namely to allow a somewhat autocratic rather than a democratic choice. Now democracy only functions intelligently if it deals with questions that can be intelligently answered in terms of majority opinion. Obviously the type of government this country wants is a question which can thus be answered. A majority cannot express an intelligent opinion about calculus, or musical modes; or the emotional effect in mural design, of muting a weaving open spiral with a crowded composition, constructed on horizontals and perpendiculars. Obviously. The award — in a competition — of a jury is the majority opinion of a selected group. It is always more intelligent than its dullest member. It is never as intelligent as its most intelligent member. A jury always tends toward a mean — the mediocre. Its value is that it insures against complete nullity. It never can select the best.

The precedent, then, was established of selecting artists, in

Photo by Robert Imandt

AUTHOR WORKING ON
CENTURY OF PROGRESS MURAL

AUTHOR WORKING ON JUSTICE MURAL   Photo by Robert Imandt

DETAIL OF JUSTICE MURAL

DETAIL OF JUSTICE MURAL

Photo by Robert Imandt

the great majority of cases, through a jury rather than by direct appointment; and furthermore, in the great majority of cases, by competitions rather than on the basis of an established reputation. The selection on this competitive basis has one great, outstanding, obvious merit, for which Bruce has the thanks of American artists. It continually holds open the door for fresh talent and younger, unknown painters. It prohibits one small group — as was the case — from getting all the gravy. On the whole it is the best contribution of the Section.

A competition rarely insures the choice of the best submitted entry. Why? Because the selection is made by a jury. The selection therefore is probably never the best. It may be very bad. Often the juries for political reasons are third-rate juries. The Section knows it and of course the artists know it. Second, even if the award of the jury were an intelligent one, it would only demonstrate that the artist selected was clever enough to win a competition. He might be a third-rate muralist and win a competition. Rivera and Orozco could never win a competition because they have not the specific — and quite unessential — faculty of polishing up convincing sketches. The situation is totally different in architecture. The plans, together with the specifications, are the precise originals — in another frame or dimension — of the building itself. The blueprints have almost the same relation to the building that a lithographic stone has to a print; that a plaster mold has to a bronze replica; that a musical score has to a piano recital. The perfect method, then, in appointing artists, is to award by competition in the majority of cases, in order to constantly exploit new talent and younger men; and in a few circumstances to commission directly, so as to insure the most intelligent selection of the best artists.

In final analysis, however, outstanding achievement is due to outstanding administrative intelligence and never simply to a framework of selection. The President and Hopkins and Bruce and Cahill have had intelligence, integrity and a human, democratic, social vision. But even these men are only the expression of something which is very much bigger. I believe it was bound to come. At any rate the force was to some degree dammed up, ready for discharge.

Originally the relief work and the decoration of federal buildings were carried on by the Section of Painting and Sculpture. At present the relief work is operated by the Federal Art Project under the Works Progress Administration. The two sections have split apart, not without considerable rivalry and jealousy. It is a pity. Each section should complement the other, and often they work at cross purposes.

Their objectives are profoundly different; and yet each is essential to a well-rounded art program. The Section is part of the Procurement Division, that department of the Treasury the function of which is to buy — furniture, cement building blocks, oil burners, asbestos shingles. Obviously the Procurement Division has the outlook on life of a grocer. Its one aim is to get a reliable standard of quality. It deals in its purchase of art as it deals in the purchase of soap, blotting paper or toilet fixtures. Its obsession is that it will be cheated in a bargain; the *quid pro quo* is its guiding moral principle. The Procurement Division handles artists with the same delicacy with which it handles building contractors and dry-goods salesmen. It surrounds itself with triple defenses of vouchers, inspections, performance bonds and delay. I am not saying the Section has this mentality; but the Section is under the Procurement Division. This is as stupid and wasteful an organizational relation for art as if our battleships were designed and constructed by a Department of Fine Arts. Now the aim of the Section is to obtain the finest quality of art — to produce a Michelangelo. That is what will justify it in the eyes of the taxpayers or of the none too sophisticated congressmen. And its esthetic credo is that the Michelangelos created the Renaissance and that fine murals will create culture in America. With this belief in mind and because it operates under the Procurement Division, which is in a constant night sweat lest it be cheated, the Section severely censors the artists. For this reason it rarely gets their best work.

Now the objective of the Federal Art Project is to put unemployed and needy artists to work intelligently. It rarely expects to obtain great art; it does expect to use its art to the greatest social advantage, whether in teaching fifty thousand New York slum children, in circuiting art exhibitions through the Bible belt or in providing outstanding frescoes by distinguished artists for Sing Sing inmates or the immigrants at Ellis Island. Its esthetic credo is that if one creates a cultural background, art will follow. It wasn't Michelangelo that created the fifteenth century but the fifteenth century that created Michelangelo. The Federal Art Project rarely censors its artists. It has not got the bureaucratic facilities to do so, as only a small fraction of relief funds can go to office overhead. So the Project often gets very bad pictures, and occasionally the best an artist is capable of. *But it is the first time in history that many thousands of artists are working completely without censorship, without even the indirect censorship of the art dealer or of the collector. I believe this is the most quickening impulse in painting alive in the world today. I believe that it will form a record of the deepest value to the psychologist or art critic of future generations.*

Maurice Sterne once said to Calvin Coolidge, of blessed memory:

"Mr. President, America is the only civilized country in the world without a Minister of Fine Arts."

"We have one, Mr. Sterne; Secretary Mellon."

"I didn't say Finance, Mr. President; I said Fine Arts."

Someday we shall have a Department of Fine Arts. It does not fundamentally matter how the organization is created. But it should unite the functions of these two federal art agencies and it should not operate under the Grocery Department of the Treasury. And I pray to God — for the sake of the national defense — that it will not take over the design and construction of our superdreadnaughts. Although of course — as Mayor La-Guardia would say — "We politicians know better." [1]

Such a Department of Fine Arts should have the power, at its own discretion, as in every other civilized country in the world, to nationalize a work of art, a painting, a sculpture, a public building. We have a Conservation Department to preserve our forests. We should preserve our art, too. Not only Rivera's fresco in Radio Center, Mr. Rockefeller; but that beautiful old Georgian mansion in Charleston, South Carolina, that was torn down by your wreckers — over the protests of hundreds of Charlestonians — to make way for your Socony filling station.

I had been asked to prepare, in conjunction with the architect, thematic mural subject matter for the Justice Building. This had been a most congenial study, for it gave me the occasion to express the social message of those democratic liberals, artists, forward-moving beings, whose credo I felt could be stated in clear patterns on a wall. Always I must keep an eye to the size of the grain which could be sifted through the sieve of censorship. But as Justice Stone put it, "One can express a deep and moving theme without entering the realm of the controversial."

On three lower landings of the stairwell where I was to paint would be panels showing man, woman and child, emancipated through justice. Logically, crowning this, would be the concept of society freed through justice. I chose as my theme the belief that "the sweatshop and tenement of yesterday can be life planned with justice of tomorrow." Stanley Reid, the Solicitor

[1] By the provisions of the message of the President of April 25 under the terms of the Reorganization Act of 1939 the above organizations have been modified, as of date of June 25, 1939. The Works Progress Administration which contains the Federal Art Project and the Buildings Branch of the Treasury which contains the Section of Fine Arts have been placed under the newly created Federal Works Agency. The setup for the program outlined by the author is, therefore, almost complete, since it needs only the administrative sanction of the new administrator.

General, asked if I might substitute "ordered" for "planned." Such is the evocation of terror sounded by this frugal word. I was all too happy to accept his emendation.

Painting *al fresco*, on plaster of lime and sand, is probably as old as the use of mortar in surfacing masonry. I own myself a bit of red Pozzuoli wall, which I had filched from the ruins of Herculaneum. It is as brilliant as if it were painted yesterday. Yet the Greeks and Egyptians used fresco hundreds — thousands — of years before Pompeii and Herculaneum were buried in the laval ashes of Vesuvius.

All colors in ultimate form are powder and require a binder to make them adhere to a surface. Oil, mastic and other varnishes are among the best binders, though comparatively late comers in the field. Glue or honey is employed as a binder in water color. In tempora the use of those mysterious colloids, egg, casein, and skimmed milk, is almost as old as fresco painting. With frescoes, strictly speaking, no binder is used with the color. It is inherent in the lime wall surface. When marble or limestone — calcium carbonate — is burnt, carbonic acid is released. The stone, burnt or oxidized, becomes calcium oxide. Mixed with water — calcium hydroxide — and sand, it slowly re-absorbs carbonic gas from the air and becomes again calcium carbonate or limestone. The colors, then, do not adhere through a foreign binder to a hostile surface. They have become actually, through a chemical transformation, the glowing transparent surface of a reconstituted marble wall. The idea generally held that in frescoes the color penetrates the wall is nonsense. The colors used are earth and mineral, often with a basis of silicate or sand, so that they are homogeneous to the plaster surfacing itself, which is sand and lime.

Certain materials, owing to their brilliancy, their durability, their resistance to climatic changes, to the very qualities of their composition, are eminently suited to wall decorations, are intrinsically mural media. From the earliest times colored marble, precious stones, and later tiles, mosaics and stained glass were used to enhance the color and the surface design of the wall. All these media have far more brilliancy and durability than oil paint. It, however, has one tremendous advantage, its plasticity. It is infinitely better adapted for painting a picture than stained glass or even mosaics. Fresco painting has not quite the plasticity of oils; but it is only a little more rigid and circumscribed in its use. It has not the luster of stained glass, but it can match the transparent glow of a fired ceramic or of the semi-precious stones. In a sense the fresco color is fired. The slow surface oxidation over a period of fifty years continually adds to its beauty.

Every medium calls for its peculiar technique, inherent in its nature. Generally speaking no white is used in fresco painting, the white plaster wall surface showing through the transparent superimpositions of color wash. Since, then, there is no binder until the process of oxidization has set in, only a very little color, mixed in water, may be used at a time; and consequently each tone is built up by hundreds of small superimposed strokes. This is the classic method of Piero, Giotto and Michelangelo. This apparently rigid and formal treatment has two manifest advantages. A very great surface brilliance and transparency is obtained which is never possible with the opaque use of mixed white. It is a physical phenomenon that light refracted through color from white is more brilliant than light refracted from color mixed with white.

Again, if color be mixed with white, there will be, let us say, one hundred gradations visible to the naked eye, yet if the same tone is matched by a series of superimposed glazes there will be perhaps ten times that number of visible gradations. It will be more necessary with opaque media to run the whole gamut of color tone to give solidity to the rendering of a white egg or of a black billiard ball, so that the shadow of the white egg will be black and the high light of the black billiard ball will be white.

Yet by painting in transparencies and without exhausting the gamut of values, a white egg or a black ball may be rendered with equal solidity and yet count as a spot of white or of black in the frame of the color design. The artist can thus use white, black, red, etc., as component parts of a color patchwork design, not simply to render the solidity of form in all its atmospheric coloring.

I was happy in painting a mural, under conditions which could never be more auspicious, the theme of which lay close to my philosophy and had some slight bearing on the manifest problems of our generation. Today the central stage for such experiments was Washington. I could, then, while I worked, and between hours of working observe the profile of the players. My brother Francis had been chairman of the National Labor Relations Board, and through him and other friends I met many of the chief actors. Through Ned Bruce I had known Harlan Stone. His salty New England accent, his direct, male approach, were all that was most finely traditional and upright-standing in his own state of New Hampshire. His language, directed as much at certain fellow members of the court as at "William M. Butler, et al., Receivers of Hoosac Mills Corporation," drew much of its whiplike sting from its New England understatement:

Courts are not the only agency of government that must be assumed to have capacity to govern. Congress and the courts both unhappily may falter or be mistaken in the performance of their constitutional duty. But interpretation of our great charter of government which proceeds on any assumption that the responsibility for the preservation of our institutions is the exclusive concern of any one of the three branches of government, or that it alone can save them from destruction is far more likely, in the long run, "to obliterate the constituent members" of "an indestructible union of indestructible states" than the frank recognition that language, even of a constitution, may mean what it says: that the power to tax and spend includes the power to relieve a nation-wide economic maladjustment by conditional gifts of money.

Bill Bullitt, too, would be back from Moscow or Paris, in and out, restless, effervescent, a little boyish in his skepticisms, violent in his abuse, enthusiastic in his hero-worships, dogmatic and intelligent. Here and there one might catch a glimpse of Secretary Hull, grave, pale and brittle, with all the courtesy of the pre-Civil War South, yet sometimes with difficulty concealing, even in an opera box, the hard, implacable violence of the Tennessee mountain people. On those occasions when I met the Secretary of Labor I might be puzzled by the stiff, professorial manner, — more of seasoned timber in her ribbing than of the pliant willow, — the conglomerate accent, the splendid vitality, the unyielding idealism, the New England mysticism, the womanly warmth and the ferocious appetite of the politician; violent, suppressed, noble in spots — like so many New Englanders. In the corridors of the Treasury one met Henry Morgenthau, Jr., hurrying with a grim leather satchel of debits and credits clutched protectively to his side. He would relax only, one supposed, if one could ask him for advice for the treatment of three thousand evergreens, bought some years before from his New York Conservation Department and suffering, it would seem, from the white pine blight.

Governor Winant, at that time head of the Social Securities Board, I saw only once. It was at a somewhat noisy and ill-assorted dinner of semi-notables where one felt that each guest by himself would have proved requiting, but that the combined intellectual expression was an empty and noisy buzz, accompanied by too much gesticulation and flapping of wings. The question had been reduced to some administrative or organizational policy, depending on highly statistical information. Opinions were being shouted, two and three at a time. Governor

Winant very modestly begged to differ and produced in the gravest and gentlest voice certain very technical figures. For a moment the guests stopped talking to listen, and he continued through a hushed and dominated silence to pile up from all possible sources — Germany, Belgium and England — facts and statistics, which seemed for all his gentleness to have the impact of body blows; and to leave the corpse of the opinion with which he had begged to differ quite flat and lifeless on the floor of the arena.

Stuart Chase had given me a letter to Bob LaFollette. We met or dined once or twice together. Nothing of the spread-eagle, of the soapbox orator about him. Rather Latin-looking, those large, dark, melting eyes. He was young and earnest and polite. One heard of his driving energy and of his political sagacity. Once I had expressed to him in no unmeasured terms the disgust I felt at those bodies of veterans, the great majority of whom had never volunteered in any spirit of service or patriotism, but always had been reluctantly drafted, had never been to the front, had never perhaps been overseas, had indeed worn a uniform, and in return been well paid and fed; and, now, loud-pedaling on this super-patriotism and super-Americanism, were clamoring by class legislation for their special dish of gravy, for having exercised the privilege of serving their country.

"Certain commercial, industrial and financial interests," he said, "had got this country into an unholy war solely to protect their own vested interests. The government of the country represented the people. The government had passed and enforced laws which drafted millions of ignorant and unwilling men. These men had forfeited their jobs, had lost their youth, had never recovered their outlook on life. They were of the lost generation. Our government was guilty of an irreparable injury. It was under obligation to repair that injury. Nothing in terms of money could ever wipe out that obligation."

As he spoke his hands trembled and he was swept along in a

(285)

gust of fury. One might differ with his logic. One could not doubt his sincerity.

Perhaps the Congressman who most defied one's conception of the politician was Maury Maverick. It was not that he went about without a hat, was an amateur of the circus and at the moment a teetotaller. For this one could hardly label him a freak; and freaks were traditionally at home in Washington. It was not his complete Irish impudence which could impel him at a cocktail party, on seeing Secretary Perkins and Justice Stone, coming up the steps together, to shout warnings to the latter that he was moving in subversive company, and then elbowing his way back to the Secretary to bellow in her ear that if she were to expect congressional backing she must cease flirting with even the youngest of the Nine Old Men. Such antics were charming since he carried them off. He had his Southern prejudices and Texan vanities. When I had told him how the only Texans I had known as a class still slung Colts from their belt straps and sometimes carried notched rifles he drew himself up: "We Mavericks don't tote guns. 'Cause we're not scared. We're men." This also fitted into one's conception not only of a Southerner but even of a congressman. Once he admitted that he had at first somewhat feared meeting me; suspicious partly on account of banker Nicholas Biddle whose reputation since his tilt with Andrew Jackson had always been unsavory among the farmers of the Southwest, suspicious also about the "queer Latin habits and possible stigmata of decadence of all you artists." But this mistrust was not only a congressional and Texan but an all-American state of mind. What completely upset my prejudices, was that the politician was honest, not just in his dealings with others, but actually in his own mind toward himself.

All these men and women who played the game of politics had common earmarks that seemed essentially non-political. None of them were stiff or had the least false frontage. They were young at heart and could always be appealed to in terms of youth or generosity, never in terms of venality. They drank cocktails; but like men whose minds and bodies were in training they drank sparingly. They were well-read and, what surprised one most, they were witty. They talked shop, but no more earnestly than artists or art students or ski enthusiasts. I had always believed that notwithstanding the fat things in life which I had missed, I had had much good conversation, yet here the talk was as provocative as it ever had been under the palm trees in the Pacific; and certainly more general in scope than about the sidewalk tables before the Dôme or the Rotonde on the Boulevard Montparnasse in Paris.

My hours of work were long. I often started before dawn during the winter months and sometimes painted on until six or seven o'clock in the evening. But I had never felt effort so requited. After climbing up the ladder to the scaffolding and adjusting my arc light and various bowls of color, I first carefully pounced the outline of my day's work through the pricked tracing paper, and set up about me the sketches of heads and hands, where I could most easily study them. Depending on the height of my work above the flooring, I must stand, sit or crouch on the boards. I gathered myself in a concentration of purpose and began my day's stint. I experienced a feeling of elation, of mastery of my medium, of faith in the outcome of the two years' preparation and work.

That year's preparation had originally been somewhat jarred by the senescent jibber-jabber, the tortoiselike withdrawings into the darkness of their own confusion and the sudden elephantine thrusts of my former friends, whom we jestingly alluded to as the Nine Old Men without their Three Dissenting Liberals — the Fine Arts Commission. Now after a full year's rest, during which they had approved the organization of the Section and of my commission under it to paint a mural, they returned, like nine

old geese, refreshed by their long nap and measure of corn, to
the scene of their former disputations. I had finished my sketches,
and they had been approved by the Section, by the Supervising
Architect and by the Director of Procurement. The Old Men
were now asked, as a last formal ritualistic courtesy, for their
opinion. After due rumination and cud-chewing they brought
up a considerable belch of mephitic disapproval. "The sketches
submitted are disturbingly busy," they averred, "in both pattern
and scale. They are too big for the allotted spaces — they are
out of drawing and are crude and harsh in color, and even grotesque — the subject selected deals primarily with social rather
than legal relations. Therefore it would seem to belong to the
Department of Labor rather than to the Department of Justice.
The artist has chosen a style somewhat French and very Mexican — a style popular today because of its novelty, but intrinsically un-American and ill-adapted to express American ideas
and ideals. . . ."

There you have it. There were a couple of pages in all. In
spots quite imbecile, quite without meaning. That phrase, for
instance, about a sketch "busy in scale" was worthy of the
Jabberwock. The pent-up disapprobation about "a style somewhat French and very Mexican" was a trifle incoherent. And then
that sideswipe at the Department of Labor — perhaps an inch
or two below the belt. That's where I belonged — Bolshevist!
Meaning, however, glimmered through the awkward and outraged wording. The style and color and drawing and choice of
subject matter and treatment were not those of the American
Academy of Rome and therefore "intrinsically un-American";
more especially in a "modernization of American architecture
based on classical precedents as adapted by Thomas Jefferson
and by him made popular throughout the Republic." A little
windy that last sentence; but it would seem to include everything and leave no loophole of escape for subversive ideas in
either architecture, mural painting or political economy.

We were all rather staggered by these heavy thrusts. My work was held up for several months. The Section was dripping with night sweats. The Procurement Division pulled in its chin in the most dignified way. The Commission of Fine Arts must be given a further opportunity to express an opinion. Wires were pulled. Precedents were studied. I indulged in a complete nervous collapse and retired to the west coast of Florida. On November twenty-sixth the Commission briefly reiterated its former opinion, with a last toothless fling that the "house gable as a large central motif is unfortunate" — and two weeks later the Director of Procurement authorized me to proceed with my painting "in accordance with the terms of your contract."

All this pother then for nothing; and hardly worth recalling if it were not an example of the misunderstanding of contractual relation between artist and client, which cuts to the root of all creative effort. I believe that a painter should have — and is denied — the same relation that exists elsewhere between employer and employee, between buyer and seller: the relation namely of a rigid statement of specifications by the employer or buyer and of complete freedom of execution by the employee or seller. And I think in justice it should be said that this relation is as little understood by the artist as by his employer. When our government buys blankets for our army or cement for construction work, it rigidly specifies the qualities of weight, durability and strength that must be maintained. On the other hand it does not interfere with the manufacturer in the production of the materials. When the artist of the Italian Renaissance signed a contract, the specifications were outlined. A certain saint in blue, another in red, a portrait of the donor to the right, landscape and angels in the background; the quality of the canvas, the colors, the varnish all determined. But the employer neither interfered with the artist nor censored his individual creative expression in the execution of his work. This of course is exactly the relation today between a contractor-architect and his client. And this relation the artist must insist on. Otherwise he becomes an apothecary filling a recipe; a grocer, a cook, a professional potboiler.

This, then, was my general indictment of the Fine Arts Commission: that it operated outside of its proper function in censoring in detail an artist's particular solution of his problem; in censoring his general style, although that style was the basis of his selection; in daring to dictate what — either in thought or in method of thinking — was un-American. There was a specific indictment, if anything more serious: that through this extra-judicial usurpation of power it had actually for about a generation — that is approximately since its creation — prevented any real expression of American art in Washington. The function of the Commission, if not to plan, at any rate was to bring order into planning. Washington to me was beautiful — where every city in America was chaos — because it had this order. But order is not censorship. Censorship in this case was the rigid insistence on a particular style, the deadest of the world we live in: a weak, thin-blooded, sugar-coated imitation of the French Beaux Arts-Prix de Rome, which in itself is the last vulgar, middle-class death agony of the pseudo-classicism of David, which even in 1800 was a dry, papier-maché, schoolboy conglomeration of bad Poussin and seventeenth-century Italian decadence; of helmets and urns and fasces and white triumphal bulls and chariot wheels and little cuty girls with budding breasts and French empire dresses. That was the dried-up tit that we painters were given to suck on; in the sonorous verbiage of the Commission, the "already established tradition built up by its pioneers and fostered by the American Academy at Rome, which was chartered by Congress for that purpose and which has brought forth a younger, more liberally-minded and murally trained modern talent." O yeah?

I have spoken of the influence that the depression was to have upon the full maturity of American art. Had it happened earlier its impact might have been crushing; but our art had the maturity to withstand the shock. One effect of the depression, which had given new vitality, had been the federal patronage of art. Another influence of major importance was the growing social awareness of American artists.

This social awareness had manifested itself in different ways. One was the obvious organization, unionization, co-operative efforts of artists for mutual economic protection. There has been nothing on the same scale since the Middle Ages. It couldn't happen in the same way in Germany or Russia, because there the collectivization would be forcefully imposed from above. Here the unionization was spontaneous and from below. The Artists' Unions had about five thousand members; the Artists' Congress, about eight hundred.

These artists' organizations were not merely concerned with their own economic problems: the rental fee, higher wages, shorter hours, improvements of contracts, censorship, lay-offs, racial discrimination. These were wholesome trades-union manifestations. The political activity of the painters, however, was a more curious phenomenon. Why at the Congress and at the Artists' Union meetings should there be prolonged cheering at the mention of the C.I.O.? Why protest the antics of Boss Hague in his bailiwick across the Hudson? Why pass resolutions endorsing Labor's Non-Partisan League? Or the Farm Labor Party? Or the re-election of Congressman Vito Marcantonio? Why invite Gorman of the Textile Workers or John L. Lewis or Maury Maverick to speak at annual meetings? Why should the Union in 1938 so pride itself on obtaining a C.I.O. charter? Why should a small group of muralists become the first A.F. of L. affiliate of the Brotherhood of Painters, Paperhangers and Decorators?

Artists were learning to deal in politics. They had written a Federal Art Bill, obtained the backing of every liberal organization and of most liberals in America; they had lobbied in Washington, testified before committees, obtained a press, written a

(291)

Department of Fine Arts into the consciousness of Congress. The Coffee-Pepper Bill was leaky in spots, not the best that could be written or enacted. The important fact was that it had been done solely through the growing social consciousness of artists and by the political pressure of the liberal artist groups.

The first exhibition of prints organized by the Artists' Congress was an interesting example of this trend. The exhibition had been organized in 1936. It was open to all American artists, and was to appear simultaneously in thirty American cities. The jury was excellent. There would be wide publicity. The participants could work in any medium and choose any subject. There was but one stipulation. The subject must be "America Today." I had been asked to review this exhibition for a Colorado Springs paper in conjunction with an excellent showing of contemporary French art, which appeared simultaneously at the Colorado Springs Fine Arts Center. The latter had all the familiar names: Picasso, Dufy, Matisse, Segonzac, Pascin, Chagal. Out of curiosity I analyzed the subject matter of the two groups and arrived at these findings.

Of the one hundred contemporary American prints seventy-four dealt with the American scene or with a social criticism of American life; six with strikes or with strikebreakers; six with dust, sand, erosion, drought and floods. There were no nudes, no portraits, and two still lifes. Out of the hundred not one could be said to enjoy, reflect, participate in our inherited, democratic-capitalist culture in the sense that Velasquez, Goya and Titian seem at home in their courtly life; John Singer Sargent in his British upper-class milieu; Manet and Renoir in their respective upper and lower nineteenth-century bourgeoisie.

In contrast to the socially critical attitude of the American group, there was not one example among the Paris contemporaries that was preoccupied with life, let alone social problems. The Paris artists were interested only in art: art for art's sake.

This was the direction of American art in these recent years and the depression had given impetus to the movement. But it was essentially an American impulse.

These artists, apart from social awareness, organizational pre-occupations, and some political sense, were beginning to develop as a body a moral sense, an ideology, wider in scope than their narrow esthetic problems of tri-dimensional form, abstract design or proper mural media. Never before to this extent had there been so spontaneous a reaction; against war and fascism; against the cynical rape of Ethiopia; the arrogant butchery of Chinese civilians; the disemboweling of women and babies by the blackshirted "knights of the air"; against racial discrimination and the censorship of freedom of expression and freedom of thought.

Sporadically these protests had occurred before, a hundred years back and more. Witness Goya and Daumier; the *Assiette au Beurre* in 1895 and the *Masses* in 1915. Then they were the exceptional, now the general expression of all the best liberal art of our day; of all save the arteriosclerotic elders who wrapped in the traditions of the American Academy of Rome, shuddered at the eruption of government relief and trades-unionism into the gentility of the past, and cast back longing glances at the golden age of the white bulls, the muses floating in cheesecloth, and the ephebic laborers with attic pectorals and Howard Chandler Christy profiles.

Not since the Armory Show of 1913 had there been such a sense of power, such a wave of optimism. Hitherto we had been individuals, purists, artists; with our individual aims and preju-dices; ready to give one friend a shove, or to knife another in the back. Here we were a body with an identical faith; identical objectives; identical hates. Men who previously had hardly nodded grasped each other warmly by the hand. The speakers were cheered because each one proclaimed the faith, the fears of us all. We were happy in the solidarity of liberal art. We were un-beaten. We had faith. We were young.

Because the previous year I had suggested a motion to the National Society of Mural Painters, of which I was the President, that our members should take no part in the art exhibitions attendant upon the Olympic games, I was asked at the open meeting of the Congress to speak on the same topic.

"Such a resolution is only effective," I said, "if we, ourselves, clearly understand the basis of such a protest and its practical significance in our life and growth as American artists.

"As with many of us, my own art development had its roots in Europe. Twenty-five years ago I studied in Germany and in Italy. I have today the deepest respect and gratitude for the high professional standards of art and for the liberal inheritance which these two countries have given us. I am personally happy that a few of my closest friends are German and Italian artists.

"The truth of the matter is this: Any nation has within its body both the seeds of liberalism and the germs of bigotry, suppression and hatred. Italy had its Renaissance. Today it has in it the seeds of science and enlightenment. Germany has given us its music and philosophy. Today it has in it the seeds of liberal progress. America has had its William Penns; its Franklins; its Paines, its Jeffersons and Justice Holmes. It has also in its heritage witch hangings, Ku Klux Klans, Vigilantes and lynchings. Today they are with us. Tomorrow they can ride us in the saddle.

"As individual artists we have been invited to participate in an exhibition by a government which sponsors the destruction of all freedom in art. This invitation directly challenges the professional code of ethics of American artists. If no such code exists, it is urgent that we adopt one. As a Congress of American artists we can emphatically state our attitude toward such an invitation.

"Our protest is not against a form of government, which to us as Americans is abhorrent; not against Germany or Italy as such. As realistic American artists we protest against participation with a government which sponsors racial discrimination, the censorship of free speech and free expression, and the glorification of war, hatred and sadism.

"There is an urgent need today that we align ourselves with such policies as we feel necessary to our professional self-preservation. There is a living danger, today greater than ever, that the germs of intolerance may so infect our system that the ends and conditions of life which are most essential to us as artists may be smothered in the general sickness of our social system.

"I therefore move that whereas the present German government, judged by the statements of its own leaders, has suppressed freedom of religion and freedom of thought, and

"Whereas they have exiled, or caused to live in exile, many of their greatest scientists, writers and artists —

"Be it now resolved that the Members of the Artists' Congress will take no part in the exhibition of paintings to be held in concurrence with the Olympic games of 1936; and they further urge all other American art societies and individual artists to refuse to exhibit in Germany, as a protest against the spiritual intolerance and suppression of free thought which the present German government not only condones but openly boasts of."

This resolution was unanimously adopted.

Art and the Creative Impulse

For this I offer many thanks to immortal and sovereign God; because in this world, vast and complex, he has proffered me this little beacon, my ambition in the noble art of painting; so unique in merit that no other gift seems to me more glorious nor more worthy of respect.

MICHELANGELO

DURING recent years I had been asked occasionally to lecture on contemporary phases of modern art. This gave me the occasion to clarify my own thoughts. Esthetics is, of course, like any other art or science, a fiction projected from the brain, itself a work of art. It has no more to do with painting than has religion.

What, in final analysis, is the fundamental quality of art, of beauty, of the creative process? To what degree is this quality inherent in art and beauty, and to what degree is it inherent in the mental attitude, in the prejudices and preconceptions of the audience?

The historical, social and psychological approach has taught us that no act is in itself necessarily good or bad. Its goodness or badness fundamentally depends on its social use in a given culture or civilization. This is true in the realm of esthetics.

If we examine history we note in matters of art, as in matters of morals, that no two epochs or individuals could ever agree

(296)

as to what was art or what had beauty. Greek culture was unknown in the Middle Ages. The Renaissance rediscovered and
enthroned classic art with an enthusiasm which would have been
incomprehensible to Giotto and Cimabue. The Renaissance despised ogive architecture, which it considered barbaric or Gothic.
Rembrandt and Vermeer were almost unknown a hundred years
after their death. The romantic nineteenth century sniffed at the
coldly uninspired perfection of Racine, of David. Thirty years
ago we should not have tolerated Léger and Brancusi. There is
no *a priori* test or standard of art and beauty.

*Art, I take it, is a re-creation, a revaluation, a reaction to, a
critique of life, expressed subconsciously in a given medium with
a certain rhythm.* It is this critical reaction to life which chiefly
concerns me; but there is always rhythm, or something like it,
in our minds, in our ears, in our pulse beats, which distinguishes
poetry from a cry of joy or distress. Art is distinguished from
non-art by this rhythm, pulse or abstraction.

Art is of course one of the greatest sources of enjoyment in
life. It is also the best gauge for understanding and evaluating
the outlook and mind of other great civilizations. If it were not
for our ability to capitalize on memory and transmitted knowledge, we might never have advanced beyond the civilization of
cavedwellers.

The creative impulse is subconscious, intuitive, imaginative.
It bridges the gap of logic. It feels, it sees, it understands. It
never thinks, if by thought we mean the rationalizing process.
At first blush this may seem absurd. Does not a writer, an architect, a scientist think? And may he not be a creative artist? I do
not mean that artists do not think. I mean that the quality of
their mental process which is creative is arrived at through the
imagination; intuitively, subconsciously.

Now although the intelligence, the logical or rational process
— whatever you may wish to call it — does not subconsciously
create or imagine intuitively, yet it can of course, and does so

(297)

chiefly, concern itself with technique, with the laws of design, composition, color, drawing — that is, with the manner of artistic performance. It is this distinction between the creative content and the manner of execution which is so little understood by either critics or the public. Let me then, for clarification, use the analogy of powder and the gun barrel, the former being very obviously the creative impulse. Now all the powder in the world, if uncanalized, will perhaps blow a pea across the road; and yet the most perfect gun barrel without an explosive has no power to move or strike whatsoever. The purpose and importance of the barrel, then, is to allow an equally explosive force to strike the bull's-eye at the greatest possible distance. When we are analyzing an artist's color or composition or design, we are probably talking about the barrel. There is not much we can say about his creative instinct except that it is there. And certainly as an artist I must take this for granted and concentrate my intelligence on the condition of my firearm. As General Putnam said: "Trust in God and keep your powder dry."

Although the arts are a different field from the exact sciences, yet in such fields, as well, one's approach may be creative. Indeed the use of this expression is as common as is also the statement that a great tennis player, a criminal lawyer, a cook is a *very real artist*. Half jokingly we are using the word in the essence of its significance. We exactly mean that this particular agent is subconscious and intuitive and therefore imponderable in his approach, or strategy; and that his accomplishment is not only the fulfillment of a useful, material purpose, but also the expression of what Dewey would call an experience for its own sake; what I think of as a revaluation of life in a certain medium. When Justice Holmes wrote *The Common Law*, his work transcended a textbook and became the expression of an artist's philosophy. Pepys kept a diary and Walton wrote a complete almanac and guide for fishermen. Yet the importance of each work is not its immediate, useful purpose, but its ulterior significance as art.

Art and the Creative Impulse

The many hundred cigar-store Indians, the carved weather-vanes, the wrought-iron and patch quilts, which Holger Cahill insists are the first examples of great American art, were created for one end — a material one — and now fulfill another, that of the criterion of the artistic and mental outlook of a vanished culture.

Perhaps all this may sound rather dry-as-dust, legalistic and metaphysical; and, as I said, esthetics has no more to do with painting than the Athanasian Credo. But in all humility I think it worth while for an artist — or a stockbroker for that matter — once in a while to work out his own Athanasian Credo. If mine may help the layman to approach with a little less fear and a little more humility — and consequently with a little more enjoyment — a work of art which he may not, any more than an artist, entirely understand, then I believe this chapter has its justification.

Little Man What Now?

If democracy wishes to make its undoubted moral superiority over fascism effective and challenge its pseudo-socialism, it must adopt in the economic as well as the spiritual domain as much of socialistic morality as the times make imperative and indispensable. . . . Everybody who would consider it a great human disaster, if in this historical struggle of the world philosophies, democracy should succumb for lack of adaptability, must desire as one desires a necessity that liberal democracy will develop into social democracy, from the economic as well as the spiritual point of view. "What is really new in our world," said the Belgian Vandervelde in answer to the Condottiere of the Palazzo Venezia when he was again prophesying that all Europe would become fascist by tomorrow, "what is essentially and actually new in the world is social democracy."

THOMAS MANN: *The Coming Victory of Democracy* [1]

WHEN I left Washington, where I had been so happy in my work and in what seemed to me the center of political intelligence and political liberalism in America, I taught art for a year at the Colorado Springs Fine Arts Center. This lovable and gracious town is a compound of various social strata. It was largely founded by English polo players, boasts the second oldest country club in America, and in certain aspects is more English than Boston and more Tory than the Philadelphia Main Line. Yet again, it and Denver are among the only frontier towns left in America. Its every other obituary in the papers is filled with prairie schooners and Indians. Cowboys still drive the "dogies" through the outskirts of the town; Leadville, Central City and Cripple Creek are all within a morning's drive. Colorado was

[1] Alfred A. Knopf, Inc.

(300)

FRANKIE LOPER, FRIEND AND EX–SLAVE OF
PRESIDENT JEFFERSON DAVIS

"DULCE ET DECORUM EST PRO PATRIA MORI"

written into history by Civil War generals, prairie scouts and pioneers in Conestoga wagons. Peter McCall Keating, who had shown me almost forty years back in the Ojai Valley in California how to throw a lariat and fasten the diamond hitch, recalls a running fight along the Avenue Cache-la-Poudre, as the sheriff stood by with folded arms and a man staggered in his saddle and plunged into a pool of blood in the gravel under the cottonwoods. Yes, the history of Colorado is the history of the pioneer; yet from the start it was also the history of the labor struggle in America. From the long view the Ludlow Massacres would have an equal importance with the pistol duels on the steps of the courthouse. Yet the element in Colorado Springs which struck me as most American was neither the socialites, the pioneers, the miners or the farmers, but the co-eds to whom I taught art on weekdays and with whom on Sundays I went skiing on Pike's Peak.

The Metropolitan area of New York City comprises in population one tenth of America. Yet I had always known New York to be as un-American — in many aspects — as Czechoslovakia. One forgets that even the eastern seaboard is not America. To feel the pull of the current, we Easterners must cross the Mississippi, the Panhandle and the Rockies. To get a bird's-eye view one must stand above the timber line.

Mountain climbers and skiers all know that above timber line moral character changes. It takes stoutness of heart to get there. But at a certain elevation, you have a smile for a stranger, you share your sandwiches, you lend a shoulder to a car, if the hubs are in a snowdrift — and you leave your key in the switchboard. That's the West. That's the reason I like it. That's what I hope America is — above timber line.

Living for a year in the shadow of Pike's Peak, among these social contradictions — or incrustations — of pioneers, workers, socialites and co-eds; breathing the air close to timber line; far removed from the somewhat self-conscious liberalism of Mount

Airy Road, Croton-on-Hudson; the art and heat of New York, the politics and heat of Washington — I was sometimes lonely. I had time to do a little thinking — to clarify or simplify the spiritual readjustments and violence of the past few years. First of all I must face one or two questions: this question of HATE, which I thought was buried with the War, twenty years ago, under hundreds of thousands of small wooden crosses. Then this thing called class loyalty, which I had also supposed history had buried in 1789, in 1776 — in 1683 for that matter. I must define a little more accurately the artist's participation in these hates, these disloyalties, these wars for democracy and against fascism.

First, then, a word or two as to this HATE which many feel toward Roosevelt and the ideals of his social program. It is not a question, mind you, of mistakes. You do not hate mistakes. You hate intentions. You hate the intention of his social democracy. You criticize mistakes. People don't criticize Roosevelt and his program. They hate them. At my thirtieth class reunion at Harvard last June I said to George Minot: "Most of our class, even the liberal ones, the ones that lived in the Yard, not the Gold Coast boys, are pretty violent in their HATE."

He said: "Oh, yes, I suppose ninety per cent."

I said: "And judging from the parades yesterday at the Harvard-Yale baseball game,. the undergraduates are pretty violent, too?"

He said: "Oh, yes, ninety per cent too, I suppose."

"And your profession, George, the doctors?"

"Well," he said, "of course there are a few of us — I don't like everything he's done, mind you, I think he's a bit crackpot — but, well of course practically all of my profession are very violent."

I said: "George, that's interesting, isn't it? Because generally speaking he is conceded — don't you think — the most popular president the country has had in the past hundred and forty years. Somebody must like him."

George said, "Oh yes, farmers, underprivileged, and Negroes."

I said: "And artists."

George said: "Yes, of course, artists, writers, intellectuals. Only numerically these aren't so important."

I asked Van Wyck Brooks the same question. He said: "It's not any different from what it always was. They hated Wilson, they hated Theodore Roosevelt just as violently. The chief difference is that Franklin Roosevelt is actually doing — here and there, now and then — what Wilson and Theodore Roosevelt threatened to do for the farmers and underprivileged."

I said: "I suppose you're right. Qualitatively — at any rate — the HATE is the same. But not quantitatively. There was always an element of liberalism, an element of sport, an element of dissenters. But now along certain lines, capitalist lines, professional lines, social lines, the cleavage seems almost universal. One wonders to what degree these groups — social, professional, economic — are in a state of flux and readjustment; and whether their members hate what to them is the symbol of their own decay."

I said to Stuart Chase: "But isn't it funny though that they hate one whom Thomas Mann quite rightly praises as 'a conservative statesman.' Of course he saved them when they had their pants down. And he wiped their behinds. I suppose that is why they hate him."

Stuart said: "Yes; but there is another reason. It isn't the money. He let them save that. But it's the irresponsible power. They will never have it again to the like degree. And so they had to find a scape-goat for the hate. For a while it was Rex Tugwell. He took it on the chin. Now it's Roosevelt."

I shall quote — with the permission of the *American Magazine of Art* — a few paragraphs from a letter which appeared in its Correspondence Column.

An American Artist's Story

To the Editor:

After looking at the reproductions of Biddle's frescoes for the Justice Department Building, Washington, I can no longer restrain myself from writing you about the aid and comfort being given Communistic propaganda by the expenditure of taxpayers' money through the Federal Art Project for the portrayal of alien themes on the walls of our public buildings. . . .

Why did Mr. Biddle deface the walls of the Justice Building with characters from New York's ghetto? Was he trying to impress us that the building is a possession of the Jewnited States? Why must people have monstrosities, indiscriminately pushed together in foul smelling tenements, that reek of vermin in the abstract, placed before their eyes on the walls of buildings that should reflect the dignity of that portion of society which it represents?

These Biddle frescoes are but another example of the poisonous pattern of Moscow being forced down the American throat, and it is the type of thing that is bringing, not a widespread appreciation of æsthetics, but rather a degeneration of public taste. If propaganda is the aim of the F.A.P., it might be well to remember that there are real artists who by means of beauty can arouse sufficient sympathy to tear apart one's heart strings. But the type of propaganda portraying vicious, horrible, nauseating scenes does not excite compassion — it excites revulsion.

One of the fundamental truths of nature is that foul, abhorrent things betray by their shape, color, sound or aroma that they are poisonous or otherwise dangerous, hence all living things avoid them. Also a truth is the fact that agreeable things betray themselves in like manner. . . .

The one truth remains. You cannot socialize art. There have been many chosen, but few will survive the back-swing of the pendulum of genius. Human reason will rebel and those timid souls who have been reticent about ridiculing the defamation of our public buildings by artistic frauds, because they feared they might be guilty of *social injustice*, will sweep these monstrosities from the face of the earth — preserving only enough to show future generations what saps we taxpayers are.

This poisonous doctrine of "social justice" — a fraudulent term for Communism — has permeated our art schools and art museums. The only art that is acceptable today, therefore, is not art at all. It is hideousness personified. It is Moscow propaganda. It is the essence of foulness and incompetence. And its constant encouragement means the death of craftsmanship — the very life-blood of artistic expression.

These radicals who realized their inability to reach the heights of technical perfection naturally sought the shortest way. The results are everywhere apparent. Hundreds of thousands of yards of perfectly good canvas; square miles of copper; mountains of marble; miles of good plaster; tons of paint and ink have been destroyed to allow "freedom of expression" to an army of morons and nitwits who have nothing to express and could not express it if they did. . . .

When will the American public have satiation of this orgy of disgusting, horrible, madhouse creations? From the Renaissance to Whistler, art improved; then it began to deteriorate until today the stuff called art is nothing but a bad copy of the lowest Congo Negro symbolism lacking, however, a reason for being — one thing the Congoite did have.

For the love of art, please give your readers something sometimes, that will not irritate the entire nervous system. Let's go back to sanity.

Yours for art's sake,

——— ———

In the early spring of 1937, I was asked if I would take part, as one of the original sponsors, in a National Conference on Constitutional Amendment, which was to meet in Washington on March eighteenth. Since Dr. Charles A. Beard, Senator Hugo L.

Black, Stuart Chase, Lloyd K. Garrison, John L. Lewis and Maury Maverick were among the sponsors, I was flattered; and I had every intention of making a motion from the platform and going down to history. However, on the fifth of February the President stole our thunder and shortly thereafter the conference was abandoned. It was, then, with more than an academic interest that I listened on various occasions over the radio to the controversy. I had read Parrington, Thurman Arnold's *Symbols of Government* and Edwin S. Corwin's *Twilight of the Supeme Court*; and I had my own views. But I could not help wondering how and what that most balanced of men, Justice Stone, a good Republican, felt through it all. I wrote and asked him. In a sentence, in one biblical quotation, he summed up all that had been intelligently said on the matter during six months of eye-gougings, wrist-twistings and kickings between the groins. In this inquiry concerning HATE, it is pleasant to end up on a note of sanity.

Supreme Court of the United States
April 8, 1937.

DEAR MR. BIDDLE:

Many thanks for your kind note.

These are, indeed, exciting days, but I go my way, doing the day's task, and render unto Cæsar the things that are Cæsar's, by letting the political arm of the Government decide whether they want six new judges or are content with nine. Whatever happens or doesn't happen, I am convinced that a little of the universal solvent of Time will settle most of the difficulties which beset us just now.

With kind regards to you and Mrs. Biddle in which Mrs. Stone joins,

HARLAN STONE

And this thing called class allegiance — am I a traitor to my class? As I am in the minority of my class, I suppose it is they who will render the verdict. It doesn't bother me. I shall plead guilty and accept the indictment without a twinge. It would be a much more serious matter, for instance, if I were a traitor to my country, to my profession, to my beliefs. But I don't think my class is important at all. In fact one would have great difficulty in defining it. Perhaps it only exists in clear-cut profile as a violent emotional symbol. And I take a naughty pleasure in the thought that I am a traitor to violent emotional symbolism.

If my class means such American citizens as are eligible to the Somerset, Knickerbocker, Philadelphia or Baltimore Clubs and to the various Assemblies, then it is a completely negligible fraction of America, either numerically, politically, intellectually, financially or socially. If my class means Americans whose forefathers were of colonial stock, then at a guess it includes about forty-five million of us, all the way from Georgia crackers and Sing Sing inmates to the White House. If my class means Anglo-Saxons and members of the Protestant Episcopal Church — well, we just won't go into my feelings about that sort of a grouping. If my class refers to the social-economic group defined by a ten-thousand-dollar income, a country club and manicured fingernails — well, I'm not eligible on any count. No; my class is without any clear-cut meaning — unless it be a large and somewhat amorphous classification of all those whose political, social, artistic and moral habits, minds and tastes are thoroughly repugnant to me.

Many of us who are indicted as being traitors to our class are accused of dishonesty. At the bar of public opinion should I say something to establish our honesty — that of artists, human beings with my background, that feel the way I do? A couple of years ago at Saunderstown I was discussing with an old family friend, an old girl friend of my brother's, his work as Chairman of the National Labor Relations Board. She said: "I think Francis is so attractive, and so swell and so intelligent. It's a pity he's not honest." I said: "What do you mean he's not honest?" She said: "Oh he couldn't be, with all this professed interest in workmen. He wasn't brought up with workmen. They're not his class. He can't really be interested in them."

Last spring I was lecturing at Rochester. I spent the evening with old friends, Harper Sibley, the former President of the United States Chamber of Commerce, whom I had known as a boy at Groton, and his wife. He reminded me that I had introduced him to Georgie Farr. She was fourteen years old and the most seductive charmer I had ever known. I had a secret crush on her. She subsequently married Harper. Georgie has lost none of her charm; and is very religious and social-minded. I was telling her about the Artists' Congress and she said: "I think its terribly interesting; and I suppose I understand why you're so violent about Hitler; but all that interest in workmen and socialism and Labor's Non-Partisan League can't be honest. After all they're artists."

That I believe is the consensus of opinion. If you're a gentleman or an artist, you can't be honest.

Now, as to Francis' honesty. He said to me once something like this: "Oh yes, I do pretty well under capitalism; my firm did pretty well during the depression; but I read books; I have some intelligence. It may not always be just this way. I rather think when Randolph's my age, capitalism, as we now understand it, may be a thing of the past. And even suppose we were to have some sort of socialism, I can't get jittery over it. I don't think on the whole that it would necessarily be worse than the past five years. And of course, if it should be socialism — which I rather doubt — I needn't worry about providing for Randolph."

His honesty wasn't even involved — merely his intelligence.

Maury Maverick said to me: "You see we're all human. Me and Rockefeller and J. P. Morgan. And its human to want to provide for your children. Now they do it one way, John D. and J. P. — with occasional tear-gas bombs and wrist-twistings —

and I do it another — making speeches. I think when my children are my age, capitalism, as we know it, may have gone. I'd rather be riding on the wave than behind it. So I'm trying to bring about what I believe will leave my children economically best provided for."

Maury's honesty wasn't involved either; just his intelligence.

Francis and Maury presume to be of the age we live in. So do artists and, very occasionally, gentlemen.

Now artists, in addition to reading the newspapers, and having some little selfish interest in productive capacity, business cycles, rental fees, hourly wages, board, bread and water, are supposedly sensitive beings; supposedly have emotional reactions to life. During the past ten years they have seen at close range, studied, noted down, drawn and painted the facts of life about them — the drunkards in the speakeasies, the men on park benches; the gold-miners among the slag, the refuse, the brothels, the saloons of Cripple Creek or Leadville; the farmers living in the sand and among the seared crops and the starving cattle of the Dust Bowl; the moral wrecks among the little businessmen, the big businessmen, the upper brackets of finance and society. They have seen and studied and drawn a million faces in the bread-line of life. Faces do not lie. Faces are the artist's clinic; his stock in trade; his professional equipment. If during the past ten years he has not been appalled, shocked, wounded by the tragic and unnecessary human wastage which he reads in these human documents, then I aver not that he is without intelligence, which is obvious, not that he is mentally dishonest, which I believe, not that he is inhuman, which is probable, but that as an artist he is completely without sensitivity, completely blind. So much for the honesty, then, of an artist, of a human being, who is capable of a feeling of sympathy or of understanding for something which lies beyond his immediate interest, outside his particular class, outside of his own skin. So much for the sensitivity of someone who is not professedly a molusk.

(309)

My brother as a lawyer, Maury as a politician, are interested in providing security for their children. Neither of them looks forward with any great terror to an economic condition in America which is not capitalism in the sense in which we know it. Assuming that my son Michael John should grow up to be an artist, I too, who have little love for capitalism, as it currently operates, can only look forward with unmixed pleasure to a greater and stronger *social democracy*. For I should like him to have a wider and more intelligent audience; to enjoy a more common democratic and universal faith; to depend on a greater economic security; and in his work to evidence a more vigorous and wholesome American appeal than was generally possible for the artists of our generation.

Am I, then, a communist? No, of course not; but have I communistic or socialistic leanings? I believe in free parks and free drinking water, which is communistic — "to each according to his need" — and free schooling which is socialistic — "from each according to his ability." [The quotations are from Lenin.] I believe first, last and always in democracy. Stuart Chase would say: "That word is meaningless. Define the referent." Roughly speaking I call democracy relying for what you want on the ballot box, not on machine guns. William Penn more or less got a religious democracy on its feet in Pennsylvania. Jefferson and the rest of them established in our constitution the conception of political democracy. But democracy is never an end in itself. Civil liberty or freedom of expression is an end. Democracy is a means. Our forefathers realized that political tyranny might be a bar to personal freedom. Some of us now realize that economic tyranny is a bar to personal freedom. So what? As Louis Adamic puts it, America is somewhat incongruous in a state of political democracy and economic despotism. I suppose we shall have to see a good deal more socialism before we secure something like social democracy. How much more socialism? Don't know. Neither does anyone. The less the better. But as much as is necessary to give the greatest amount of spiritual freedom to the greatest number of the people. In theory it's as simple as that.

Here my communist friends answer in rebuttal: But if you admit the need of economic socialization to secure individual freedom, a real Bill of Rights, a real democracy, why not admit that communism — not necessarily Stalinism or Trotskyism or even Communism, that is the Russian party method — is the logical, honest, unequivocal answer?

Professor John Chipman Gray, in opening his course on evidence in the Harvard Law School at the turn of the century, used to say that of all the methods devised by men to inquire into and arrive at the truth, the English jury system — as it had gradually emerged from the medieval trial by sword, by fire, by water, by the oath of twelve good men and true, peers of the assize — was probably the most irrational, slow and inaccurate. "It has one undeniable virtue, however," old Professor Gray would conclude his opening lecture. "Under the jury system and under the Common Law body of the rules of evidence, it is perhaps more difficult than under any other known system to hang an innocent victim."

Professor Charles Beard put the same thought to me once even more graphically: "There is no question about it that a fast motorboat has more speed than a dory. Now if a dory runs upon a reef — well, it slides off, but if a fast motorboat hits a reef — well, there you have the weakness of some of these fast, logical European systems." Trial, and approval or rejection, is another definition of democracy. Not very scientific, rapid or logical. But you don't hang so many innocent people and you avoid total shipwrecks. It's a question of preference. My American prejudice — and answer, in surrebuttal, to the communists.

Three or four years ago I read Turgenev's *Father and Sons*. Only then I realized that all this Union Square slibber-slobber about party obedience, boring from within, the class war and so on — which had seemed so foreign and un-American to me — was part of the philosophic heritage of the young Russian intellectual almost three generations ago. To us — to most of us — it was a lot of foreign jibber-jabber. I was convinced more and more that it couldn't be settled in those terms here. Later I read Vernon Louis Parrington's *Main Currents in American Thought,* and then for the first time I understood the other side of the picture: how from the very beginning America had inherited two great streams of European thought. They had formed and molded all that seemed most American in us. They had fused in the new American environment. Rather, these two streams of thought had been given new shape by the pressure and impact of new surroundings. They had created under pioneer-democratic conditions a new mind, a new temper. One of these influences stemmed from Calvinism, Hume, Locke, James Harrington and the Puritan revolution of 1648. Being a revolt against religious absolutism, royal feudalism and the Crown Courts it emphasized religious individualism, political freedom and the protection of property rights against the Crown. This current had dominated New England Puritanism for two centuries. It was the small change of the Revolutionary patriots. It was written into the constitution and the fabric of the nation. Here had been the headwaters of the best of the conservative tradition in American thought today. *American Conservatism was not begotten during the normalcy of Harding, Coolidge and Hoover.* The other current of European thought flowed against our shores at a somewhat later period. It came from Montaigne and the French Encyclopedists, Rousseau, Voltaire, Condorcet, Diderot and the idealists of 1789. Based on the principle that property rights may be subordinated to human rights and on a belief in education and democracy — since it believed in humanity — it was the source from which Sam Adams, Ben Franklin, Tom Payne and Jefferson slaked their thirst. It inspired the

Bill of Rights, which to date is our most revolutionary doctrine. *Radicalism in America was not born of the Russian Revolution.*

Here is my only purpose for this historical digression, which
I may have stated a little crudely, a little inaccurately. Even the
clearest and coolest of our critics are too close to the heat of
their political passions to see events in their true perspective —
from the long view of history. When I read Parrington it
shocked and delighted me to realize that the Supreme Court issue had been chewed over and debated by Sam Adams in 1760;
and finished forever by Roger Williams, who in 1640 declared
that a judiciary not responsible to a popular assembly was a menace to democracy! I read Beard's *Economic Interpretation to the
Constitution* and learned to what extent the color of the constitution had been affected by the fear of cheap money of the "Sixty
Families" and the fear of cheap land by the real-estate interests
of the day. I began to realize that the political violence which
many of us construed as the evidence of an impending collapse
was also the recurrent assertion of two dominant streams of
thought that have made up the fiber of our being, but which may
— since we are still a young and growing nation — again in the
future as in the past result in diverse expansions or contractions,
readjustments and growing pains.

One suggests to one's radical Union Square friends a course
of reading in early American history and a little more junketing
about America. A similar diet and some little firsthand acquaintance with American labor would not, I think, increase the blood
pressure of our arteriosclerotic elders. What neither the radical
intelligentsia nor the conservative low-brows realize is that intellectually and politically labor is essentially conservative. Here is
an example. I had wanted for a long time — and am still very
desirous — of establishing a closer and more pragmatic relation
between the left-wing, socially conscious, liberal artists and left-
wing labor, as, for instance, industrial unionism. Such a relation

(313)

I know will help both. It will give the painter an artistic and emotional outlet for his political credo. Today the field of the radical cartoonist is almost confined to *Fight* and the *New Masses*, which unfortunately are read and seen largely by the intelligentsia and the radical cartoonists. But labor would profit even more by such a relation. Industrial unionism is under a cloud. It needs to be sold to the country. Propaganda? Of course. Education? Art is always more convincing than fireside chats. I had talked the idea over with various Washington friends. Two or three of us — Ben Shahn among the number — went round one afternoon to C.I.O. Headquarters. We met John Brophy and some of the leaders. John L. Lewis was away in Pittsburgh. On the way over I was admonished: "Better not mention the I.L.D. or the *New Masses*, George; it will frighten them." "And Ben, I shouldn't say anything about art propaganda in Soviet Russia." "And by the way, George, avoid such words as 'radical,' 'left wing' or 'proletariat.'" We had a long talk with Brophy. I think we sold him an idea. The seed is still underground. Someday it may germinate. At first we were up against a wall of silence and suspicion. I could see they thought us subversive. I took the bit in my teeth. I didn't quite speak the truth. I talked in terms they could understand. The idea behind what I said was true. I said: "Listen. The best art is good salesmanship. Always has been. How do you suppose Uncle Sam enlists soldiers? High-brow cartoons about seeing Hawaii. How do you suppose Uncle Sam sold Liberty Bonds in 1917? High-brow art. James Montgomery Flagg and Charles Dana Gibson. The artists are there. It's up to you to use them. You want to unionize workers. You want to sell yourself to the country. You'll be surprised to find how many artists on the *New Yorker*, earning perhaps fifty thousand a year, are deeply interested in what you are doing: Peter Arno; maybe Thurber; maybe Soglow. Why not use them?" That's the way I peddled left-wing art to radical labor. I talked in a language sufficiently conservative not to scare the wits out of them; and sold them an idea which someday may germinate.

To many it will appear that the American artists today are pathetically bogged down in a morass of social dilettantism, of political verbiage, of pseudo-ethical sentiment. Many would prefer to see us back again — if not among the apples and swaying bottles of the Cézanne-Coolidge era — at least on our cobbler's bench, fitting the form to the last. We won't — we can't — go back to the Ivory Tower, to Art for Art's sake. The pendulum has swung the other way. The tide is on the flow. I, too, believe that we should tend our own woof, but we can keep the pattern clear. In America there is far too much of the petty shopkeeper's preoccupation with technical values — good painting and drawing as an end in itself; and too much preoccupation on the other hand with passionless and anæmic statements of social utopia. *Technique is not the end of art: nor is life, for that matter, but only its raw material. What the artist feels about life — his experience of it — is the only warranty of his validity as an artist.*

My only plea — in mitigation of what to some will appear an unwarranted dalliance in alien fields — is that the artist should not desensitize his aptitude for living — for experiencing life — by a refusal to take the mental consequence of envisaging a better and happier world than that we live in.

The critic a hundred years hence may speculate how the painter, living through these ghastly, honor-soiled days, could sit quietly before his easel, and meticulously, flawlessly finish his snow scene, his flower piece or his "Mariposa with a Red Scarf." He will speculate, too, how little artistic gunpowder is found among much of the *New Masses* art and propaganda of such ilk. He will concur with Edmund Wilson that an artist could have served Loyalist Spain more efficaciously by dropping bombs from an airplane than by drawing third-rate cartoons for *Fight*. What escape from this dilemma is there for the young man whose nerves have not been callused by memories of, and participation in, the

Great War of yesterday? Is it perhaps this: that a sensitive being must find some escape, or sublimation, for the horror he feels about him, and that this sublimation need not necessarily be a further statement of more hatred, of more evil?

This is not merely *an escape.* It is the artist's proudest challenge to humanity. The future will not judge our generation and civilization solely by the wrecks, the lies, the cruelty which they have perpetrated. It will understand and judge them too by the protest of our artists — whether their language is couched in terms of escape, of hatred or of love. It is imperative, then, for artists to remember — no matter how strong is the pull of their moral allegiance, the call of their political faith — that only such protest as is cast and hammered in the clear, hard language of art, will survive at all our tears, our laughter and our cries of pain.

Life today in America is often colorless and drab; often without design or texture. It can be brutal, ignorant and cruel.

It can be beautiful.

THE END

"Our senses will applaud the world again,
But who can clap life into murdered men?"

IN MEMORIAM:
SACCO AND VANZETTI

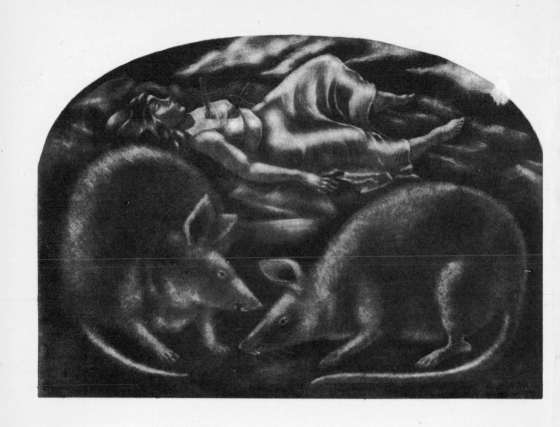

IN MEMORIAM: SPAIN   HITLER: "Let her bleed awhile longer."
                                        MUSSOLINI:

INDEX

Index

Index

Index

(323)

Index

Index

(325)